GOVERNORS STATE UNIVERSITY LIBRARY
W9-AAT-620
3 1611 00167 1103

The Therapeutic Relationship

Recent Titles in
Developments in Clinical Psychology
Glenn R. Caddy, Series Editor

Strategic Health Planning: Methods and Techniques Applied to Marketing and Management
Allen D. Spiegel and Herbert H. Hyman

Behavioral Medicine: International Perspectives, Volume 1
Don G. Byrne and Glenn R. Caddy, editors

Behavioral Medicine: International Perspectives, Volume 2
Don G. Byrne and Glenn R. Caddy, editors

The MMPI: A Contemporary Normative Study of Adolescents
Robert C. Colligan and Kenneth P. Offord

Adult-Child Research and Experience: Personal and Professional Legacies of a Dysfunctional Co-Dependent Family
Robert E. Haskell

Behavioral Medicine: International Perspectives, Volume 3
Don G. Byrne and Glenn R. Caddy, editors

Reprogramming Pain: Transform Pain and Suffering into Health and Success
Barry Bittman, M.D.

Personal Construct Therapy: A Handbook
Linda L. Viney

The Natural Limitations of Youth: The Predispositions That Shape the Adolescent Character
John J. Mitchell

Distance Writing and Computer-Assisted Interventions in Psychiatry and Mental Health
Luciano L'Abate, editor

Beyond Psychotherapy: Programmed Writing and Structured Computer-Assisted Interventions
Luciano L'Abate

Intimate Relationships and How to Improve Them: Integrating Theoretical Models with Preventive and Psychotherapeutic Applications
Luciano L'Abate and Piero De Giacomo

The Therapeutic Relationship

Listening and Responding in a Multicultural World

Ira David Welch

Developments in Clinical Psychology
Glenn R. Caddy, Series Editor

Westport, Connecticut
London

Library of Congress Cataloging-in-Publication Data

Welch, Ira David, 1940–
The therapeutic relationship : listening and responding in a multicultural world / Ira David Welch.
p. cm.—(Developments in clinical psychology)
Includes bibliographical references and index.
ISBN 0–275–97626–2 (alk. paper)
1. Psychotherapist and patient. 2. Clinical psychology. 3. Listening. 4. Counseling. 5. Cross-cultural counseling. I. Title. II. Series.

RC480.8.W448 2003
616.89'14—dc21 2003042892

British Library Cataloguing in Publication Data is available.

Library of Congress Catalog Card Number: 2003042892
ISBN: 0–275–97626–2

First published in 2003

Praeger Publishers, 88 Post Road West, Westport, CT 06881
An imprint of Greenwood Publishing Group, Inc.
www.praeger.com

Printed in the United States of America

The paper used in this book complies with the Permanent Paper Standard issued by the National Information Standards Organization (Z39.48–1984).

10 9 8 7 6 5 4 3 2 1

Copyright Acknowledgments

. . . to Chris,

. . . counselor, educator, artist, and searcher

and

. . . to Rik, Marsha, Michael, and David

. . . for friendship, guidance, and good times at the lake

Contents

Part III: Responding Skills

Illustrations

Tables

Figure

Preface

It remains something of a mystery why listening is such an undeveloped skill in the ordinary commerce of American life. We are a rushed nation increasingly comfortable with sight and sound images that bombard us from radio, television, and computers. It takes time to listen and, perhaps, that has been what increasingly has led us to rely upon "professional listeners," with whom we entrust our intimate fears and unfulfilled hopes. It was against this backdrop that I wrote this book.

Professional counselors and psychotherapists are the trusted confidants of a community that has found the ordinary means of networking, studying, talking with friends, and even turning to family unsatisfying in clarifying and resolving what troubles it. Yet, in my experience over the years, I have come to realize that even those of us who want to be servants to the emotional needs of others are ourselves products of a culture in which good listening skills are not a natural development of our experience. Listening is a skill that must be learned and practiced.

As I reviewed other works devoted to training counselors and psychotherapists, I was struck by the lack of a thorough approach to the skills of listening. It was as if the profession had made an assumption that listening was, of course, important and, at the same time, a given. Sometimes the section on listening in books devoted to therapy skills would be limited to a few paragraphs pointing out the importance of listening, making the assumption that the reader already knew the skills of listening, and then quickly moving on to a more thorough treatment of theory and responding skills. My experience in working with beginning counselors and psychotherapists over the years, however, has taught me that this is an assumption we cannot make safely. We all live in the experiential world, as diverse and multicultural as it is, in which we all are exposed to the rapid pace of life, including radio, television, the overstimulating experience of shopping malls, and the rapid exchange of information in the communication age, which teaches us the opposite of careful listening and reflection—foundational skills of counseling and psychotherapy. The common social experience of using ritualized greetings and responses (e.g., "Whatssup!"; "How ya doin?") without actually listening has to be discarded in the therapeutic relationship, and new skills must be learned in their place. A major difference between this book and others in the field is the focus on listening. It represents the result of years of training others to listen and respond and in teaching others the components of listening skills. It has often surprised me that students come to therapy without a real understanding of why and for what they are listening. As the students and I struggled through learning responding skills, a model of listening began to form, and I increasingly began to teach systematic listening skills as the foundation for responding. While the first section focuses on listening, responding skills are given an equally thorough discussion in the later sections of the book. Much of what I have said about listening skills is true for therapeutic responding as well. Therapeutic responding suffers somewhat from the same cultural limits addressed above. Many of us have learned more to suppress our genuine responses in the name of manners or courtesy and have not developed the skills necessary to respond to another's need empathically, genuinely, and respectfully. We have learned to respond with questions and advice—skills that have their usefulness in arenas other than counseling and psychotherapy, but do not serve therapists and clients well at all. So, training in the skills of listening and responding becomes a matter of unlearning some of our societal listening and responding habits and replacing them with more effective therapeutic skills.

This book is for those beginning therapists who are starting to master the fundamentals of effective work with others. It provides a model of listening and responding skills that forms the foundation for understanding others. I have tried to provide the reader with a solid framework of listening and responding skills grounded in research and theory that is supported through the best thinking of scholars and trainers in the field. This clearly is meant to be a training work that is practical, useful, and understandable while, at the same time, scientifically and theoretically sound. What I have not done is advocate any particular theory of counseling or psychotherapy over any other. I believe the listening and responding skills described in this book are important and essential for any therapist, regardless of his or her theoretical orientation. My own background, which is influenced by humanistic and cognitive-developmental assumptions, obviously may slip through from time to time, but my intention remains pure: to describe skills needed by any therapist. In addition, this is not a work that focuses on counseling and psychotherapy research, design, methodology, and evaluation. It is more in the practitioner's than the scientist's vein. Further, it is not a text that focuses on assessment or diagnosis. The purpose of this book is to focus the student on the skills of listening and responding that contribute to building an effective therapeutic relationship with clients.

I have attempted to draw the reader's attention to diversity and multicultural issues throughout the book. I am indebted to my colleague, Dr. David M. Gonzalez, who coauthored with me chapter 9, "Diversity and Multicultural Concerns." In addition, I have highlighted in chapters throughout the book those aspects of diversity and multiculturalism that seemed most pressing for that particular topic.

Finally, in the appendix, there are practice exercises to aid the reader in mastering the skills of listening and responding. I believe deeply in the training model in which beginning counselors and psychotherapists meet with clients, videotape the session, and view the tape with a training group and a supervisor (direct observation has even more power, I believe). Using these practice exercises, especially in a training group, can be helpful as the student practices and develops his or her therapy skills.

Some material included in the chapter references are not cited specifically in the chapter. I thought these citations would be useful to the reader and chose to include them.

I am hopeful that this book will serve its purpose of teaching fundamental, sound, and essential listening and responding skills. Psychotherapy is an endeavor to which I have devoted my professional life, and I have a stake in its effective practice. It is a noble profession, and if this book helps along the way, then its purposes have been well met.

Acknowledgments

Certainly, no work such as this comes to life through the efforts of a single writer. While my name alone appears on the cover, there are many who contributed their time, effort, and support throughout the writing.

I express my appreciation and gratitude to:

my wife, life partner, and best friend, Marie, who endured the many weekends when I wasn't a good companion; even then, she continued to listen and respond

our sons Dave and Dan, all grown up now and who welcome us into their homes

my students at Howard University, who read and critiqued the manuscript as it evolved, especially my graduate assistant, Lenora McClain, and the members of my Ethics class and the Introduction to Counseling and Psychotherapy classes

my clients over the years, who continually inspire me to live a life of courage

my teachers throughout my academic life, who, in ways great and small, paved the way for this book

my editors at Greenwood Publishing, especially Debbie Carvalko and Arlene Belzer, who worked hard and long to bring this book to press

and I have saved for last; a special "thank you" for my colleagues—Dr. Christine Breier, Dr. David M. Gonzalez, and Dr. Anne Richards—who contributed in so many different ways to the completion of this book

Part I

Listening Skills

Chapter 1

The Role of Listening in Counseling and Psychotherapy

"He words me . . . he words me." How eloquent! Cleopatra condemns Octavius Caesar in Shakespeare's *Antony and Cleopatra* (Act V, Scene 2). He will not listen. Shakespeare's Elizabethan English might trouble our ears in today's modern world, but Cleopatra's frustration is a present-day reality. "It is a rare thing in human relationships to be listened to" (Martin, 1983, p. 18). Contrast Cleopatra's experience with a bit of old Scottish wisdom, "His thoughts were slow, his words were few, and never formed to glisten. But he was a joy for all the clan, for you should have heard him listen!"

We explain the rattle somewhere in the front part of our car to an auto mechanic who nods his or her head knowingly and returns our car to us the next day with the rattle still vibrating. We explain our symptoms to a physician who is rushed and aloof. For many, calling a customer service representative is no better than talking to an answering machine with preprogrammed replies to any question. In each of these daily irritations, we experience the annoyance and exasperation of being misunderstood and dismissed. These people aren't deaf, of course. They hear, but they do not listen. Listening transcends hearing. Hearing describes sensation. Listening involves an underlying motivation of attending, alertness, and a desire to understand. We might, for example, hear a noise, but we listen for any indication of danger. Or we might overhear a conversation, but we are moved to concentration if we recognize our names. We know what it means to be listened to and, correspondingly, we know what it means to be ignored, interrupted, disregarded, and misunderstood. We know what it means to be listened to as opposed merely to being heard.

These everyday examples pale when we consider what brings many clients to the offices of counselors and psychotherapists. Among the reasons is the unspoken complaint that no one (no one!) will listen to their stories. No one in their personal world acts as if they have the time or the patience to listen. In the aftermath of turmoil, the injured and victimized yearn to revisit the situations, events, and causes of the disarray in their lives. Many share a common experience. They seem to wear out the patience of friends and relatives who tire of listening. The common responses seem to be "I have heard it all before" and "get on with your life." While we seem willing to allow time for physical injuries to heal and willing to change the bandages from time to time, we simultaneously seem to believe that the injuries of the psyche do not require time to heal. Some even seem to be intolerant of the notion that emotional injuries require the time and the psychic equivalent of cleaning wounds and changing bandages.

Listen to this story:

> A runaway youth has fallen in with a gang of thugs and terrorists who have captured a Great Teacher for cruel and nefarious purposes. He watches as they torture and seek to humiliate the Teacher. Touched by the Teacher's courage and inner strength, the youth shyly approaches the old Teacher. The Teacher says, "How can a face so young wear so many burdens?" The boy replies, "So, you can talk." The Great Teacher replies, "And I can also listen. Some say that the path from inner turmoil begins with a friendly ear. My ear is open if you care to use it." (Welch, 1998, p. 33)

As the author notes, these are "profound words. We should not be deterred from recognizing them as such merely because they come from a movie about sewer-dwelling, mutated, reptilian comic book characters and are spoken by a giant rat! Regardless of the source, these words do carry wisdom with them. An open ear can begin the process of healing for a troubled person" (Welch, 1998, p. 33). Some, perhaps many, would view the sentiment above as overly maudlin. Others might be offended at the apparent flippancy by introducing a comic book character into a serious discussion of the importance of listening in our lives. I am risking those negative judgments to make the following point. Many in our society carry heavy burdens. It isn't the case that we do not know the remedy. A comic strip character can tell us the cure, "The path from inner turmoil begins with a friendly ear." Fromm-Reichmann (1950) made this case powerfully some years ago in her advice to psychotherapists:

> "The psychotherapist must be able to listen." This does not appear to be a startling statement, but it is intended to be just that. To be able to listen to another person in this other person's own right, without reacting along the lines of one's own problems or experiences, of which one may be reminded, perhaps in a disturbing way, is an act of interpersonal exchange which few people are able to practice without special training. (P. 7)

McKay, Davis, and Fanning (1983) would supplement Fromm-Reichmann's statement by adding "and it can make a person feel valued and can free that person to explore new thoughts" (p. 18). That is the premise of this book. Listening can begin the process of helping others bear the burdens they carry.

LISTENING

Listening to others stretches along a continuum from inattentiveness to deep concern. Long (1996), for example, discusses types of listening. She argues that there are five basic types of listening, ranging from nonlistening to empathic listening. *Nonlistening* refers to when a person is hearing another but is not mindfully paying attention. *Pretend listening* refers to when a listener gives the appearance of listening with eye contact and other signs of attentiveness, but his or her mind is occupied with other concerns. This might be labeled "false listening" or even "manipulative listening," depending on the motives of the listener. *Selective listening* simply refers to when a person is attending to only part of what the speaker is saying. A common form of selective listening is acknowledging only the intellectual parts of a person's story and ignoring feelings or emotions. *Self-focused listening* is centered in the listener. It is the form of listening we use when we are using the speaker's words as a bridge to what we want to say. We listen for an opportunity to interrupt or listen halfheartedly as we organize our own thoughts. *Empathic listening* refers to when a listener is focused on the speaker's meanings (even vague, hidden, suggested meanings) and seeks to understand the person at many levels, including intellectual and emotional. Long concludes that in a given day we might practice several or all of these types of listening. As a matter of therapeutic importance, empathic listening and selective listening are useful skills. Nonlistening, pretend listening, and self-focused listening have no apparent therapeutic value.

Listening is not a passive process. "Being quiet while someone talks isn't real listening" (McKay, Davis, & Fanning, 1983, p. 14). On the other hand, as Patterson (1985) notes tongue in cheek, "Someone has suggested that with beginning counselors adhesive tape might be more useful than recording tape" (p. 103). Some have used the terms "active" and "passive" in an effort to capture the importance of attending to the meanings clients give to their experiences. Active listening is a concept that describes a situation in which the listener is not merely attending to what another says, but actively is trying to understand the meanings of the other (Rogers & Farson, 1980). Passive listening may demonstrate courtesy, but does not make a real attempt to understand anything other than the manifest content of another's speech.

A colleague and I have used the words "compassionate" and "polite" to define this difference (Welch & Gonzalez, 1999, p. 130). Even while one may listen courteously, polite listening tends to be self-serving. Polite listening may be separated into two categories—genuine and false. Genuine polite listening is sincere, and the listener is seeking some gain, such as information or insight. An interested student in a class might be an example of a genuine polite listener. False polite listening occurs when a listener has no real interest in what another person is saying, but seeks to give the false impression that he or she does. This is the listening style of confidence tricksters and some sales people, and it can be found in every singles bar in the United States.

McKay, Davis, and Fanning (1983) alert us to the danger of appearances by what they label as "pseudo-listening." While they identify the goals of "real listening" as understanding, enjoying, learning, or helping, pseudo-listening has different, more self-serving goals:

> The intention is not to listen, but to meet some other need. Some of the typical needs met by pseudo-listening are:
>
> 1. Making people think you're interested so they will like you
> 2. Being alert to see if you are in danger of being rejected
> 3. Listening for one specific piece of information and ignoring everything else
> 4. Buying time to prepare your next comment
> 5. Half-listening so someone will listen to you
> 6. Listening to find someone's vulnerabilities or to take advantage
> 7. Looking for the weak points in an argument so you can always be right, listening to get ammunition for attack
> 8. Checking to see how people are reacting, making sure you produce the desired effect
> 9. Half-listening because a good, kind, or nice person would
> 10. Half-listening because you don't know how to get away without hurting or offending someone. (P. 14)

Burley-Allen (1982) also discusses the disingenuous appearance of listening. She describes her style of false listening through the *faker*, whose goals are to gain or please; the *dependent listener*, who seeks to meet personal needs through the vicarious experience of the speaker's narrative; the *interrupter*, who merely uses the speaker's tale as a launching pad for a self-serving end; and the *self-conscious listener*, who is so self-absorbed that his or her internal dialogue blocks any real listening. Finally, Burley-Allen identifies the *intellectual* or *logical listener*, who disdains anything other than factual content.

Compassionate listening, by contrast, is centered in concern for the welfare of the client. It is purposive listening in which the goal is to understand not only content but also feelings, emotions, and/or meanings. The difference between compassionate listening and polite, pseudo-, or disingenuous listening lies at the heart of psychotherapy and the "path from inner turmoil." When clients come to psychotherapy, they come not for courtesy, but for a compassionate hearing of their story. Compassion alone, of course, does not make a psychotherapist. The willingness to listen may well be driven by compassion, but effective listening is a skill. A psychotherapist is a person who has not only an open ear, but also a trained one. Egan (1998), for example, identifies four requirements for what he labels "complete listening." We must listen for *verbal descriptions* of experience. We must listen (observe and read) for *nonverbal behavior*. We must listen to *context*, or for the relationship of the person in the environmental and social settings of life. We must listen for *sour notes*, or elements of the client's story that might need to be challenged. Long (1996) provides a similar description in her explanation of "total listening," which includes attending, hearing, explicit comprehension (the face value of the communication), implicit comprehension (nonverbal and deeper communication), understanding, and remembering.

It is the blend of compassion with training that characterizes an effective psychotherapist. The nature of that training occupies the substance of this book. Training in listening includes the skill of recognizing important content. How one differentiates vital content from less crucial information should not be simply a matter of guesswork. Clients do not come to psychotherapy to be the subjects of trial-and-error methods and strategies. They come for the expertise of the therapist. Expertise in listening is essential to effective listening and understanding. Thus, the training of psychotherapists includes strategies and methods of identifying meaningful content buried within a narrative.

It is a widely accepted belief among psychotherapists that clients do not say what they say, and how they say it, by accident. Many years ago, Johnson made this point about the importance of language in psychotherapy: "The language of distress might be part and parcel of the distress" (Johnson, 1946, p. 16). The words, tone, inflection, and gestures clients use to express themselves frequently carry more meaning than the clients may recognize initially. Listening skills help the therapist identify and clarify vague meanings for the client and pave the way for the understanding both of the therapist and client.

LISTENING SKILLS

McKay, Davis, and Fanning (1983) list twelve blocks to effective listening that prevent our understanding of another person. If we compare, mind read, rehearse, filter, judge, daydream, identify, advise, spar, want to be right, derail, or seek to placate, then genuine understanding is blocked.

Egan (1998) warns of the "shadow side of listening" and points out a variety of listening errors. *Evaluative listening* is when the listener judges the speaker even as he or she speaks. The speaker is right or wrong, moral or immoral, genuine or false, pleasant or abrasive. *Filtered listening* screens what is said through social, cultural, religious, moral, or other sieves that prevent the meaning of the speaker from being heard. *Labeling*, from either some social perspective or even a diagnostic perspective, can act as a filter that prevents the person from being understood. *Fact-centered listening* (rather than person-centered) focuses on content, information, and details and, in the process, may miss the heart of the issue. *Rehearsing* what we want to say as another speaks prevents understanding. This can be an early block for beginning therapists as they struggle with finding the proper response or as they internally ask themselves, "What should I say to this client?" *Sympathetic listening* interferes with understanding. If I sympathize with a client, then I "feel" what he or she is feeling and I am prevented from seeing beyond the pain, discomfort, or psychological blocks of the client and can be of little help. Sympathy plays an important role in human relationships, but it is has limited helpfulness in a counseling relationship.

PURPOSIVE LISTENING

The skills of listening include those that help to identify both content and meaning (feelings, emotion). Some years ago, I was taught that the first paragraph in any news story gave the reader six important pieces of information: who, what, when, where, why, and how. This journalistic guideline is one aspect of purposeful listening. When one listens with purpose, by purposively listening for the five Ws and H, what initially might seem to be a rambling and chaotic narrative can provide important and clear material. The principle of purposive listening teaches that one listens for intensity and frequency as clues to meaning, feelings, and importance for clients. Simply put, listening for intensity means listening for emphasis, inflection, and/or amplitude. Frequency refers to repetition. Using these two guidelines of purposive listening, one can make sense of apparent confusion and disorder.

Words alone do not carry the full meaning of human intention. If a therapist focuses merely on words (i.e., content alone), then much of the rich, perhaps even vague and disguised meaning of the client will be missed. What is apparent quickly to fledgling psychotherapists is that, when they focus on content alone, the therapy is bland, superficial, and weak. What seasons therapy, just as it does life itself, are the emotions, feelings, and/or meanings we give to our experiences.

Content alone reminds one of the old *Dragnet* television series in which Sergeant Joe Friday would intone with flat affect each week, "Just the facts, Ma'am." The show was notorious for its cardboard characters, and any therapy that focuses on "just the facts" will be similarly stiff and two dimensional. In addition to listening for content, the psychotherapist learns to identify the underlying meaning, either vague or apparent, in the client's story. In seeking to identify and clarify emotional meaning, psychotherapists learn the skill of listening for dramatic, affective, metaphoric, and symbolic words, inflections, and gestures that are the language of expression. They reveal more deeply held convictions about the content being verbalized. There may be a world of difference between two ways of telling the same story. "I don't like my job" is bland and dry. "My job is like a desert filled with snakes and scorpions!" is rich, metaphoric, and symbolic. One can imagine the client's feelings about the dangers and poisonous climate of his or her workplace. Such language can be viewed as a guide to more deeply held feelings and meanings.

In order to be an effective listener and understand the meanings clients are trying to express, a psychotherapist must attend to the nonverbal communication of the client. We are an animated species. We speak and listen to one another in a "hidden cultural grammar" that Hall (1966) has suggested is a mere 10 percent verbal. Other research suggests that nearly two-thirds of any human communication is conveyed nonverbally (Birdwhistell, 1970). In order to understand a human being, we must listen not only to what is spoken, but also to what the body says. We speak with our hands, our eyes, our shoulders, our feet, and, indeed, our entire body. Our bodies are articulate and expressive. Think about this scene: A client tells the therapist of her continued love for her husband and how much she wants to stay in the marriage. She says, "I want to stay with my husband," and, even as she says it, her head moves back and forth, from side to side. While her words say one thing, her body gives another signal.

It is important to use caution when interpreting both language and nonverbal communication. There might be a subtle difference between interpreting and inferring, but it is within that difference that the helpfulness of psychotherapy may be measured. Interpretation stems from the beliefs and, more frequently, from the theoretical orientation of the therapist. Inference comes more from the experience of the therapist and is a deduction that can be checked for accuracy with the client. Combs and Gonzalez (1994) offer the example of a ball heading for someone's head. When the person ducks, an observer may infer accurately that the person ducked because he or she didn't want to be hit by the ball. It isn't an interpretation; it is an inference and can be checked out. Understanding another is not a matter of interpretation so much as it is a matter of clarifying whether what the client wants to communicate is understood properly.

In my teaching I give students this paradoxical statement to emphasize the importance of listening, paying attention to nonverbal language, and not being overly interpretative: "All behavior is symbolic, except when it is not." This requires discussion, of course. It is meant as an attempt to create cognitive dissonance in the minds of students to force them somehow to reconcile the apparent contradiction in the rule. It is in the discussion that a truth emerges: In order to understand another person, we have to pay attention to everything he or she says, both verbally and nonverbally. Listening is a holistic enterprise. We have to pay attention not only to words, but also to any inferred meanings that may be present. In this attempt to understand, we simultaneously have to avoid telling the client what he or she thinks, feels, or means. Our task as psychotherapists is not to explain clients' behavior to them, but rather to understand collaboratively what is vague, undifferentiated, and, perhaps, even presently unknown to the client. In the situation above, for example, what is the client communicating when she moves her head back and forth, from side to side? I don't know precisely, but I do recognize that gesture. It is a gesture, typically in the United States, that signals "No." A negative message. It might also mean "I don't know" or "I'm not sure." What it should signal to the psychotherapist is the client's incongruence, uncertainty, and ambivalence about what she is saying. Her words are saying one thing, and her body another. Minimally, this requires exploration in order for any understanding and clear decision making to take place. This form of exploration includes more than mere words; it includes a holistic, thoughtful, and empathic clarification to discern the client's intent.

It is equally important to remind ourselves as psychotherapists that it is not the therapist alone who is interpreting and listening. Clients are keenly attentive to the words and nonverbal behavior of the therapist. They observe, infer, and interpret. They listen and evaluate. Gazda, Asbury, Balzer, Childers, and Walters (1977) point to the credence clients give to nonverbal messages. They indicate that, "when verbal and nonverbal messages are in contradiction, the helpee [client] will usually believe the nonverbal message" (p. 93).

Listening *is* a holistic enterprise. It is born from compassion, concern, and deliberation. It is enhanced by therapeutic purpose and matures in the development of skill. The skill of listening includes attending to content, underscoring expressive language (emotional language), and staying open to symbolic nonverbal expression.

DIVERSITY AND MULTICULTURAL CONCERNS

Each of us lives in three worlds simultaneously. First, we live in our individual world. Our uniqueness may stem somewhat from a matchless combination of genes, but, more likely, comes from personal construction. Our individualism, our idiosyncrasies in thought and behavior, may deviate only slightly from the thoughts and behaviors of our friends, or we may differ in some extreme and live on the fringes of society. The great difficulty of approaching people from a position of generalization is that whatever may be true in the general certainly may be false in the particular. This is the world of the individual.

Culture represents our second world of experience. Culture implies a group of people who share and maintain an agreed-upon and recognizable set of values and behaviors. Thus, culture may be used to identify a set of values and beliefs that range from a single family to a national group. The United States is home to a bewildering array of cultural groups from nations, religious groups, and ethnicities all over the globe. This rainbow nation includes red, white, black, brown, and yellow people who, regardless of their color, have been here for hundreds of years. We are a nation of immigrants. Even our indigenous people, who have been here for thousands of years, apparently wandered over from Asia on a land bridge into a fertile, empty land, which they made home. When we figure in gender and sexual orientation differences, the United States of America represents perhaps the most diverse, multicultural society in the history of humanity.

In such a climate of diversity, where new cultures mix with older, established ones, there is little wonder that conflicts and frictions occur. We have struggled as much as any society with concerns of respect, acceptance, integration, and maintenance of cultural integrity. Each of us is born into a cultural home with teachings, values, accepted truths, and behaviors that we learn and incorporate into our thinking as natural and right. Brought up in the bosom of culture, it is sometimes a wrenching, transcendent experience to learn that others view the world differently and that their claim to understanding carries as great an argument for truth as our own. This is the world of diversity and multiculturalism.

Each individual human is born into a family that is even larger than culture. We are born into the human family. Whatever differences we may create in our struggle for individualism, or whatever learnings we may inculcate from our culture, we still are one human group. Whatever surface differences seem apparent pale before the biological truth that we are one. We are separate and different from all other species on Earth, and we are linked indivisibly to all other members of our species. Our languages may be different, but the processes that created those languages are the same. We may practice different rituals, but the processes that created those rituals are the same. Our external countenance may be different, but at our genetic center we are the same creature. This is the world of universality, the final of our three worlds. The skill of listening must be tempered by the knowledge that people live in each of these worlds simultaneously.

SUMMARY

Take a moment to review the references for this chapter. You will realize that publication dates span a period of over fifty years. It is not that we have learned nothing new in those fifty years, but it is true that the role of listening in counseling and psychotherapy has remained remarkably consistent across time. Listening is, as Welch and Gonzalez (1999) phrased it, "the fundamental skill." Effective listening is the key to empathic understanding, and empathy is the heart of psychotherapy. The skills surveyed in this chapter, and given more in-depth treatment in the chapters that follow, are the bedrock of effective counseling and psychotherapy. Techniques, strategies, and manualized treatments are wasted in the absence of foundational skills that enhance listening and critical understanding. It is one of the purposes of this book to teach the fundamental skill of listening.

REFERENCES

Birdwhistell, M. L. (1970). *Kinesics and context.* Philadelphia: University of Pennsylvania Press.

Burley-Allen, M. (1982). *Listening: The Forgotten Skill.* New York: Wiley.

Combs, A. W., & Gonzalez, D. M. (1994). *Helping relationships: Basic concepts for the helping professions* (4th ed.). Boston, MA: Allyn and Bacon.

Egan, G. (1998). *The skilled helper: A problem-management approach to helping* (6th ed.). Pacific Grove, CA: Brooks/Cole.

Fromm-Reichmann, F. (1950). *Principles of intensive psychotherapy.* Chicago: University of Illinois Press.

Gazda, G. M., Asbury, F. S., Balzer, F. J., Childers, W. C., & Walters, R. P. (1977). *Human relations development* (2nd ed.). Boston, MA: Allyn and Bacon.

Hall, E. T. (1966). *The hidden dimension*. Garden City, NY: Doubleday.

Johnson, W. (1946). *People in quandaries: The semantics of personal adjustment*. New York: Harper.

Long, V. O. (1996). *Communication skills in helping relationships: A framework for facilitating personal growth*. Pacific Grove, CA: Brooks/Cole.

Martin, D. G. (1983). *Counseling and therapy skills*. Prospect Heights, IL: Waveland Press.

McKay, M., Davis, M., & Fanning, P. (1983). *Messages: The communication book*. Oakland, CA: New Harbinger.

Patterson, C. H. (1985). *The therapeutic relationship: Foundations for an eclectic psychotherapy*. Monterey, CA: Brooks/Cole.

Rogers, C. R., & Farson, R. E. (1980). Active listening. In P. V. Lewis & J. Williams (Eds.), *Reading is organizational communication* (pp. 276–291). Columbus, OH: Grid Publishing.

Welch, I. D. (1998). *The path of psychotherapy: Matters of the heart*. Pacific Grove, CA: Brooks/Cole.

Welch, I. D., & Gonzalez, D. M. (1999). *The process of counseling and psychotherapy: Matters of skill*. Pacific Grove, CA: Brooks/Cole.

Chapter 2

Establishing a Climate of Listening

Listening has both physical and psychological prerequisites. In counseling and psychotherapy, the climate of listening is not left to chance. It is an environment created purposefully to help clients enter into a trusting and facilitative relationship. As it is with any profession, however, good intentions are not sufficient for effective practice. A set time, a planned setting, and an attitude focusing on the needs of the client forms the foundation for effective listening. While listening is the fundamental skill, attending skills are the prerequisites necessary for effective listening.

Sommers-Flanagan and Sommers-Flanagan (1993) remark that "it is refreshing to find a concrete principle in the fields of psychology and counseling upon which virtually everyone agrees . . . attending behavior, and in a more general sense, the importance of the art of listening well, is spectacularly uncontroversial" (p. 53). There is agreement among counselor educators and authors not only about the importance of attending and listening, but also in their descriptions of attending and listening skills.

THE ATTENDING SKILLS

Attending skills are presented in a number of ways by several authors (Brammer, 1988; Burley-Allen, 1982; Capuzzi & Gross, 2001; Carkhuff & Anthony, 1979; Egan, 1998; Hackney & Cormier, 1988; Ivey & Ivey, 1999; King, 2001; Lauver & Harvey, 1997; Long, 1996; Martin, 1983; Sommers-Flanagan & Sommers-Flanagan, 1993; Verderber & Verderber, 1989). The most widely accepted is, perhaps, Egan's (1998) summary of the attending skills captured by the acronym SOLER.

SOLER

This acronym provides a basic course in preparing to listen to a client. It focuses on the use of the body to indicate interest in what the client is saying.

Attending skills are largely nonverbal clues that can be read by clients and that indicate to them the therapist's interest and concern. SOLER is explained as follows:

S This stands for sitting in such a way that the therapist and client are Square, face-to-face.

O This indicates a posture that is Open. Practically, it means not crossing the arms tightly across the chest or crossing the legs so that they form a wall (a barrier) between the therapist and the client.

L Lean forward slightly, as do others who are deep in conversation and genuinely are interested in what is being said. In a research study conducted many years ago, Genther and Moughan (1977) found that clients evaluated therapists who leaned forward as more attentive than therapists who sat upright.

E While Eye Contact carries different meanings for different cultures, it is reasonably safe to assume that at least some eye contact is expected for intimate conversations throughout a variety of cultures.

R Use the body for personal contact and expression. A therapist is not a statue. Clients can read a Relaxed presence as a sign of competence.

V^3B

In another presentation of attending skills, Ivey and Ivey (1999) present four characteristics of successful attending that extend SOLER into verbal behaviors as well as nonverbal attending. The acronym of V^3B is used to capture the concepts of visual eye contact, vocal quality, verbal tracking, and body language:

Visual Eye Contact: Ivey and Ivey (1999) pointedly recommend that "if you are going to talk to people, look at them" (p. 28). They are respectful of the cultural cautions concerning eye contact but still view eye contact as an essential part of attending behavior.

Vocal Quality: This is meant to draw our attention to the notion that "how" we say "what" we say carries importance as well. Tone, inflection, and pace all have the power to influence clients as we are talking to them.

Verbal Tracking: The client has a story to tell. Don't change the subject. Stick with what the client is saying.

Body Language: This includes leaning forward, having an attentive face when listening and an expressive face when speaking, and making gestures that invite open communication.

Ivey and Ivey (1999) indicate that these behaviors have a common goal. The purpose is to reduce therapist talk and provide the client with an opportunity to tell his or her story openly and with as much detail as necessary. Practiced with an openness to both individual and cultural differences, these general recommendations for attending set the stage for effective listening and understanding.

Egan's (1998) recommendations plus Ivey and Ivey's (1999) contributions have substantial support among counselor educators teaching the importance and skills of attending.

Eye Contact is recognized as being essential to effective attending (Brammer, 1988; Capuzzi & Gross, 2001; Egan, 1998; Ivey & Ivey, 1999; Lauver & Harvey, 1997; Long, 1996; Martin, 1983; Sommers-Flanagan & Sommers-Flanagan, 1993).

Vocal Quality also finds substantial support (Brammer, 1988; Capuzzi & Gross, 2001; Ivey & Ivey, 1999: Lauver & Harvey, 1997; Martin, 1983).

Verbal Tracking is advised by a number of writers (Capuzzi & Gross, 2001; Hackney & Cormier, 1988; Ivey & Ivey, 1999; Lauver & Harvey, 1997).

Body Language appears to be supported universally as having an important role in establishing the recognition of attending (Brammer, 1988; Capuzzi & Gross, 2001; Egan, 1998; Ivey & Ivey, 1999; Sommers-Flanagan & Sommers-Flanagan, 1993).

Touch receives less support but is recognized by some writers as an important part of attending (Capuzzi & Gross, 2001; Egan, 1998; Welch, 1998; Welch & Gonzalez, 1999).

Distance and Space are concerns that are recognized as contributing to the psychological climate of attending (Capuzzi & Gross, 2001; Carkhuff & Anthony, 1979; King, 2001; Lauver & Harvey, 1997; Long, 1996). This has to do with how close one sits to the client and the size of the counseling room. The general recommendation here, given individual and cultural differences, is that chairs are placed face-to-face and about an arm's length, or slightly less, apart. The room should allow for some movement and space to walk a bit, if desired.

Just as there are recommendations for what to do, there are recommendations for what to avoid. Negative attending can be seen in either totally avoiding eye contact or in being "shifty-eyed." An embarrassed catching of the eye or looking away rapidly when eye contact is made can be disquieting for clients and does not help to establish trust. Turning away from or sitting at an angle to a client can convey an unwillingness to face the person head-on. Leaning back or away from the client can convey a sense that the therapist is trying to get away or back off from the client's concerns. If we fold our arms across our chest and cross our legs in front of the client, then it is possible that we will be seen as armored, or blocking. It might look as if we are trying to make a barrier between the client and ourselves. Each of these behaviors—avoiding eye contact, sitting at an angle, leaning back, and wrapping our arms and legs around ourselves—should be avoided. If you consider two different portraits of a therapist, one open and square and one wrapped up and sitting sideways, it becomes apparent which would be viewed as more interested and concerned.

These attending behaviors all are displayed in a counseling room. The physical setting contributes to an atmosphere of attending and listening. It is an environment that deserves some attention and one where both the therapist and client should feel comfortable.

THE PHYSICAL SETTING

Consider this scene: You go to a therapist who greets you from behind a desk. He rummages through a mound of papers on the desk and takes out a manila folder, asks you to sit down in front of the desk, and looks at the folder while he asks you questions and makes notes with a pen from the National Rifle Association. As you are talking, the computer buzzes in the background, and the telephone interrupts the interview twice. The therapist spills his coffee as he reaches to answer the phone.

Question: What would be your willingness to disclose important and vulnerable situations and events to this therapist?

This is obviously a caricature, but contrast it with a different portrait.

Let's just say for the sake of argument that the first therapist decides to leave human service work and go into firearms manufacturing. You decide to come back, and the agency refers you to a new therapist. As you enter the room you see that the desk has been moved so that it faces the wall. The room is neat, and there are two chairs set up in the front of the room. There is a coat rack, and on the walls hang French Impressionists' landscape paintings. The computer is turned off, and the therapist is disconnecting the phone just as you come in the room. The therapist extends her hand and says, "Hello, my name is Sally Morris. Come and have a seat." She indicates one of the two chairs in the front of the room and takes a seat across from you. Your folder is on the table next to you. She says, "I've read your folder from your last visit, but I thought it would be important for you to tell me what brought you to counseling." She leans forward slightly and extends her hand in an inviting gesture signaling you that this is your time.

Question: What would be your willingness to disclose important and vulnerable situations and events to this therapist?

These images are exaggerated and startlingly different from each other, yet they make a point. We do know which one is inviting and which is not. So do our clients. What is the physical setting we want to create?

It should be a room where you are comfortable. Within very loose guidelines, it should:

- *Be pleasant.* The room should be clean, fresh, and neat.
- *Be comfortable.* Furnish the area with comfortable, straight-backed chairs rather than deep, cushioned chairs. Chairs should be as similar as possible. Avoid a specific "therapist's chair" that is higher, has wheels, or other differences that may indicate power or authority.
- *Have minimum visual distractions.* It doesn't need to be stark, but it should not be decorated extravagantly.
- *Be reasonably quiet.* Auditory distractions can be as problematic as visual ones.
- *Be roomy.* To the extent possible, have room for clients to stand and move around some, if they need to do so.
- *Have folders, pads, and pens.* These should be available on a side table.
- *Have tissues.* These should be in plain sight and within easy reach.
- *Have clocks.* At minimum, there should be a large clock that can be seen easily by both the therapist and the client. It is better to have two clocks, so that the therapist doesn't have to look around to see the time.
- *Have a telephone.* Set it so that it doesn't ring during sessions.
- *Have no computer.* If a computer is unavoidable, it should be silent.
- *Be private.* The most important consideration is that the counseling room ensures that what is said cannot be heard beyond the confines of the room. It should not be a shared office, one with a partition between office mates, or one with openings above the door, or one with any arrangements that threaten privacy.

The purpose of this list of course, is to describe an environment in which clients can feel that their issues are considered important, that a time and a place are set aside for them to tell their stories and be understood. Clients need to be reassured that they can relate the important events of their lives without fearing that some passer-by might overhear what they are saying. They need to be able to do this in an atmosphere reasonably free of distractions. It is hard enough to talk about sensitive issues without having to compete for attention with visual and auditory interruptions. It may not be possible to achieve all these qualities in some work settings. So do the best you can to create an environment that is welcoming and encouraging.

PSYCHOLOGICAL PREREQUISITES

While attending skills mostly have to do with arranging such things as the physical setting and with observable verbal and nonverbal behaviors, there are some psychological considerations that bear examination. In SOLER, for example, the *R* representing "Relaxed" clearly has to do with the appearance of the therapist. Psychological preparation for a therapy session may well include relaxing or, as Long (1996) recommends, "centering." This means preparing to enter the room relaxed, at ease, and ready to listen to the client's narrative. Lauver and Harvey (1997) list four major skills involved in attending:

1. Setting your focus on the task of attending.
2. Using nonverbal attending and accepting responses.
3. Using verbal accepting responses.
4. Using brief, on-topic, open leads. (P. 59)

The first of these is obviously not a behavioral goal so much as it is a psychological one. It is a matter of mind. It is a matter of will. It is a matter of determination to attend conscientiously to the needs of the client.

Verderber and Verderber (1989) itemize steps in the attending process which include the following:

1. Adopt a positive listening attitude
2. Get ready to listen
3. Adjust hearing to goals of the client
4. Make the shift from speaking to listening
5. Listen without interrupting
6. Eliminate physical impediments

The first four items are clearly psychological steps. A positive listening attitude does not have as much to do with behavior as it does with a mental set toward listening with a particular goal in mind. Getting ready to listen has physical aspects to it, but it also includes relaxing, as we have seen above, and, perhaps, clearing one's mind to attend. Item 3 might refer to preparing to sublimate one's own goals to those issues of importance to the client. Item 4 is similar in this regard. It is a mental set of saying to oneself, "I am here to listen, not to talk."

Miars and Halverson (2001) recommend a set of self-attending skills for listening to clients effectively. They write: "Counselors who are aware of their own values, beliefs, and assets are much more likely to find it easier to 'be with' clients, help clients explore personal issues, and facilitate client action. Therefore, the self-attending skills are extremely important for each person who wishes to be an effective counselor" (p. 59). These skills, according to Miars and Halverson (2001), include the following:

1. *Self-Awareness*. The philosophical teaching to "know thyself" is the point of this skill. Therapists need to be reasonably aware of their beliefs, attitudes, values, fears, and biases. They need to know and be comfortable

with who they are. They need to be aware of their counseling approach and comfortable with the strategies and techniques they use.

2. *Centering and Relaxing*. "A significant level of relaxation . . . in the therapist will help clients relax as they face the stress and challenges of the counseling process itself" (p. 60). In addition, they add, "With a keener focus than is common in most human interaction, the counselor is better able to empathically understand the client's problems and concerns" (p. 60).
3. *Humor*. Miars and Halverson (2001) note that "humor can provide a means of connecting with clients, and counselors need to affirm any humor presented by their clients" (p. 60).
4. *Nonjudgmental Attitude toward Self.* Another way of saying this is that it is important for therapists to be forgiving of themselves when they make mistakes. It might mean being able to laugh at one's foibles and move on to correcting them. A story from my training days recognizes this point. A therapist is giving a demonstration with a client who says, "I worry about my looks." The therapist replies, "I had noticed that your nose is sort of large." The client took on a startled look and said, "I wasn't talking about my nose." The therapist ended the demonstration, and, when he met with the observers afterward, there were a number of comments about his serious therapeutic error. He replied, "Sometimes, I make mistakes." He had left it behind and already was moving on.
5. *Nonjudgmental Attitude toward Others*. This is the skill of suspending one's judgment, especially until the client is able to tell his or her story fully, and an empathic understanding is presented and accepted by the client. This is a matter of respect. Judgment implies that one knows better, and that is a dangerous assumption to make before one has invested some energy into understanding another's point of view.
6. *Genuineness*. This represents the struggle each of us faces as we strive to be naturally and simply who we are. Effective therapists do not play a role or seek to imitate some image of an effective therapist. They strive to know themselves and use that self to be a helpful agent for others.
7. *Concreteness*. Miars and Halverson (2001) note that the "effective use of concreteness keeps the counseling session productively focused and aims at making vague experiences, behaviors, and feelings more specific" (p. 62). Clients frequently come to therapy with vague and undifferentiated concerns. Focusing and clarifying are important goals, and the therapist's own self-awareness can serve to avoid blind alleys based on the therapist's undifferentiated needs. These psychological concerns need to be addressed before one meets with clients; they are a matter of the therapist's own self-examination and willingness to confront personal issues that might interfere with effective practice.

SUMMARY

Attending skills are a prerequisite to listening. They form the psychological and physical groundwork for being able to listen to and understand the complexities that often accompany client concerns. The mastery of attending skills serves several vital purposes in the counseling relationship.

First, attending skills reassure clients that the setting is reasonably safe and nonthreatening. Second, attending skills invite the client to participate with the therapist in an *open* dialogue in which a free exploration of issues, problems, and dilemmas can take place. Third, the attending behavior and attitude of the therapist helps build trust for the continued development of a therapeutic relationship.

This foundation represents the necessary base for listening. Grounded in the attitude of attending, engineered in the physical setting, and practiced in verbal and nonverbal presentations, the therapist is able to listen effectively and move toward an empathic relationship with the client. These early achievements promise a successful outcome for clients as they gain the skills necessary to cope with the issues, problems, or dilemmas that brought them to therapy.

REFERENCES

Brammer, L. M. (1988). *The helping relationship: Process and skills* (4th ed.). Englewood Cliffs, NJ: Prentice-Hall.

Burley-Allen, M. (1982). *Listening: The forgotten skill.* New York: Wiley.

Capuzzi, D., & Gross, D. R. (Eds.). (2001). *Introduction to the counseling profession* (3rd ed.). Boston, MA: Allyn and Bacon.

Carkhuff, R. R., & Anthony, W. A. (1979). *The skills of helping*. Amherst, MA: Human Resource Development Press.

Egan, G. (1998). *The skilled helper: A problem-management approach to helping* (6th ed.). Pacific Grove, CA: Brooks/Cole.

Gazda, G. M., Asbury, F. S., Balzer, F. J., Childers, W. C., & Walters, R. P. (1977). *Human relations development* (2nd ed.). Boston, MA: Allyn and Bacon.

Genther, R. W., & Moughan, J. (1977). Introverts' and extroverts' responses to nonverbal attending behavior. *Journal of Counseling Psychology, 24*, 144–146.

Hackney, H., & Cormier, L. S. (1988). *Counseling strategies and interventions* (3rd ed.). Englewood Cliffs, NJ: Prentice-Hall.

Ivey, A. E., & Ivey, M. B. (1999). *Intentional interviewing and counseling: Facilitating client development in a multicultural society* (4th ed.). Pacific Grove, CA: Brooks/Cole.

King, A. (2001). *Demystifying the counseling process: A self-help handbook for counselors.* Boston, MA: Allyn and Bacon.

Lauver, P., & Harvey, D. R. (1997). *The practical counselor: Elements of effective helping*. Pacific Grove, CA: Brooks/Cole.

Long, V. O. (1996). *Communication skills in helping relationships: A framework for facilitating personal growth.* Pacific Grove, CA: Brooks/Cole.

Martin, D. G. (1983). *Counseling and therapy skills*. Prospect Heights, IL: Waveland Press.

McKay, M., Davis, M., & Fanning, P. (1983). *Messages: The communication book*. Oakland, CA: New Harbinger.

Miars, R. D., & Halverson, S. E. (2001). The helping relationship. In D. Capuzzi & D. R. Gross (Eds.), *Introduction to the counseling profession* (3rd ed., pp. 50–68). Boston, MA: Allyn and Bacon.

Sommers-Flanagan, J., & Sommers-Flanagan, R. (1993). *Foundations of therapeutic interviewing*. Boston, MA: Allyn and Bacon.

Verderber, R. F., & Verderber, K. S. (1989). *Inter-act: Using interpersonal communication skills* (5th ed.). Belmont, CA: Wadsworth.

Welch, I. D. (1998). *The path of psychotherapy: Matters of the heart*. Pacific Grove, CA: Brooks/Cole.

Welch, I. D., & Gonzalez, D. M. (1999). *The process of counseling and psychotherapy: Matters of skill*. Pacific Grove, CA: Brooks/Cole.

Chapter 3

Therapeutic Listening

Listening means, literally, attending to sound. We might listen to music on the radio as we drive or from a CD as we cook dinner. In both of these examples we listen and attend to the sound, but it is simultaneously true that we are not considering seriously the meaning of the music. There is a second meaning of listening, which is hearing "something with thoughtful attention" (*Webster's Ninth New Collegiate Dictionary*, 1983). It seems clear from these definitions that when we listen, sometimes we merely hear. At other times we not only hear, but also consider, ponder, and think about what we have heard.

A number of authors have sought to describe this phenomenon in counseling (Capuzzi & Gross, 2001; Egan, 1998; Welch & Gonzalez, 1999). They have used such terms as "active listening" to define this thoughtful listening and to separate it from "passive listening," where listening means only attending to the sound (i.e., words) and not the meaning. Welch and Gonzalez (1999) have laid out a four-part listening model that "teaches how to identify content and discern meaning" (p. 130). This chapter develops and extends that model.

Listening is guided by our purposes. If our purposes are vague and undifferentiated, then listening will be diffuse and unfocused. At a party we may drift from conversation to conversation, group to group, person to person, and, in all of the talk, not give thoughtful consideration to anything anyone says. We may listen to their words and reply to their superficial meanings with superficial replies of our own. We may sit in a classroom as the lecture drones on, and our thoughts may take us to the grocery store, to the test in the next class, or to the party on Friday.

If our purposes are clear and distinct, then our listening will be sharp and intense. Purposes, of course, can be for good or ill. The listening skills of confidence tricksters are no less refined than those of a psychotherapist. What separates them is not so much their skill as their purpose. The purpose of this chapter is to define, explore, and discuss "therapeutic listening."

Therapeutic listening is an example of the second meaning of listening, in which the listener gives "thoughtful attention" to what is being said. What, then, is the purpose of therapeutic listening?

PURPOSE

There are many theories of counseling. These theories differ widely from one another in their specifics, and it is not the intention of this book to focus on the differences among theories. Instead, let's consider what commonalities these theories share in their approaches to the counseling process. Here is a global definition of the purpose of psychotherapy that many, if not all, theories share: to enter into a particular kind of relationship in which the outcome is expected to be the relief, resolution, and/or solution to issues, problems, and/or dilemmas for clients. The nature of that relationship may be characterized, at least with major agreement among theories, by empathic understanding, a commitment to the standards of therapeutic practice, and a respect for the client's struggle.

Empathic Understanding

There is no uniform prescription for the relief of human suffering. Common problems, obviously, often have common sources and common strategies for resolution. Yet, one does not have to practice as a therapist for long before a client appears and gives lie to what was thought to be a commonly understood life problem. Human beings are easily the most complex psychological creatures on this planet, and we can find more ways to foul up our lives than reasonably can be counted. *The Diagnostic and Statistical Manual of Psychiatric Disorders* (APA, 1994) is growing ever thicker as disorder after disorder is added in an effort to describe and catalog psychological dysfunction.

As psychotherapists, we are confronted with a challenge that remains constant across time, theories, and persons. We must understand each client individually, uniquely, and separately. No psychotherapy proceeds in the absence of a reasonable understanding of what the issue, problem, or dilemma is for the particular client. An empathic understanding is multilayered.

Content. Content is something like the definition of a noun. It represents the names, dates, places, and things of the client's narrative. Content reveals the events, situations, and context of what brought the client to therapy. It is the surface of the client's motivation for coming to therapy. It is the most easily understood aspect of a client's narrative.

Emphasis. Emphasis represents the importance a client gives to different topics within his or her story. Some issues and problems have greater weight and intensity than others, and clients will reveal these relative weights even when they themselves sometimes don't recognize that one issue is more important to them than another.

Value. Value represents the emotionality of the content. Clients come to therapy knowing that they are troubled. They may not be clear at all about what the trouble is or what the source of the trouble is. They may be guarded or defensive, and an empathic understanding may help clarify for clients those elements in their stories that they have expressed with greater emotion.

Congruence. It may seem strange, yet it is frequently true that clients may be so out of touch with their own feelings that they are unaware of when they describe their lives with and without emotion. Therapeutic listening has as one of its purposes the recognition and acknowledgment of emotional expression. The clue to congruence is often nonverbal expression. Words may seek to communicate one meaning while the body may disavow what is being said and/or seek to communicate another message. The recognition of congruence is the recognition of the correspondence between verbal and nonverbal messages.

It is the sum of content, emphasis, value, and congruence that contribute to an empathic understanding of clients. Each adds to the message something that, if missing, would distort or confuse the listener. The purpose of therapeutic listening is to attend to and recognize each as it appears in the client's story.

Standards of Practice

Every psychotherapist commits him-or herself to both the principles and standards of professional practice. The form this takes is often a commitment to the ethics of one of the disciplines in which psychotherapy is practiced, such as psychology, counseling, or social work. There is more to it than that, however. It also encompasses an attitude that the therapist will present him- or herself without guile or subterfuge. The client can assume reliably that the therapist's purposes are clear, above board, and trustworthy. In the colloquial, "what you see is what you get." Psychotherapy is designed to offer a relationship in which the psychotherapist strives to be open, trustworthy, forthright, and without airs. In psychotherapy, the therapist is striving to be what is missing in the client's life: a reliable source of genuine feedback about how the client presents him-or herself. To use a metaphor, psychotherapists are striving to be the one for whom Diogenes is searching—an honest person.

Respect for the Client

Clients are people in turmoil. Their struggles can range from a roommate who is messy to one who committed suicide. Clients may be in a situation where they can't seem to get a date or in a marriage of twenty years that is breaking up. Whatever their situation, they do not need to be judged, criticized, or discounted. Psychotherapy is a process in which one can reasonably expect that issues and problems will be given thoughtful, respectful consideration. Respect is conveyed by an attitude that shows an understanding that the issues or problems are real for the client and that, for whatever reason, their solution or resolution currently lies outside the options the client sees as available. In a climate of respect, options can be explored, evaluated, selected, and exercised.

STRATEGY

The purpose of therapeutic listening is to enter into a particular kind of relationship with clients. It is a relationship characterized by empathy, standards of practice, and respect. These are the goals. What is the plan by which a psychotherapist will pursue these goals? Again, theories differ with respect to how the therapeutic process is described. The plan or model offered below represents an attempt to describe a common understanding of the therapeutic process. It may differ descriptively from others', but the themes described seem congruent with the processes described in many therapeutic models. Therapy begins with the unknown and proceeds, sometimes awkwardly and sometimes with startling precision, to develop strategies to cope with the identified issues, problems, or dilemmas the client brings to therapy. The model below describes this process as (1) exploration, (2) understanding, and (3) action.

Exploration

When clients come to therapy they come for two reasons. First, they come because they are in psychological distress. Second, they come because they have exhausted their knowledge, networks, and the relief those sources have provided for them. Typically, clients know they are in distress and they know they don't know what to do about it. Surprisingly and frequently, what they don't know is the problem! Exploration is the stage in psychotherapy in which the client and the therapist seek to uncover or discover what the problem actually is.

> Carl is a 55-year-old management executive. He is married with three children. The first two are now adult males, and the third, a female, is in her midteens. His wife works outside the home. Carl recently was promoted and he has spent an increasing amount of time at work. He reports feeling depressed and he has been taking antidepressant medications prescribed by his family physician. He has been spending more time at his spa exercising because, he reports, his physician recommended that exercise could also help with depression. He has been depressed for more than six months and he is afraid that his job is going to suffer unless he can get over his depression. He says that he has been able to work in spite of his depression and that, so far, he thinks that his work has not been affected. He points to his recent promotion as proof that his job hasn't been hurt.

Exploration is the stage of therapy designed to answer the question, "What is the problem?" What is the problem with Carl? He would insist that the problem is that he is depressed. Yet, people aren't depressed without a reason. In fact, as we review Carl's story, we can see that it isn't at all clear why he is depressed. It is clear that he is receiving treatment for his depressed feelings. He is taking antidepressants and he is exercising. It is also clear, so far at least, that he isn't feeling relief from either of these treatments. As we will discuss later, the content of Carl's narrative leaves out many important details. Exploration will invite him not only to fill in those details, but also to look at the values and meanings that accompany his story. Part of Carl's lack of effectiveness in dealing with his struggle is that his efforts may well be directed in the wrong place. Carl considers his depression to be the problem, but it might be that it is a symptom. His efforts to cope with his depression (drugs and exercise) aren't providing any relief because he isn't coping with the actual problem at all.

While there isn't any clear indication of what Carl's problem is, there are some clues in his narrative that could begin to guide an exploration. Consider what is missing. Carl spends time talking about his depression not affecting his work and no time talking about the effect on his family. In fact, what he reports is how much he is away from his family (at work and at the club), but he offers no information about the time he spends with his family. There is no indication of how the two older children are doing or where they are living. He says nothing about the third child other than her age and barely mentions his wife at all except to say she also works outside the home. An initial reading of this narrative would suggest that exploration might take some time.

The purpose of exploration is to avoid the mistake that Carl's family physician made in treating the symptoms without any understanding of the source of Carl's depression. While we don't have any better idea at this point what the source of his depression is, an exploration of what is missing from his narrative will begin the process of movement toward an effective solution or resolution. As discussed above, this will involve an exploration of content, emphasis, value, and congruence.

In Carl's story, we are faced with a number of unknowns. Clearly, without a better understanding of the facts of Carl's life, the plan for therapy remains open. Exploration, as the word itself suggests, means examining the unknown. Most therapy begins here and moves toward greater clarity and understanding.

Understanding

Exploration is meant to answer the question, "What is the problem?" The next stage of therapy is meant to answer yet another question. Once both the client and the therapist know what the problem is (or, what the problems are), then another question presents itself: "Why is it a problem?" Let's return to Carl for a moment. Let us suppose that exploration revealed the following:

> The two older children have left college and live at home. They both work but live at home. Carl has tried to talk to his wife about this but he reports

that she is perfectly happy with the situation. He doesn't want to confront the boys and stays at work and goes to the club so he won't have to deal with the situation at home.

So the problem begins to unfold. Carl is unhappy because his two older boys have returned to the nest and he isn't getting support from his wife about his concerns. Why is this a problem? On the one hand, it is understandable. Parents expect kids to move out and find lives of their own. On the other hand, many families have children come home from college and move back into the house for a time until they can afford to move out on their own. And, many of those families have no trouble with it and even enjoy having their children back in the house. So why is it a problem for Carl?

This phase of therapy is directed at answering that question to Carl's satisfaction. He is feeling depressed because he has two adult sons living at home and doesn't feel supported by his wife in wanting the sons to move out on their own. The therapy now begins another form of exploration in which the client has to struggle with understanding why the problem he is facing is such a problem for him when it may not be for others. We don't know, of course, what the answer will be for Carl. It is important to recognize that this *why* question is raised not to find an explanation for his behavior or a motivation but to provide a personal understanding of the reason the issue he is facing is a problem for him. Hopefully, it will lead to a highly individual and personal reason that the client can accept and with which he can live. Often, such reasons have to do with a client's value system. That is, there is a conflict between some situation or event in the client's life and some value he or she holds. Let's speculate about Carl's situation addressing issues that could be explored in the therapy. Carl might believe that

—Life is hard, and if people are going to survive, then they have to learn to live on their own

—Children should be out of the home by age 18

—His children lack confidence and are afraid to move out on their own

—If he lived only with his wife, then their relationship would improve and they could have a more meaningful life together

Obviously, any of these, or even others, could be the underlying reason for Carl's discontent. Each could be the source of his depression and each has a different resolution. The importance of answering the *why* question is that it provides the foundation for the next phase of therapy. Without a clear understanding of what the problem is, it is impossible to understand why it affects the client as it does. And, without a clear understanding of why it is a problem, it is exceedingly difficult to develop an effective plan of action.

Action

The action phase of therapy answers a third question: "What do I do about it?" It might be worthwhile to note that it is not at all unusual for psychotherapy to terminate after the second phase of therapy. Once the problem has been identified and an understanding of why it is a problem is clear, clients often are able to cope effectively on their own without the need for supportive therapy. People aren't stupid and once they know genuinely what is wrong and why, they are able to use their existing resources to cope effectively. Often a clearly defined problem and an understanding of it allows options, solutions, and resolutions to present themselves.

It is equally true that clients often still need help in identifying solutions to clearly identify and understand issues and problems. When the client still needs to be in therapy after the exploration and understanding phases, then the action phase can permit an even more collaborative relationship in which the client and therapist jointly seek to develop solutions, resolutions, and relief from the issues and/or problems facing the client. Strategies of problem solving are important in this phase of therapy, as goals and expected outcomes are defined clearly. There is a key difference between this phase and the first two phases. In the first two phases, concretely, the outcomes are unknown. Both of these phases require open-ended exploration. In this phase, the problem is known, and strategies can be developed to achieve specific outcomes.

TECHNIQUES

The techniques of therapeutic listening are explored in greater detail in chapters 5, 6, 7, 8, and 9. Briefly, the techniques of listening for content, emphasis, value, and congruence provide the therapist with the tools necessary for exploring and understanding clients' stories.

Content can be understood by using the W^5H principle. This is a matter of listening for Who, What, When, Where, Why, and How. As one listens to a client's narrative, the characters, situations, and events of the story can be given coherence and order.

Emphasis is understood through the I/F principle. Clients emphasize important issues and themes through Intensity and Frequency. A topic that is underscored by tone or volume invites deeper exploration. Similarly, a topic that is repeated time and again also invites the therapeutic listener to explore.

Value is revealed through the DAMS principle. The emotionality, depth of meaning, and closeness to self are all ways of expressing the value or power the content has for the client. Clients express their more powerful issues and problems Dramatically. They express topics that have greater effects in their lives with greater Affect. They express topics that are difficult to explain to themselves and others through Metaphor, and Symbol. Drama, Affect, Metaphor, and Symbol represent the language of emotion and reveal those issues of greatest sensitivity for clients.

Congruence describes the correspondence between verbal and nonverbal messages. When the verbal message and the nonverbal message are congruent, this signals that the message is more likely to represent the genuine attitudes, beliefs, and values of the client. When the verbal and nonverbal messages are discordant, this invites the therapist to further exploration.

SUMMARY

Therapeutic listening has as its purpose the goal of entering into a particular kind of relationship with clients. It is a relationship in which the therapist seeks to understand the client not only at the surface content level, but also at the meaningful level of emotions and meanings. It is a relationship that is characterized by empathy, standards of care, and respect.

Therapeutic listening leads to an unfolding relationship in which different questions are answered as the therapy progresses. The first phase of therapy is characterized by exploration, when the problem is identified and clarified. The second phase of therapy is concerned with understanding why the issues or problems are troublesome for the clients. The final stage of therapy is the action phase, in which the client seeks to resolve the problem that has been identified, clarified, and understood.

Specific techniques that aid in exploration and understanding of content, emphasis, value, and congruence can bring order and structure to the sometimes vague and disjointed narrative clients present in therapy. In subsequent chapters, techniques for understanding content are presented, techniques for listening for emphasis are discussed, techniques for identifying value are examined, and the importance of congruence through nonverbal observation is presented.

REFERENCES

American Psychiatric Association (APA). (1994). *The diagnostic and statistical manual of psychiatric disorders* (4th ed.). Washington, DC: Author.

Capuzzi, D., & Gross, D. R. (Eds.). (2001). *Introduction to the counseling profession* (3rd ed.). Boston, MA: Allyn and Bacon.

Egan, G. (1998). *The skilled helper: A problem-management approach to helping* (6th ed.). Pacific Grove, CA: Brooks/Cole.

Webster's ninth new collegiate dictionary. (1983). Springfield, MA: Merriam-Webster.

Welch, I. D., & Gonzalez, D. M. (1999). *The process of counseling and psychotherapy: Matters of skill.* Pacific Grove, CA: Brooks/Cole.

Chapter 4

Content Listening and the W^5H Principle

Narratives have characters, plots, settings, history, and motivation. As clients tell their stories, therapists listen for the content to guide the therapy. The W^5H principle teaches us to listen for particular content in a client's narrative. This is the guideline taught in journalism in which the opening sentences of any news story should inform the reader of the who, what, when, where, why, and how of the story. It should be noted here that content alone is a poor guide for therapy. It is relatively important to know the details of a client's experience, but it is more essential to understand the meanings, emotions, or feelings clients give to their experiences. If we use the analogy of a play, then the script is the content. Yet the drama of theater lies in the subtleties of meaning, the nuance of a character, and the emotions it touches and invites from the audience. This chapter focuses on recognizing and understanding content. Listening for content is the most straightforward and uncomplicated form of listening.

CLIENT NARRATIVE

Below is a client narrative. As you read through this story take note of the W^5H embedded in the narrative. Take note of what is missing as well. As clients share their issues, problems, and dilemmas, they may not provide a lucid, clear, and linear description of the situations, people, and events of their lives. If we listen purposefully, then we can bring some order and clarity to understanding not only for ourselves, but also for clients. As we become aware of missing information, either we can ask for it directly or we can encourage the client to tell more of his or her story, thereby allowing other details to come out in their own time and in the client's own way. Take a moment now and read the client story. Let the W^5H principle guide your reading.

Who (The characters—protagonist, antagonists)

What (What is happening? The plot, themes)

When (History? Present? Anticipated?)

Where (The setting—home, work, other)

Why (The client's explanation, motivation)

How (The circumstances, situations, and events of the story/behavior)

Devon is an African American woman in her early sixties. She tells the following story:

> My husband passed last year. We had been married for 43 years. It was so sudden. Cancer . . . took him. He . . . it . . . he went in about six months and . . . I don't have to worry about money. That's not a problem. But . . . it's been a year, and I still . . . I'm lost without him. James did everything for me, and I . . . don't know how . . . I'm learning how to pay bills and . . . I didn't even know how to put gas in my car. I didn't know where the gas cap was . . . I pulled into a gas station and got out and just started to cry . . . when I . . . didn't know where the gas cap was. People tell me I am strong . . . I seem to be doing so . . . doing. I'm doing is about all. But, they don't know. I hate having to put gas in the car. I hate paying the bills. I miss James doing for me! And, more than that, he was the one who liked people. Invited them over. Talked to them. He was the social one. I'm more critical. He was my buffer. I have to do it all now. And, I used to love to go to movies and shows but now I . . . I come home alone and there is no James to talk about the show to. We used to have coffee . . . after the show . . . and I would criticize and he would listen and put up with me . . . and now . . . it's not the same if I go with other women . . . other widows! I hate that word! The black widow! Like some little spider! Some ugly . . . I don't know what.

As you answer the questions below remember to consider also what is missing. What detail or clarification would you need to answer one of the five Ws or the H? This is a fairly straightforward statement. The client is articulate and clear, and yet there are moments when we might want to know more. Answering the W^{5}H questions provides good guidelines for not only what is understandable, but also what needs further clarification. Answer the following questions:

Who are the characters in the narrative? ______

What is the plot/theme of the narrative? ______

When does the narrative take place? ______

Where does the narrative take place? ______

Why does the client say she feels this way (her explanation)? ______

How did the client get to where she is in her development? ______

What do we know about Devon from her narrative alone (with only the addition of her name, ethnicity, and age)? If we answer each question in turn we would get at least the following information.

Who

There are five characters in this story. Each is significant to Devon in ways that will need to be explored later in the therapy, but for the present let's be content with simply identifying them. First, there is Devon, an African American woman in her sixties. Second, there is her deceased husband, James, who died of cancer. Third, there is an anonymous group of "people" who offer advice. Fourth, there are "other women" with whom she sometimes attends social events. Finally, there is the character of the "black widow" spider.

Each of the characters in the narrative raises questions for consideration. For example, there are questions of diversity that need to be considered. What do her ethnicity, gender, and age contribute to her presently felt sense of distress? We don't know James' ethnicity and, in fact, know little about James other than that he died and, at least in Devon's description of him, seemed to be a protective and very supportive husband. The "people" in Devon's narrative are unnamed, and it might be important to know if she means strangers, friends, or family. Without reading in too much, the phrasing, distant and objective, may imply some anger or derision that needs to be followed up. The "other women . . . other widows!" are also unnamed. Does this mean that she has no female friend(s) with whom she is close and that her relationships are superficial, leaving her with no network of friends with whom to talk and ease her burdens? Finally, there is the character of the "black widow." This is both a play on words (black = African American and widow = a surviving spouse) and a powerful symbol. The importance of symbols is explored later in this book. For now, it is sufficient to recognize its insulting and demeaning use here ("ugly").

It certainly requires time to search for the meanings each of these characters has in Devon's narrative. Each character contributes to the meanings Devon holds about her experience and each has a separate story to tell. As the therapy unfolds, each character may require time to reveal its contribution to Devon's distress. What is missing? There is no mention of relatives, especially children (we would know this from the intake information but it is missing from the narrative). There is no mention of a minister. Spirituality in the lives of clients is now receiving new attention in the field of counseling and psychotherapy. It would be worthwhile to explore whether this omission in Devon's narrative is significant.

What

The most obvious theme in Devon's narrative is grief. She is mourning the passing of the most significant person in her life. James was the hub in her wheel of life. James' death has altered her experience of life. A major part of this seems to be her sense of being unfulfilled when doing alone what she and James once shared—going out to the theater or movies and then talking about it over coffee afterward. She comes home now to an empty house.

There are subthemes that might hold deeper meanings as the therapy unfolds. The major subtheme is that her husband took such care of her that she had to do little in the way of social planning, finance concerns, automobile maintenance, and the like. She says clearly, "I miss James doing for me!" What meaning does this have for her? Is it merely inconvenience or, perhaps, a deeper, more substantive recognition about her life? Another metaphor that certainly bears looking into is the story of putting gas in the car. Both metaphors—"empty house" and "putting gas in the car"—are descriptive ways of portraying human experience and can be the sources of profound understandings for the often-submerged meanings people give their lives. Metaphors will be discussed in greater detail in chapter 6.

When

The time of Devon's grief is the present. As she reflects on her life, she brings in the past, but there is not much discussion of past events. Devon's psychological distress is felt in the present. Her husband's death is the precipitating event for her distress and it is what brought her to therapy. Three mentions of time in the narrative may need some discussion: "he went in about six months," "my husband passed last year," and "we had been married for 43 years." So we know that her husband died only a year ago and that he died quickly after many years of marriage. What is significant about these times is that continuing grief after one year following a long relationship is not unexpected or complicated (complicated in the sense that it is abnormal). This raises the question of what brought Devon to therapy? What pressures is she facing in her life that might be contributing to some idea that her grief is unusual or wrong? It might signal that there are other concerns in her life, in addition to her normal grief, that need to be brought into the therapy.

What is recognizably missing is any mention of the future. This seems an important consideration for the course of therapy as Devon struggles to find a way to live in the world without her husband.

Where

The settings revealed in Devon's story are expected, with the exception of two that are missing and the general lack of a rich involvement in the venues of life. Her story reveals a gas station, the movies, and home. There is no mention of a place of worship or support. These noteworthy settings can play important roles in the lives of people. The fact that Devon doesn't talk about either might suggest that she has little in her life to provide meaning now that her husband is gone. The overall picture of the settings of Devon's life reveals a general lack of involvement. Is this merely an oversight as she describes her feelings of distress or is it an accurate picture of her life? The answer to this question will contribute to the focus and direction of therapy.

Why

Devon's personal explanation of her distress is the loss of her husband. She says, "I'm lost without him." She is grieving the death of her husband. He died a year before, and she is experiencing the loneliness and lack of satisfaction that has come intruding into her previously contented and secure life. She is being forced to take care of herself, whereas previously "James did everything for" her. She now has to deal directly with life's events, while, prior to James' death, he acted as a "buffer" for her, and she was relieved of dealing directly with the daily trials of life. She is feeling not only the pain of James' death, but also the demands of managing her own affairs. While she is aware of the pain of her grief and of the aggravation of her daily transactions, she may not be aware of other meanings contributing to her felt distress. She "hates" doing the daily, routine obligations required of each of us. This might be a direction the therapy could take as Devon struggles to understand her meanings and feelings surrounding the widening impact of her husband's death in her life.

How

As Devon tells her story, it becomes increasingly clear that James might be described as caring and attentive or as overprotective, perhaps even controlling. He took care of everything. We know little, if anything really, about James. We don't know, for example, whether he viewed his wife as incompetent, weak, or unhelpful or he simply believed that a man's role was to take care of things. Whatever the case, what we do know is that, as Devon's married life unfolded, she became less and less in charge of dealing with the daily chores of life. "James did everything for me." Now she not only is faced with grief, but also is coping with her anger ("I hate having to put gas in the car"; "I hate paying the bills"). She finds herself with inadequate mechanical skills, social skills, and emotional skills to cope with her newly demanding life.

As the therapy proceeds, her recognition that her grief is normal may permit her to focus on other aspects of her life. The continuing dissatisfaction she is experiencing in life can be examined as she comes to terms with the need to be in the world as an autonomous, interdependent person who no longer is so wholly dependent on another to take care of her. Whatever direction the therapy takes, it seems clear that the process of at least one aspect of her grief will need to be explored, and that is James' taking care of everything, which left Devon ill-prepared to face life on her own.

SUMMARY

Listening for content is the most basic and clear-cut listening skill. Yet, as we have seen above, it is still possible to glean rich, meaningful, and pointed suggestions for the therapy from content alone. As other chapters explore the deeper meanings of affect and attribution, the stories clients tell reveal themselves as trustworthy paths to understanding and ultimate problem solving with clients. No single domain—content, affect, or nonverbal behavior—alone can lay claim to providing the whole meaning of a client's experience. The individual listening skills associated with content, nonverbals, and affect can be mastered. Each of these skills contributes to an understanding of the expressed experience clients bring to therapy and, when combined, they act to reveal the nuanced, multifaceted, and multilayered meanings clients assign to cope with the issues, problems, and dilemmas of their lives.

REFERENCES

Brownell, J. (2001). *Listening: Attitudes, principles, and skills.* Boston, MA: Allyn and Bacon.

Fernald, P. S. (2000). Teaching students to listen empathically. In David E. Johnson and Mark E. Ware (Eds.), *Handbook of demonstrations and activities in the teaching of psychology, Vol. 3. Personality, abnormal, clinical-counseling, and social* (2nd ed.). Mahwah, NJ: Lawrence Erlbaum.

Helgesen, M., & Brown, S. (1994). *Active listening: Building skills for understanding.* London: Cambridge University Press.

Kratz, D. M., & Katz, A. R. (1995). *Effective listening skills.* Columbus, OH: McGraw-Hill.

McDonald, P. A., & Haney, M. (1988). *Counseling the older adult: A training manual in clinical gerontology* (2nd ed.). Lexington, MA: Lexington Books.

Sproston, C., & Sutcliff, G. E. (1998). *20 training workshops for listening skills.* Amherst, MA: HRD Press.

Chapter 5

Listening for Emphasis and the I/F Principle

Clients talk. Sometimes they ramble. They might look pleadingly at the therapist for guidance. Sometimes they present themselves with utter confusion. They might struggle with genuine befuddlement over how and what to bring into therapy.

Sarah was a wife and mother in her midthirties when she came to therapy. She was verbal and articulate as she sat tensely in her seat. After completing some paperwork, the therapist began the exploration of what brought her to counseling.

Therapist: Sarah, how can I be of help?

Client: I . . . well, I don't know. Well, I mean, I know but . . . I just don't know where to start.

Th: Uh-huh. A number of things, perhaps.

Cl: Yes. I'm happy, I mean, you know, I have a good husband and kids and, really, everything is just the way it's supposed to be. Do you know what I mean?

Th: It's like the American Dream—married with children.

Cl: Yes, and I'm happy except, I don't know, I'm discontent or unsettled or something. My husband has a good job and we have enough money. We aren't rich, but we have enough. He spends a lot of time at work, but we still have quality time.

Th: Uh-huh.

Cl: And, I get along with his parents—our in-laws. The kids, Michael and Aaron, are doing well in school and have friends. My husband has his friends, too. He gets along well with my parents, too. Sometimes I call my husband at work just to say "hello," and he likes that. So all our relationships seem to be going good. My husband plays softball, and the family likes to go to the games, and so that takes some time, too. I have friends too, but I like being with my family. My husband likes family things but he is a little more involved with things outside the family than I am. Is this what I'm supposed to be talking about?

Th: Talk some more about your relationship with your husband.

Let's stop here and ponder a question: Why did the therapist ask Sarah to talk more about her husband? Where did that response come from? Isn't the therapist leading the client now? Hasn't the therapist selected the topic and, perhaps for theoretical reasons or for some other reason, chosen to focus on her relationship with her husband? That might not be what the client wants to talk about at all, and hasn't the therapist taken over the direction of the session?

These are, of course, important questions. They deserve answers because it is decidedly the case that therapists do not want to set the direction, take over the session, arbitrarily pick a topic, or simply explore all of the material a client brings into therapy. If we were to ask the therapist what guided the request to talk more about her husband, he or she might say, "The client indicated that she needed to talk more about her husband."

THE PRINCIPLE OF FREQUENCY

We aren't talking magic or giftedness or mind reading. We are talking about a skill. What the therapist would mean by his or her explanation is that he or she was following one of the principles of purposeful listening. The particular principle involved here is labeled "Frequency." If we examine the narrative above, then we discover that, while relationships with children, in-laws, parents, and friends are all mentioned, the client's relationship with her husband is brought up frequently. She says:

- I have a good husband
- My husband has a good job
- He spends a lot of time at work
- My husband has his friends, too
- He gets along well with my parents
- I call my husband at work
- My husband plays softball
- My husband likes family things but he is a little more involved . . . outside

While the phrases themselves don't reveal anything startling, the frequency of them may show that this is an area of concern and requires more exploration. The principle of Frequency reminds us as therapists that the issues that trouble us come up frequently. Even when we want to hold back, important issues have a way of popping up when we talk for a while. They reoccur. Listening with purpose, then, means paying attention to those frequently reoccurring issues and, as therapy evolves, themes as they emerge during the therapeutic relationship. In this session a tentative theme might be that the client is feeling some neglect in her relationship. Embedded in her discussion of her relationship with her husband are hints that he might not be spending enough time with her to meet her needs:

- He spends a lot of time at work
- My husband has his friends, too
- I call my husband at work
- He is a little more involved . . . outside

These might all be clues to a felt sense that she is feeling neglected by her husband. It is important, as well, to take note of what is not being said by the client. While she mentions the names of her children, she does not talk about her husband by name. As we listen for frequency, we also listen for omissions. What could such an omission mean? This also presents itself as worthy of exploration.

In the short time the client has been talking, we have taken note of three important things: the frequency of her husband in her narrative, the possibility of feeling neglected, and a puzzling omission. It is far too early, of course, to conclude with any certainty that the primary issues are with her husband and that the theme is a feeling of neglect. These are hypotheses, however, that invite exploration. The recognition of these issues, themes, and omissions requires that we listen further. It requires that we listen with purpose. It is not merely a matter of passively sitting back and permitting the client to talk without interruption. It is a matter of being attuned to the possibility that an issue may be repeated and being alert for that, noting when it happens, and responding when it is appropriate.

Just as with any principle, the principle of Frequency can get complicated as major and minor issues and subthemes present themselves. Even when these emerge, the skills of attending to, noting, and organizing based upon frequency gives structure and a degree of order to what initially may sound chaotic and disorganized. Another level of complication of frequency is that issues and themes may be subtle. The reoccurring issues and themes may not be as apparent as they are in the example above and can occur throughout a session rather than within a paragraph. Further, the reoccurring issues and themes may be repeated across several sessions, rather than within one session. This highlights the importance of taking progress notes and recording issues and themes noted in a session so that, as we review our notes, we can identify those patterns. It highlights the importance of audio/video recording, especially in training, so that the skill of listening for frequency can be honed.

Listening for frequency is helpful in identifying important meanings in the client's narrative. Frequency alone, however, doesn't lead us always to the identification of important issues and themes for clients.

Here is a classic: Doug sits sullenly in his chair and glares at the therapist.

> Th: How can I be of help?
>
> Cl: I guess we're supposed to talk about me, and I know I have a lot of problems. I could talk about just being angry all the time or not being appreciated. My wife is trying to help. I guess we could talk about my damned job and my arrogant, obnoxious boss [he raises his voice] who is just riding me all the time. I don't know, maybe just talk about life in general not being very satisfying for me.
>
> Th: Let's spend some time talking about your job and the boss.

THE PRINCIPLE OF INTENSITY

Uh-oh! Here we go again. The directive therapist has selected what he or she thinks is important from the laundry list the client has brought in. It is obvious that the client has said that issues in his life include his anger, lack of appreciation, his wife, his job, his boss, and "life in general." He has brought in seven issues, and the principle of Frequency does not give us a clue about which of them is more important because the client hasn't repeated any one of them. So what led the therapist to select the issues of job and boss as ones that merit further, or at least initial, exploration? Again, it isn't giftedness or even intuition. The therapist might say that the client identified the important issue and that the therapist simply invited him to explore it further. What is at work here is the principle of Intensity. The client emphasized his job and his boss by using a mild expletive and raising his voice. This quality of inflection and pitch often identify more sensitive issues in a list of concerns. Sometimes a client will lower his or her voice.

> Cl: Oh, everyone in our family gets along so well. I mean everyone. Well, mother sometimes is a little problem [he whispers]. But, really we are just the most agreeable family.

This is an example of underemphasis that brings the issue of the mother into the session. What is so secretive about the mother that it requires a hushed tone? It bears repeating again and again that this is not a matter for interpretation, but rather a matter for exploration.

Intensity reveals itself in a variety of ways. Look at this example of client talk:

Cl: Two things brought me in: my relationship with my grown children and a deep sense of dread about my life.

Which do you think you would respond to as a therapist? While the principle of Frequency can become subtle and complex, the principle of Intensity is one that we all can identify readily. In this clear example, it isn't hard to recognize that the use of words like "a deep sense of dread" are more powerful (intense) that common, everyday language. The use of emphatic, powerful words themselves is one guide for identifying important issues for clients. Sometimes, the words themselves are ordinary, but the tone or pitch will emphasize the importance it has for the client.

Cl: Everything is going okay. My *boyfriend* might be a problem.

Her emphasis of the word "boyfriend" can serve as an invitation to explore her relationship with him further.

Nonverbal behavior can intensify a message, as well. A client might roll his or her eyes as he or she talks about a relationship, and another might slam a fist down on the arm of the chair. Nonverbal language can serve to emphasize what the client is trying to express verbally.

Cl: Oh yeah, I'm angry [he grits his teeth and balls his fingers into a fist].

Whether nonverbal clues confirm or disconfirm a verbal message, they can serve to provide intensity. The intensity clue would serve as a guide to what message would be more fruitful to explore in more detail.

Intensity can help therapists make decisions about whether a client's denial of an issue or downplaying the importance of an event, for example, can be taken at face value or requires more exploration.

Look at the difference between the two clients presented below as they indicate they are ready to move on to another issue:

Cl 1: I am feeling pretty confident that I understand this. I think I can deal with it.

Cl 2: Look, I think this is a dead horse. I don't think we need to beat it anymore. I get it. I don't need to talk about it anymore. I don't think I can talk about it anymore. I just want to move on to something else and stop talking about this.

In the first example, the client seems calm and reasonably confident that he or she has the skills necessary to cope with the issue. The second client protests too much. It is the need to belabor the point that there is no further need to talk about the issue that intensifies the issue and alerts us to the need to stay with it for a while longer.

Consider this analogy: Imagine you are walking along a beach and occasionally exploring the sand with a bare toe or kicking over a piece of driftwood as you stroll along admiring the gentle breeze and sound of the waves. You are appreciating a scene of beauty rather than walking along with a metal detector that sounds a beep and gives an indication of the mass of the metal object below the surface. Appreciation of the value of recognizing intensity as a clue to underlying importance for clients can serve in much the same way as a metal detector. Intensity can identify the underlying value an issue plays in the life of a client. It signals us and invites us to spend some time with the issue to see its relevance in the life of the client.

SUMMARY

These two principles of listening—Intensity and Frequency—are valuable aids as we listen with guided attention to the stories clients have to tell. Both the frequency with which an issue is mentioned and the intensity it is given can help therapists identify, organize, and prioritize the sometimes confusing and chaotic stories clients bring to therapy. As we listen to what is said, it is important to recognize that frequency includes the concept of omission. It is sometimes important to recognize what is not said, as well as what is.

Intensity = Affirmation and Denial

Frequency = Inclusion and Omission

It is important to recognize too that we can pay attention not only to what is left out, but also to what is denied. Intensity, including both affirmation and denial, and frequency, including inclusion and omission, are supportive skills that increase our ability to understand and empathically respond to clients.

REFERENCES

Brownell, J. (2001). *Listening: Attitudes, principles, and skills*. Boston, MA: Allyn and Bacon.

Fernald, P. S. (2000). Teaching students to listen empathically. In David E. Johnson and Mark E. Ware (Eds.), *Handbook of demonstrations and activities in the teaching of psychology, Vol. 3: Personality, abnormal, clinical-counseling, and social* (2nd ed.). Mahwah, NJ: Lawrence Erlbaum.

Helgesen, M., & Brown, S. (1994). *Active listening: Building skills for understanding*. London: Cambridge University Press.

Kratz, D. M., & Katz, A. R. (1995). *Effective listening skills*. Columbus, OH: McGraw-Hill.

McDonald, P. A., & Haney, M. (1988). *Counseling the older adult: A training manual in clinical gerontology* (2nd ed.). Lexington, MA: Lexington Books.
Sproston, C., & Sutcliff, G. E. (1998). *20 training workshops for listening skills*. Amherst, MA: HRD Press.

Chapter 6

Listening for Expressive Information and the DAMS Principle

The language of emotion is not bland. It is spicy, fiery, intense, and expressive. Listen to the difference between two clients who both report that they are angry:

> Edward: Yes, I think I am a little angry.
>
> Aaron: I am fuming!

Edward is speaking the language of politeness, of manners, of control. Edward is intellectualizing and distancing. If Edward is steaming, he certainly isn't telling us with his words. While therapists would listen respectfully to Edward, it is clear that his words provide little direction or substance for the therapy. He has identified a feeling, of course, but he has identified it so mildly that it lacks conviction. It is a thin, unseasoned, and tasteless soup. Clearly, Edward's therapist will have to listen even more intently to his story to seek the topics and meanings that would bring him to therapy. There is little motivational drive in the comment, "I think I am a little angry." Having said this, it also should be understood that neither Edward nor his statement are being devalued in this analysis. Edward's content and style are respected. What is being discussed here are verbal clues to the drives and goals of clients' lives that bring them to psychotherapy and that open the door of understanding for the listener. What clients say is what they say. The stories they tell are the stories they tell. The language they use is the language they use. Counseling/psychotherapy is not an endeavor aimed at correcting the ways in which clients struggle to understand themselves and to make themselves understandable to others. It is a process in which a professional listener strives to understand and clarify the life stories clients bring to therapy. Edward's story (or, in this case, short sentence) initially offers little to the listener. It does not offer a clear direction. It doesn't invite inquiry and it provides no confidence that this is what brought him into the therapeutic relationship.

Aaron, on the other hand, is speaking the language of expression. He is alerting the listener that his anger is hot, bubbling, and steaming. He is ready to erupt, perhaps. He is "fuming!" Take a moment to create a vision of what the word "fume" means. Let your senses recall the meaning. Does it call to mind the smoke and stink of some chemistry lab or the fumes of gasoline spilled from the pump? Fumes come from some volatile mixture of ingredients. Thus, the use of this word depicts the sensation of smoldering beneath the surface, being ready to burst into flame. Aaron has expressed himself fluently and powerfully. He has provided the listener with clear evidence that the content and meaning of his narrative need further exploration. As we shall see below, in this single sentence he has offered a convincing invitation to spend more time with this specific emotional content.

What are the guides for understanding expressive language? How can a therapist know that Edward's statement carries less emotional content than Aaron's with any confidence other than that of his or her own intuition or guesswork? One guideline we have explored already is the I/F principle (Intensity and Frequency). Aaron's statement carries some intensity and the therapist's trained ear would register the emotional charge behind his words.

DAMS PRINCIPLE

Another principle of listening provides the psychotherapist with a method of discriminating what content carries expressive power. This is the DAMS principle. DAMS is an acronym for the concepts of Drama, Affect, Metaphor, and Symbol—all of which contribute to the language of the emotions (Alschuler & Alschuler, 1984; Hallock, 1989; Hendrix, 1992; Kaplan, 1994; Kennedy-Moore & Watson, 1999; Lyddon, Clay, & Sparks, 2001; Paulson, 1996; Romig & Gruenke, 1991; Strong, 1989). This is the language of passion, obsession, excitement, and fervor. It is not the language of aloofness, calm, or control. It is language that provides the listener with a thermometer. The DAMS principle alerts the listener to the relative heat of the expressed content.

Drama

When clients express their narrative in a dramatic way, they are revealing concern, anxiety, alarm, distress, and, perhaps, an intense conflict of forces in their lives. Drama in speech may be intended or unintended. It may be verbal or nonverbal. It may be real or imagined. It may be accurate or erroneous. It may be the truth or a fabrication. Whatever the case, it is a signal that the content is of more than ordinary importance for the client and it invites the therapist to an exploration with the client.

Affect

Listen to the words clients use to describe the people, situations, and events of their lives. Are the words themselves powerful and, to some extent, out of the ordinary? If a person stands before Leonardo da Vinci's Mona Lisa and says, "It's a nice picture," we know with some certainty that he or she has not been moved deeply. Language can express emotional power or it can reveal tepid, even apathetic, involvement. In counseling and psychotherapy, the therapist is listening for those issues and problems that have power for the client. When clients use unusual, out-of-the ordinary words to describe situations, events, and/or relationships, effective listeners are sensitive to the affective emphasis they have given to the narrative.

Consider the following two remarks: "He is wrong about that" and "He is a pig-headed fool!" There is a difference. The principle of listening for affect sensitizes the listener not only to the overt and obvious affective language of clients, but also to the nuances and subtleties that characterize clients' narratives.

Metaphor

In metaphoric or figurative language, a word or phrase is used to connect one object or idea to another. For example, "My father is drowning me with money, but I am thirsting for attention." I remember, even after so many years, a high school class in which the teacher introduced the concept of metaphor. She read from the poem, *The Highwayman*, by Alfred Noyes: "The road was a ribbon of moonlight." Later, in college, an instructor ventured the opinion that this was perhaps the most famous metaphor in literature. I could see the image then, and I can see it now. In my mind's eye I can visualize the dim outlines of a narrow, winding path stretching out across a wooded hollow.

"In my mind's eye" is a metaphor that captures some reality for you, the reader. It indicates to you that I will be using some description that involves imaging or visualization. You may even use your own imagination as you read the descriptions in this paragraph. It is just so in therapy. Client metaphors invite the therapist to explore the images the client is providing and provide another path to understanding the client's experiences, situations, and life struggles.

Such images remain with us. They inform the memory. We know when a speaker uses metaphor that he or she is trying to tell the listener something that goes beyond the mere description of an issue, event, or relationship. The speaker is trying to give more than the facts. He or she wants us to know something of the experience he or she had, as well as the tangible content. Metaphor is another signal of what is important for the client. As I write this, I remember a statement made by Carl Rogers (1984), who said, "anytime a client begins to speak in metaphor, I know something important is happening."

Symbol

A symbol is a visible sign of something invisible, something that stands for or suggests something else. For example, a lion is a symbol of courage, and the heart is a symbol of affection or the seat of the emotions. As used here, symbol means any object that has some literal, often physical meaning that may represent something psychologically for the client. Even ordinary words used in a particular way may take on symbolic meanings for clients. Look at these two different ways of describing a belief about others: "My sister is a *woman* who has ways of getting what she wants," and "My sister is a *lady* who has ways of getting what she wants." I am not fully certain, but I suspect that you have two different understandings of what is implied by these two different ways of expressing a belief. We might chafe at the politics of the characterizations but, as therapists, we must understand the meaning clients bring to their narratives, both explicit and implied. In the first description the speaker seems to see his or her sister as more coarse than in the second description, which implies that she is more refined in her manners. Sexual overtones may be implied. In counseling, symbols can have the effect of sensitizing the therapist to pay close attention and be mindful of the meaning and consequences of what is being said. If there is any single theorist in the history of psychotherapy who is more noted for highlighting the importance of symbols in the lives of human beings than Carl Jung, then I don't know who it is. His work on archetypes and symbols across cultures is worth any student's attention. I do not share his conviction that particular symbols hold universal meanings. I lean more toward the individual and personally significant meanings clients give to their experiences. We do share the conviction that symbols are vehicles of communication and that we ignore them at the expense of greater understanding. I do believe that there can be common meanings to common symbols, but I also believe we, as counselors and psychotherapists, have to remain open to an individual client's unique meanings. Mothers, fathers, sisters, brothers, knights, queens, "lions and tigers and bears," and any other image a client uses to tell a story can all carry meanings. Some might cut across time and culture, and some may reside within the psyche of a single client.

Our task as counselors and psychotherapists is to develop our skill at recognizing and using symbols to understand the people who come to us for help. It is important for us to recognize the possible, perhaps important, differences between a description of a relationship in which "she is like a mentor to me" and one in which "she is like a mother to me." Both need exploration, but the second may carry meanings that extend beyond teaching one the ropes of an organization or a profession and into more emotionally important areas. This is the power of symbols in the stories clients bring to therapy.

USING THE DAMS PRINCIPLE

In chapter 5 we were introduced to Devon, an African American woman in her early sixties. Let's return to her story to see how the DAMS principle may help us understand her narrative:

> My husband passed last year. We had been married for 43 years. It was so sudden. Cancer . . . took him. He . . . it . . . he went in about six months and . . . I don't have to worry about money. That's not a problem. But . . . it's been a year, and I still . . . I'm lost without him. James did everything for me, and I . . . don't know how . . . I'm learning how to pay bills and . . . I didn't even know how to put gas in my car. I didn't know where the gas cap was . . . I pulled into a gas station and got out and just started to cry . . . when I . . . didn't know where the gas cap was. People tell me I am strong . . . I seem to be doing so . . . doing. I'm doing is about all. But, they don't know. I hate having to put gas in the car. I hate paying the bills. I miss James doing for me! And, more than that, he was the one who liked people. Invited them over. Talked to them. He was the social one. I'm more critical. He was my buffer. I have to do it all now. And, I used to love to go to movies and shows but now I . . . I come home alone and there is no James to talk about the show to. We used to have coffee . . . after the show . . . and I would criticize and he would listen and put up with me. . . . and now . . . it's not the same if I go with other women . . . other widows! I hate that word! The black widow! Like some little spider! Some ugly . . . I don't know what.

Let's use the DAMS principle to review Devon's narrative. The purpose is to see what aspects of her story might give us clues for further exploration and provide us with a greater sense of understanding of Devon and her life situation. It is apparent that categories overlap. A word or sentence may be simultaneously dramatic, affective, metaphoric, and symbolic. For the purpose of examining each category, however, let's focus on the discrete words or sentences that seem to fit mostly into a single category.

Drama

There are several places in her narrative where Devon introduces a dramatic use of language. As she describes her visit to the gas station, she says, "I . . . just started to cry." Listen to what she is describing in that section. On the surface she is describing her frustration with her lack of skill. Consider also the idea that she concretely is facing one more time in her life in which James is missing. She is feeling his death again, freshly, and in the present. Remember that it is not the therapist's job to interpret for Devon what she is feeling but rather to allow her dramatic use of language to sensitize the therapist to aspects of her story that might need further exploration.

She says, "I'm doing is about all." It may be that she is trying to tell the therapist that she merely is surviving. She is just getting by but she does not see herself as moving, making progress. What this introduces for the therapist is the need to understand whether Devon has some self-imposed or introjected idea of how she is supposed to be getting along and feeling. It raises the question of what timetable or criteria she is using to measure her adjustment. It is a suggested area of exploration and clarification.

"I miss James doing for me!" Devon tells the therapist. She is expressing something in addition to her grief. There is a quality of resentment, perhaps, or of bitterness. She is angry. One issue that needs to be addressed is the source of that anger. Is it another example of her having to face the tangible absence of James' death, or is she feeling somehow put-upon by having to do those things for herself that James once did for her? Is she facing the task of becoming more independent with anger and indignation?

Devon is describing her outings with other women when she clarifies who these other women are: "other widows!" She is dramatic in her clarification of the class of the women. It suggests revulsion and disgust. What needs to be clarified as she uses the word "widow" in the pejorative is whether she applies its negative definition to herself. Is she revolted and disgusted by herself? Does she see herself as less worthy because she has become a member of a class she considers repugnant? Clarifying these questions can lead to a greater understanding of the forces that are interfering with Devon's coping more effectively with her grief.

Affect

Devon used several affectively loaded words to describe her feelings. She says, for example, "I hate having to put gas in the car" and "I hate paying the bills." "Hate" is a powerful word. It is an extreme word. Consider for a moment the experiences she is describing. She is talking about servicing her car and paying bills. Many of us might consider gassing up the car an inconvenience and, for many, it might even rise to the level of an irritation. How many of us, however, would use the word "hate" to describe putting gas in the car? Its place on the continuum of dislikes is at the extreme. It is not a feeling that accompanies inconvenient tasks. As a consequence, it can serve to alert the therapist that something other than grief is being introduced into the session. What would cause Devon to use such a powerful word to describe an inconvenience? It may be that she is angry at having to develop her independence. It might signal the need to accept responsibility for other aspects of her life that she previously has been able to ignore. If we consider some of the statements discussed under "Drama" above and some of those under "Metaphor" below, then we might see subthemes of resistance toward accepting authority and of resentment for developing independent skills, both of which need exploration and clarification.

She follows her statement about filling the car with gas with "I hate paying the bills." This may be a part of the theme we just discussed and it also may signal another theme we discussed above: It might be another concrete example of James' death. Are the bills she is paying, for example, the expenses for the funeral? This is another place in the narrative where the therapist might seek to clarify understandings of Devon's story. It makes a difference what she means here. If it is genuinely a subtheme of resistance toward developing her independence skills, then that takes the therapy in one direction. If it is another reminder of James' death, then that focuses the therapy differently.

"I used to love to go to the movies and shows." It may be that Devon is telling the therapist that her present life is not as rich as her life with James. If that is the case, then it may be a matter of loneliness and isolation. This leads, however, to the description of widows, and thus it may not be so much a matter of loneliness as another example of her resentment. It might be another guide to the subtheme of anger over having to be an independent person. Clearly she is reporting that her affective response to previously pleasurable life events has been blunted. Is this simply a matter of normal grief? This is one of the questions that attentive listening for affective language can signal to the therapist.

Metaphor

Devon's use of metaphoric or figurative language is, perhaps, a key to understanding her and her reactions to James' death. She describes his death, "My husband passed last year." This is a euphemistic way to describe death. On the other hand, Devon is an African American woman, and this is a common way in which death is described in the African American community. What it might alert the listener to is the question of whether she is using it in her cultural and religious way, or as a way to avoid facing her husband's death.

She says, "I'm lost without him." We have already discussed above the possibility of the developing subtheme of resistance to independence that this comment also might indicate. Another possibility is that it represents a metaphoric indication that she took her identity from her husband and without him she has no self. "Lost" might also imply "vanished" or "missing." We have shifted from metaphor to symbol in this discussion, and Devon may be reacting to the loss of James as the defining member of the family who gave the other members their identity. It raises the prospect of exploring the idea that Devon's identity was as James' wife rather than as a person in her own right.

These next three statements all have to do with Devon's description of her experience of the service station. She describes her lack of skill and knowledge and her feelings about the task: "I didn't even know how to put gas in my car," "I didn't know where the gas cap was," and "I hate having to put gas in the car." What is the metaphor in this group of phrases and sentences? It is important to recognize that two seemingly contradictory ideas might both be true. People may say what they mean, and their language still may be figurative. It is certainly possible that Devon is describing her reaction to having to service her car. What is sometimes harder to accept is that a person's language may be figurative with their meaning being metaphoric rather than literal.

What could be the metaphoric meaning of Devon's description? It might be worthwhile to mention the I/F principle here and invite you to determine the frequency of gasoline in this story. It turns out that "gas" is second only to Devon's husband as a topic in her narrative. Consider that "gas" might be metaphoric language. The definition we used above identifies metaphoric language as figurative language in which a word or a phrase is used to connote literally one kind of object or idea with another. What is "gas"? It has several meanings, of course, but for our purpose and for the sake of space, let's select the one that has to do with fuel—a source of energy. Now the question for exploration has to do with the metaphoric meaning of Devon's focus on fuel and her struggle with it. How much of a stretch is it to clarify with the client how she energizes herself? How does she motivate herself? She indicates that she "didn't know where the gas cap was." She doesn't know how to use her skills and knowledge so that they motivate her in the ways that her husband did in the past. She says, "I hate having to put gas in the car." The exploration is around the idea of her possible resentment toward having to be the source of her own energy, which she would have to overcome before she could be a source of independent motivation in her own life.

Are these ideas too much of a stretch for a seemingly straightforward description of her feelings about an inconvenient task? Perhaps. What would be your reaction if the images I have described above were presented as a dream? She reports her dream in this way: "I didn't even know how to put gas in my car," "I didn't know where the gas cap was," and "I hate having to put gas in the car." Would it be such a difficult supposition to believe that the images were metaphoric and even symbolic? Human beings are complex. Our complexity extends to the ways in which we try to make ourselves understandable to others and ourselves. It is worth considering, as we seek to improve our listening skills, the idea that language may carry information that disguises meaning just as we believe our dreams do. Conscious processes can be imaginative, metaphorical, and illusionary, and, if we can remain flexible and open to possibilities, then we will become better listeners.

Let's examine one last example of a metaphor in Devon's narrative. She describes one of her husband's roles in her life: "He was my buffer." Listen to that statement again: "He was my buffer." It is an interesting choice of words. What is she trying to convey to her therapist? What is the role she is trying to describe? "Buffer" is a word that has a variety of meanings. What would it mean if Devon were trying to tell the therapist that her husband was a shock absorber, for example? He would then be someone in her life who protected her from the harsher facets of life. She might not have had to deal with the mess of life. James might have done all of that if this is what the word "buffer" means in this instance. She might have meant something a bit different. She might have meant that he was a barrier. Somehow he stood between her and the outside world. In some way he prevented others from having direct access to her, which may have had some comforting effects, but he also prevented her access to others. Understood in this way, her use of the word "buffer" looks quite different. We are reminded once again that, unless a listener is open to the possibility of metaphoric language and its signal of other meanings, he or she may miss the opportunity to understand a client in deeper and more profound ways.

Symbol

Devon uses some symbolic images in her story. The most descriptive is her characterization of herself as "the black widow!" It is a description that has three levels. First, it is a literal description of herself as an African American woman whose husband is dead. Second, it is a play on words, or, perhaps, a joke. Third, it is a symbolic characterization of herself in a pejorative way.

The first description is a statement of fact, but the context reveals that she is aware of the double meaning of the phrase "black widow." The third characterization of "black widow" is also one that Devon recognizes, as she continues with "like some little spider!" She knows she is describing herself in negative terms, and her symbolic representation invites the therapist to explore the negative definitions she gives to her state of being a widow. There is something further that should be clarified: The implication that a "spider" is revolting and "ugly" is clear. What is not clear is whether or not the client is taking on another definition of the "black widow" for herself. Is she, for example, feeling any sense that she somehow contributed to the death of her husband as a female black widow spider might?

Consider for a moment the difference between describing oneself as an "African American widow" and as a "black widow." The first is a description that involves not only information, but also dignity. Any negative implications do not reside in the speaker. Within the term "black widow," on the other hand, there is a double meaning that immediately is brought to the listener and might even interfere with immediately comprehending that this is a woman whose husband has died. The image is so strong that it overwhelms the information meant to be conveyed. This is the power of symbol for both the speaker and the listener. There is a danger in symbolic communication. The images are often powerful. They are powerful for both the speaker and the listener, but there is no guarantee that both understand the powerful image of the symbol identically. The speaker may intend one message, while the listener, caught in his or her interpretation of the symbol, may perceive something substantially different. Thus, it is important that the therapist resist the temptation to interpret client symbols in the therapist's terms but instead permit the client to provide his or her own personal meaning for the symbol. It might be too easy, for example, to use some reference book to interpret the symbol of a spider or of the color black without permitting the client to give his or her own definitions and meanings for the symbol.

SUMMARY

Expressive language conveys meanings that are both more profound and subtler than descriptive language. The difference between literal language and figurative language may well be the difference between facts and emotions. Certainly it is accurate to say that the language of feelings, of sentiment, and of passion is figurative and expressive. Expressive language may be described as dramatic, affective, metaphoric, and symbolic. Such uses of language are clues to the listener that the speaker has introduced something into the story that has a higher probability of importance for the speaker than mere descriptive language.

Improving our listening skills includes not only a mastery of content information, but also the open-minded willingness to listen for and explore more figurative and expressive language. The language of the emotions often may be disguised, not only from therapists, but also from the client. The effective listener is one who is willing to hear and acknowledge that some expressive language has been introduced into the counseling session.

REFERENCES

Alschuler, C. F., & Alschuler, A. S. (1984). Developing healthy responses to anger: The counselor's role. *Journal of Counseling and Development, 63*, 26–29.

Hallock, S. (1989, fall). Making metaphors in therapeutic process. *Journal of Reality Therapy, 9*, 25–29.

Hendrix, D. H. (1992, April). Metaphors as nudges toward understanding in mental health counseling. *Journal of Mental Health Counseling, 14*, 234–242.

Kaplan, S. P. (1994, summer). Metaphor, shame, and people with disabilities. *Journal of Applied Rehabilitation Counseling, 25*, 15–18.

Kennedy-Moore, E., & Watson, J. C. (1999). *Expressing emotion: Myths, realities, and therapeutic strategies*. New York: Guilford Press.

Lyddon, W. J., Clay, A. L., & Sparks, C. L. (2001). Metaphor and change in counseling. *Journal of Counseling and Development, 79*, 269–274.

Paulson, B. L. (1996). Metaphors for change. *Journal of College Student Psychotherapy, 10*, 11–21.

Rogers, C. R. (1984). Personal communication.

Romig, C. A., & Gruenke, C. (1991, May–June). The use of metaphor to overcome inmate resistance to mental health counseling. *Journal of Counseling and Development, 69*, 414–418.

Strong, T. (1989, July). Metaphors and client change in counseling. *International Journal for the Advancement of Counselling, 12*, 203–213.

Chapter 7

Listening for Style

We talk like we walk. It is personal, identifiable, and habitual. It is a matter of style or a manner of expression with which we have become comfortable and of which we are hardly aware. Style is influenced by any number of factors (Griggs & Dunn, 1989). The nation of our birth and upbringing, or a region within that nation, can influence our speech for life. The idioms, phrases, cadence, and images we use to communicate have evolved from infancy to adulthood into our ordinary, everyday manner of speaking. Language, culture, and religion all affect our manner of expression (Milgram, Dunn, & Price, 1993). These influences on the way we express ourselves aren't limitless but they are many. In this chapter, I want to tease out three ways in which we express ourselves that can help aid a listener in understanding. These are sense modality, vocation, and avocation (or interests). It is common for people to use the senses as a way to describe their experience. A client might say, for example, "The way I see it, I'm out of focus all the time." Another might say, "I just keep hearing myself tell me I'm no good," or, "When I think about my life, my stomach knots up." All of these can be seen as attacks on the self or issues of self-esteem. Yet, each is expressed in a different sense modality. Careful listening can help the listener identify the style that characterizes a client's efforts to tell his or her story.

An accountant and an engineer might describe their experiences in very different language and yet both may be struggling with feelings of despair: "My life isn't in balance. I think I have many more credits than debits and I feel like my whole life is always in debt" and "Sometimes I think of my life like a bridge constructed with defective materials and shoddy assembly. It won't stand up to the stresses it has to bear." Our vocation can easily influence the way in which we try to express our feelings about the people, situations, and events of our lives.

Others of us might use the metaphors of our interests or hobbies to explain ourselves. Sports metaphors, perhaps more for males than females but increasingly for both, are common. "I'm don't think I'm a quarterback. I mean, people expect me to be a leader, and I don't even think I know the plays." Another person might be involved in community theater and express despair in other ways: "I find myself acting all the time. I'm don't think I know how to be real. I'm just saying lines but I don't know who I am." Sometimes, people's interests, hobbies, or avocations become such central parts of them that they become their dominant way of expression.

SENSE MODALITY

People tend to favor one of the sensory modalities—vision (sight), audition (hearing), kinesthesis (used here to mean other bodily sensations including gustation [taste] and olfaction [smell])—in the use of language to describe experience. These visual, auditory, or kinesthetic styles are tendencies we have. Most of us tend toward visual speech, but some people tend toward auditory or kinesthetic words to describe their experiences. Our manner of expression may come to be dominated by one of the sense modalities, but all of us use each of them from time to time (see Table 7.1).

Visual

The most common sense modality used to describe experience is vision. We tell one another what we see. It isn't at all uncommon to hear someone say, "Look at it from my point of view." What is important for a listener is to practice listening literally. How would understanding be aided if we, as counselors and psychotherapists, literally did "look at it" from the client's "point of view."

Read this short example and, as you read it, focus on the visual images it evokes for you. The client is a young woman talking about her experience of emptiness in her life.

> Cl: I keep having this image. I see this crane, you know, like a big machine with a long neck that lifts heavy building materials. And I see this crane swinging this huge wrecking ball, and it just smashes right into my face. And then I look at the operator and I see that it is me!

Consider the idea that the client is telling us her "sense" of her experience. She is not, in this example, telling us how it feels to be hit in the face with the wrecking ball. She doesn't describe the sound of the ball smashing into her face. Consider the meaning that using a visual description can give us. What would be different about her experience if she described it in terms of how it sounded or how it felt? She didn't. She described what it looked like. She didn't focus on the pain and she didn't focus on the sound. She described the picture of being hit in the face. The literal conclusion from her story is that her face has

Table 7.1
Language Modalities

People tend to favor one of the sensory modalities—vision (sight), audition (hearing), kinesthesis (bodily sensations), gustation (taste), and olfaction (smell)—in the use of language to describe experience. Empathy seems to be the key ingredient of a helping relationship. It has been observed that empathic therapists tend to match the language modality of the client. For example, a visual client might say, "My life is just so out of focus." A therapist who responds, "I hear you saying that your life is confusing," while accurate, would be missing this client because the response is more auditory than visual. A more empathic response might be, "The picture is hazy and you can't seem to find a way to clear it up." This respects the client's visual way of talking.

The following phrases, grouped under modalities, might prove helpful in responding to clients who evidence a preference for one way of speaking over another. While most people use mixed modalities, occasionally a client will be influenced strongly by one. The gustatory and olfactory modalities are used infrequently, so visual, auditory, and kinesthetic senses are given as examples here.

Visual

From your point of view . . .
As you see it. . . .
I see what you mean, you . . .
You just want to shut your eyes to . . .
It is hard to focus on . . .
You want to keep an eye on . . .
That seems like an eye-opener to you . . .
You're beginning to see . . .
Your goal is in sight . . .
That emotion really caught your eye . . .

Auditory

Sounds like . . .
He really bent your ear when . . .
Your inner voices say . . .
Your internal dialogue tells you that . . .
I hear you saying . . .
You went silent when . . .
It is just so noisy in your head that . . .
It rang a bell when . . .

Kinesthetic

You feel . . .
It is just outside your grasp . . .
It touched you when . . .
I have the feeling that maybe . . .
It is tough for you to . . .
You just seem held back when . . .
It feels like you have a handle on it . . .
It just slips away when . . .
That feeling really got a hold of you . . .
I have the sense that it is rough for you to . . .
I am getting in touch with . . .
See if this grabs you . . .

been destroyed. If we take a leap, then we might say that what she has described is that her identity is being destroyed. It is being destroyed by herself. This visual image leads to a decidedly different understanding of her experience than a kinesthetic reference would.

Auditory

What are the sounds of suffering? How do clients hear their anxiety, depression, anger, and despair? One answer, of course, is that they hear voices. Often the voice they hear is their own. In counseling and psychotherapy, it makes a difference whose voice clients hear as well as what it says. Listening for style can alert the therapist to both the content and identity of clients' auditory messages (Griggs, 1993). What is being discussed here is not auditory hallucinations but rather the style or metaphor clients use to describe their experience. The style they use can provide clues to how they conceptualize their issues or problems and to a deeper understanding of their experience.

If we alter the example above and use an auditory description rather than a visual one, then the meaning of the story might change. Consider how different it might be to you if the client had said:

> I have this image of a big mechanical crane creaking and groaning as it swings a huge wrecking ball right at my head. I can hear the ball whistling through the air as it swings toward me and I hear my face shatter as the ball hits. The operator is me and I hear her laughing when the ball hits.

If we examine this story, what different understandings might we come to? It might not be about her fear of the loss of identity. It sounds more complicated and somehow insulting: the crane's "creaking and groaning," the ball's "whistling through the air." She can hear her "face shatter" and the crane operator (she herself) "laughing." While all the images are important, if we focus on the crane operator laughing, we are led to an understating that insult or derision is involved in this story. This image of scorn and disrespect is different from the fear of the loss of identity in the example of a visual metaphor. The auditory metaphor leads to an understanding that the client is sending a message to herself that there is something about her that she finds laughable. We don't know what that is at this point, but it does lead to a different understanding and a different focus for the therapy.

Kinesthetic

We have seen that visual and auditory descriptions can lead to different understandings. It is no less true when clients use kinesthetic descriptions to express their experiences (Griggs, 1993). If we again alter the story above, it might read like this:

> I have this image of this big crane and it swings this huge wrecking ball right at my face. I can feel it smash into my face and the pain just explodes through my whole body when the ball hits. I sense that the crane operator is me!

In this way of telling the story, the client does not seem to be talking about the loss of identity *or* of some sense of scorn or rejection. Instead, she is telling us, pretty straightforwardly, that she feels an intense attack on the self. It seems clear, as well, that she is directing the attack. She is her own enemy.

She also could use an olfactory sense to tell the story, in which case she might say, "My life stinks." Or she might use the gustatory: "It has such a bitter taste." While it would be unusual for a client to use the gustatory or olfactory sense as a dominant way of expression, careful listening might note the occasional use of these kinesthetic modes as well.

We have looked at three different ways of telling essentially the same story. Yet, depending on the sense modality used to describe the experience, we were led to different understandings of the meaning the client is giving to her experience. Listening for the sense modality used by the client helps the counselor or psychotherapist get a personal "sense" of the experience for the client (Griggs, 1993; Griggs & Dunn, 1989; Marshall, 1985). In turn, this becomes another aid to listening and understanding.

VOCATIONAL/OCCUPATIONAL STYLES

While sense modalities are the most dominant type of style, the type of work clients do also might provide a form of expression for them. Earlier I cited the example of an accountant and an engineer as they tried to explain their senses of despair in their lives.

Truck drivers might talk about "putting on the brakes," "gearing down," "dodging road hazards," or "jackknifing the rig" in their descriptions of life events. An electrician might describe the same events as "shutting down the power," "blowing a fuse," or "mixing up the AC and DC." A mathematician might seem cold and distant as he or she explains life's difficulties in formulae, equations, and symbolic logic. Yet if the listener is aware of the client's occupation, then it is possible to use the language style in the same way one would use a metaphor for understanding.

A firefighter might describe his or her anxiety as a "flash fire"; can you see how that might carry meaning just as well as a clinical description of a "panic attack"? If a plumber says his or her life is "clogged" and he or she fears that you, as the therapist, will be like "Draino," doesn't that capture both a sense of unfulfillment and fear? Listening for and respecting occupational language adds another tool to our listening skills. Recognizing and respecting a client's occupational metaphors serve to both create trust and aid change later in the process.

AVOCATIONAL/INTEREST STYLES

People have interests outside their work. Sometimes these interests play a more powerful role in their lives than does their occupation. An office manager might be a volunteer firefighter. A retailer might be a Boy Scout leader. A mechanic might be a soccer coach. A teacher might be an artist. A sales representative might teach Sunday school. A brokerage clerk might be a storyteller in an ethnic community. In each of these examples, the language style could be more influenced by the clients' interests than by their occupation.

Just as it is important to recognize and respect clients' occupational language, it is important to listen to and acknowledge their avocational expressions.

A client might talk about what he or she collects and might say:

> Cl: I have this collection of turtles. I have been collecting them or years. I don't know, somehow that is the way I see myself now. I have this shell that covers me and I know I'm not going to get anywhere unless I "stick my neck out" . . . but, . . . well . . . I'm not sticking my neck out much.

This client is using a collection of turtles as a way to talk about his or her withdrawing and fear of taking risks. If the therapist is able to use this interest and metaphor as a way of understanding the client, then that promises a more helpful therapy.

Another client is a woman in her forties who takes ballet lessons for the first time in her life. She might describe her relationship with her husband in ways that use dance as a metaphor to bring the troublesome aspects of her relationship into therapy. For example:

> Cl: I have started ballet lessons. It's something I have always wanted to do ever since I was a little girl. I think it is so beautiful. Now I think it has so many meanings for my life. I think I am in a constant *pirouette.* Just spinning and spinning. I don't know. It isn't like I'm out of control, but I am spinning. I know what I wanted in my marriage was a *pas de deux.* We would be a couple and dance. Now I'm afraid we have become a *pas de trios.*

The client has used the language of the ballet to tell us that she is fearful her husband is having a relationship outside their marriage and yet she still has this sense of being in control, even though she doesn't see herself as advancing. She is spinning in control, but spinning nevertheless. We might not know the vocabulary of coin or stamp collecting, of ballet, or any number of other hobbies or interests that clients can bring to therapy. Yet, by listening, we can gain some meaning and understanding. It is altogether proper to have a client tell us the meaning of terms or words we don't recognize. Often, of course, we can gain the meaning from the context. In explaining meanings of terms and words, clients often explore the meaning for themselves and extend their own understanding as they distinguish the metaphor in their lives and attach it to the events that brought them to therapy.

SUMMARY

The senses we use to experience the world often are used as language to tell others what we have experienced. The sense modalities—vision, audition, and kinesthesis—are used by all of us to tell one another our experiences of the people, situations, and events of our lives. We use our jobs and their specialized languages as another way to communicate our understandings and meanings to others. Our hobbies, interests, or things we do for pleasure can become such a part of our lives that the vocabulary and jargon of our special interests become the language we use in our effort to tell others how we feel.

Clients often come to therapy confused and at their wits end. In telling their stories, they use the language and style they are most comfortable with in order to make themselves known. As counselors and psychotherapists, we can increase our listening skills by attending to the language style of clients as they express themselves using sense modalities and occupational and avocational language.

Style can carry more than content. It also may carry meaning. As we listen to clients, we can give some consideration to the importance of the style the client is using to tell his or her story. This is even more important if the client typically uses a visual style of talking but then changes to another style when talking about a new issue in his or her life. The change might well signal an out-of-the-ordinary experience that the client has processed in a different way. Such attention to style provides counselors and psychotherapists with added paths to understanding and meaning.

REFERENCES

Griggs, S. A. (1993). Counseling gifted adolescents through learning style. In R. M. Milgram, R. S. Dunn, & G. E. Price (Eds.), *Teaching and counseling gifted and talented adolescents: An international learning style perspective*. Westport, CT: Praeger Publishers.

Griggs, S. A., & Dunn, R. S. (1989, October). The learning styles of multicultural groups and counseling implications. *Journal of Multicultural Counseling and Development, 17*, 146–155.

Marshall, E. A. (1985, June). Relationship between client-learning style and preference for counselor approach. *Counselor Education and Supervision, 24*, 353–399.

Milgram, R. M., Dunn, R. S., & Price, G. E. (Eds.). (1993). *Teaching and counseling gifted and talented adolescents: An international learning style perspective*. Westport, CT: Praeger Publishers.

Scorzelli, J. F., & Gold, J. (1999, April). The mutual storytelling writing game. *Journal of Mental Health Counseling, 21*, 113–123.

Chapter 8

Listening to Nonverbal Messages

"The eye is the window to the soul." Ancient wisdom teaches us that words are not the "royal road" to genuine understanding. We communicate volumes even when we refuse to talk. "I'm not talking" certainly doesn't mean we are not communicating.

Take this short test.

1. What percentage of communication do words represent?
   a. 7%
   b. 16%
   c. 30%
   d. 42%
2. What percentage of communication does vocal tone represent?
   a. 10%
   b. 27%
   c. 38%
   d. 40%
3. What percentage of communication does nonverbal language represent?
   a. 20%
   b. 32%
   c. 40%
   d. 55%

If you selected 7 percent words, 38 percent vocal tone, and 55 percent nonverbal language (facial expressions, posture, and gestures), then you are correct (Mehrabian, 1971). Gorden (1992) reports studies that indicate as much as 65 percent of a message may be communicated by nonverbal language.

These figures seem to come as a surprise and a challenge to beginning counselors and psychotherapists. The focus, early in training, is frequently, almost

Table 8.1
Nonverbal Communication of Therapist Attitudes

Counseling Dimension	Nonverbal Behaviors Likely to be Associated with Ineffectiveness	Nonverbal Behaviors Likely to Be Associated with Effectiveness
Empathy	frown resulting from lack of understanding	positive head nods; facial expression congruent with content of session
Respect	mumbling; patronizing tone of voice; doodling engaging in or paperwork; lack of eye contact	spending time with client; full attention
Warmth	apathy; delay in responding; insincere effusiveness; fidgeting; signs of wanting to leave	physical contact; nonjudgmental empathy; attentiveness
Genuineness	low or evasive eye contact; excessive smiling	congruence between verbal and nonverbal behavior
Concreteness	shrugging shoulders when client is vague instead of seeking clarification; vague gestures used for substitute for specific verbal meaning	drawing diagram to clarify an abstract point; clear enunciation
Self-Disclosure	bragging gestures; pointing to self; covering eyes or mouth while talking	gestures that keep references to self low key
Immediacy	turning away or moving back when immediacy enters the session	tone of voice congruent with expressed mood of the client
Confrontation	pointing finger or shaking fist at client; tone of voice that communicates blame or condemnation; loudness of voice to intimidate; insecurity with self	natural tone of voice; confidence

Adapted from G. M. Gazda et al. (1984).

exclusively, on the spoken words of clients. To the extent that this is so, the focus on verbal communication alone accounts for some of the early miscues and necessary feedback received early in training. As Table 8.1 indicates, specific nonverbal behaviors may be associated with effectiveness and ineffectiveness across a broad spectrum of counseling dimensions. It is a terrific example of losing our natural abilities as we seek to master a new skill. Certainly each of us, in our personal lives, uses nonverbal messages to understand others and to gauge our own communication. It must be something near a developmental truth that as newborns and infants we respond to nonverbal cues more accurately than we do to verbal cues. It takes some time for us, as humans, to break the code and ease into the mastery of language.

The professional literature, in fact, is packed with both opinion and research that supports the notion that nonverbal messages carry more power, are more trustworthy, and bear the greater burden in communication than verbal messages (Egan, 1998; Ekman, 1992; Grace, Kivlighan, & Kunce, 1995; Highlen & Hill, 1984; Ivey & Ivey, 1999; Mehrabian, 1971; Russell, 1995; Siegman & Feldstein, 1987; Welch & Gonzalez, 1999).

It is essential to be cautious in reviewing the importance of nonverbal communications. Such cautions are appropriate in verbal communication as well. First, we live in a multicultural world. This obvious reality seems to get lost sometimes when we try to teach the skills of counseling, attending, and listening as if all clients are the same. Obviously, clients may be different both individually and culturally. In recent times, we increasingly have become sensitized to multicultural issues. So sensitized, in fact, that there can be a corresponding danger of forgetting that individuals are different within their respective cultures. So, the caution is to remember that gestures, facial expressions, eye contact, and other nonverbal clues to communication do not carry the same message from culture to culture and from individual to individual within a given culture. "Within a culture there is room for much individual variation. For instance, you may indicate annoyance by quick, jerky movements, while your partner may express annoyance by frowning, folding arms, and standing rigidly at attention. Tuning into each other's unique way of expressing feelings and attitudes helps communication" (McKay, Davis, & Fanning, 1983, p. 61). The profession of counseling and psychotherapy, perhaps more than any other, continually strives to recognize, understand, and appreciate individual differences.

Second, given the individual and multicultural diversity of nonverbal gestures, we should be extraordinarily cautious about interpreting the meanings of such acts. In a sentence: Don't do it! While in our everyday lives we continually interpret both language and gestures, in the counseling relationship it is a serious therapeutic mistake to interpret meanings. It is an altogether different matter to observe, note, and seek to understand meaning than it is to interpret and assign meaning. This difference in how we deal with both verbal and nonverbal messages from clients is central to the counseling endeavor. In counseling, clients are not told what they mean, believe, value, or intend. Instead, therapists seek to clarify and understand the meaning conveyed by words and the language of the body. It is a mistake to assign meaning based on common understandings of symbolism or even from common practice. Such a common meaning can be an initial guide for exploration, but effective therapists always leave room for the unique meanings given to language, gestures, and symbols by individual clients. Later in this chapter, there is a list of "common meanings" for some gestures. While such lists may prove helpful, I have put the caution before the list to emphasize that guidelines are not laws and common meanings are not individual meanings.

Third, not in its order of importance but merely as its place in this list, is the serious therapeutic mistake of ignoring nonverbal signals from clients. Any therapist who listens only to the words of clients misses (as we have seen above) the greater weight of the message. This is especially true when the words say one thing and the body communicates another. In such moments of discrepancy, the recommendation is that the body is a more trustworthy guide to accurate understanding (Long, 1996; Welch & Gonzalez, 1999).

Finally, as Lauver and Harvey (1997) advise, "we tend to trust people when their nonverbal messages seem consistent with the words they utter" (p. 57). Long (1996) labels this concept "consonance," which "refers to the congruence of verbal and nonverbal messages" (p. 175). While we might recognize the importance of observing, noting, and clarifying clients' nonverbal communication, we might forget to apply the same learning to ourselves as counselors and psychotherapists. It is our task to learn to present ourselves genuinely, naturally, and simply without undue awkwardness or consciousness. Early in training, of course, beginning therapists have to keep in mind a number of variables at once, and their presentation may lack the qualities of simplicity, naturalness, and congruence. At some point, however, the awkwardness must be transcended, and effective therapists find their style and presentation and wear it like a loose garment. We need to learn to be congruent in our verbal and nonverbal communication. When we are, we are better able to build trust with clients.

THE NATURE OF NONVERBAL COMMUNICATION

Body Movement

McKay, Davis, and Fanning (1983) describe the importance of body movement in nonverbal communication. Body movements (kinesics) come to have cultural and/or individual meanings that largely are learned. Body movements include such things as facial expressions, gestures, and posture. Even breathing can communicate meaning and add nuance to a verbal message. Body movements may serve to aid communication in different ways. McKay, Davis, and Fanning (1983) point out that, in addition to showing feelings, attitudes, and deeper meaning, body movements serve at least two other purposes: They can serve as illustrators or as regulators. The illustrator function of body movement is involved when we simultaneously name and point at an object. "Look at the sunset!" we might exclaim as we reach out an arm to point to the distance horizon. Or, a client might shake his or her fist and angrily declare, "My father makes me so mad." In both of these examples, the gesture illustrates the spoken words. Regulators play a different role. The purpose of regulators is to influence, monitor, or even control the speech of another. We might shake our heads "No" or hold up a hand to stop another person's comments to us. We might nod in agreement or as a sign that we are listening. We might signal for a person to keep talking by rolling our hand over and over as if to say "roll it out" or "tell me more."

Punctuation. Egan (1998) elaborates on ways in which nonverbal communication can modify or "punctuate" verbal messages. A raised eyebrow, for example, can convey disdain, while raising both eyebrows might evidence surprise. Nonverbal messages might

> *Confirm or repeat.* We might respond accurately to a client who jabs his or her finger downward and exclaims, "That's right!" A client might make a gesture like he or she is going to hit his or her other palm and then stop just short of it: "I felt so angry I almost hit him!" The gesture could be seen as confirming that the individual didn't hit the other person, as much as he or she wanted to.
>
> *Deny or confuse.* The classic example is someone who shouts, "I am not angry!" and slams his or her fist down on the table. A common example is a person who smiles as he or she talks about how angry he or she is. These are examples of discrepancies between what someone says and what his or her body communicates. It is something like an unfamiliar dog greeting us in its yard with barks and a wagging tail. We are in a quandary. We don't know which end of the dog to believe! When the words and the body are discrepant, then further clarification is required before a therapist can grasp the genuine meanings the client is expressing.
>
> *Strengthen or emphasize.* Just as a nonverbal communication might confirm a message, it also might add to it. Clients might use endearing language to talk about relationships, but if they also move their hands and place them over their hearts, then that adds power to the words. It is a gesture of closeness and intimacy. It emphasizes the "heartfelt" nature of the relationships and strengthens the stories they are describing.
>
> *Control and regulate.* We use nonverbal communication in an attempt to control the conversation or what is said in a conversation. Some years ago, I came across a story of a class that used behavior modification techniques to manipulate their professor's behavior. Every time he took a step to the right, the class would smile. Every time he took a step to the left, they would not smile, but look at him blankly. After a time, the professor was lecturing from the right hand corner of the classroom! I don't know if the story actually is true, but it makes a point. We can, and do, influence the behavior of others by our nonverbal signals. Just as we monitor and alter our own speech in response to nonverbal clues, we seek to influence others as well.

Harmonics. Ivey and Ivey (1999) discuss *movement harmonics* as patterns of movement that occur when people are in conversation. It is possible to observe the ebb and flow of movement that occurs between a therapist and a client in a relationship. These patterns may be harmonious or discrepant. A harmonious movement would include moving toward a client when the client moves forward. A discrepant movement would show the therapist leaning away as the client leans forward. Ivey and Ivey label *movement synchrony* those times when the therapist and client are involved in a pattern of movement similar to a choreographed ballet. The therapist and client move in harmony, in synchrony. This pattern might also be called *mirroring*. A different form of harmonious interaction is called *movement complementarity*. The therapist might nod as the client glances up to see if the therapist is still attending. The nod might not match anything the client has been saying but complements the client's narrative and encourages the client to continue. The opposite of these harmonious movements is one Ivey and Ivey label *movement dissynchrony*. This disparate movement pattern does not mirror the client, but instead blocks or confounds the client's narrative. An example might be a therapist shaking his or her head back and forth, signaling "No," even though the therapist might be encouraging the client verbally. This discordant signal would create confusion for the client, at the minimum, and likely would interrupt the flow of the narrative.

Space

Sitting close to or far away from another—leaning in or out—can communicate interest or indifference, respectively. In counseling, the physical arrangement of the counseling room can communicate through both the degree of privacy and the flexibility of the seating arrangement. A cramped office that forces the therapist and client to sit close together might be intimidating and create an unwelcoming atmosphere. A more roomy counseling room with flexible seating that can be moved or arranged to fit different situations and circumstances will convey a different meaning. In both cases, it is the space that is sending the message.

These qualities of the nature of nonverbal communication are all important in attending, listening to, and understanding another person's story. Movement (including punctuation and harmonics) and use of space act as clues that can be used to focus our understanding of the deeper meanings for clients. Nonverbal messages can illustrate, confirm, and—strengthen or deny and confuse—a verbal message. They provide important clues about whether, as a therapist, to clarify or to explore what is being spoken. It is important to recognize that concepts such as movement, punctuation, harmonics, and space are considerations for self-observation as well as for the observation of clients.

GUIDELINES FOR NONVERBAL UNDERSTANDING

The skills of attending apply to both verbal and nonverbal messages. Effective listening means attending to the whole of the meanings conveyed by clients. Even considering the research on the significance of nonverbal dimensions of communication, mentioned at the opening of this chapter, it would be a radical proposal indeed to suggest that the words of clients should be ignored and that therapists should listen only to nonverbal messages. Each of us, nevertheless, would be resistant to ignoring verbal messages, even with all of the evidence that words deceive us. What we want, of course, is to be able to communicate and be understood accurately. This is the argument that calls each of us, as therapists, to learn to understand nonverbal messages with the same skill we do with verbal messages.

Awareness

The focus of counseling and psychotherapy is rightly on client needs and behavior. In training, however, the focus on the self of the therapist is often necessary as a prerequisite to mastering the skills of the counseling process. The path to this kind of change begins with awareness. The mastery of many skills begins with the self. Learning to observe, note, and understand nonverbal messages is no exception, and so the first guideline to understanding nonverbal messages in others is self-awareness.

Self-Awareness. Self-awareness lies along a continuum from too little to too much. Both extremes hamper observation and understanding. If self-awareness is so high that it becomes self-consciousness, then we appear forced, phony, and awkward. If we are unaware of our values, attitudes, and convictions, then client disclosure may catch us off guard and threaten us. We might respond defensively and thus be of little help to the client. If we are unaware of our own nonverbal behavior, for example, then there is little we will seek to do to improve our communication with clients. And yet, in order to create a climate that facilitates client exploration and trust, awareness of our nonverbal behavior is as important as awareness of our verbal utterances.

Table 8.2 provides a checklist of nonverbal behaviors, including body movement, space, and vocal qualities. It also covers areas such as altering the environment prior to meeting with a client. Other areas, such as posture, eye contact and vocal quality, require at least an initial meeting before one can assess how to respond. It also calls attention to distractions that one can avoid. Remember that the point here is awareness. This checklist is meant to stimulate self-awareness as a self-observational instrument in the review of videotapes. Used as an observational instrument, it will provide a portrait of one's behaviors, showing where one might need to increase or decrease particular behaviors. The long-term goal is to be simultaneously aware and spontaneous and natural in the therapeutic relationship.

Awareness of Others. Nonverbal behavior cannot be read like a table of elements in which we know precisely what we are dealing with by its atomic weight. Both cultural and individual differences make such a concrete reading of behavior slavish and unhelpful. Table 8.3 provides a listing of nonverbal behaviors and some common understandings of those behaviors. Again, the

Table 8.2
Nonverbal Behavior Checklist

Posture	
Attending—Slightly Forward	______
Appropriate Position—Facing Client, Other	______
Relaxed	______
Hands and Arms Relaxed	______
Legs—Spaced, Flat on Floor, or Crossed and Relaxed	______
Eager and Ready to Respond	______
——	
Slouched	______
Armored—Arms and Legs Crossed	______
Sitting Sideways	______
Too Close	______
Too Distant	______
Rigid, Statue	______
Eye Contact	
Relaxed, Spontaneous, Appropriate	______
Looking at Client while Listening	______
Looking at Client while Talking	______
Observing Whole Person	______
——	
Shifty-Eyed	______
Looking Down, Away	______
Staring Intensely	______
Breaking Eye Contact Immediately	______
Looking Defiantly, Competitively	______
Staring Blankly	______
Facial Expression	
Calm, Attentive, Interested while Listening	______
Appropriately Expressive while Talking	______
Smiling Appropriately	______
Expressions—Match Client Mood	______
——	
Wrinkled Forehead (Frown)	______
Biting Lip	______
Rigid Face	______
Smiling Inappropriately	______
Disapproving/Aghast Face	______
Overly Emotional	______
Inappropriate Facial Expression (Not Matching)	______
No Facial Expression (No Change)	______

Table 8.2 (continued)

Gestures	
Gestures—Appropriate for Emphasis and Point	______
Nodding Head Appropriately	______
Symbolic Gestures	______
Gestures—for Explanation and Demonstration	______
——	
Gestures—Inappropriate or Wrong	______
Nodding Head Continuously	______
No Gestures, Statue-Like	______
Gestures—Wild or Exaggerated	______
Touch	
Greeting—Handshake, Other Touch	______
Appropriate Touch	______
——	
Inappropriate Touch	______
Sexual Touch	______
Interrupting, Crying, or Weeping	______
Vocal Quality	
Intonation	
Change of Inflection, Tone	______
Strong, Confident Tone	______
Pleasant	______
——	
Flat Monotone	______
Too Emotional	______
Pace	
Fast	______
Appropriate	______
Slow	______
Volume	
High	______
Appropriate and Varied	______
Low	______
Diction	
Precise	______
Clear	______
Pronunciation	______
Jargon, Slang	______

Table 8.2 (continued)

Nonverbal Distractions	
Fiddling, Twiddling	______
Smoking, Drinking, Chewing Gum	______
Tapping Finger, Foot	______
Touching Hand, Finger to Head	______
Scratching, Rubbing	______
Unusual Hand Configuration ("Steeple," etc.)	______
Playing with Hair, Beard	______
Trembling	______
Environment	
Lighting	______
Chair Arrangement	______
Appropriate Chairs	______
Neat, Clean	______
Casual	______
Warm	______
Cheerful	______
____	
Desk or Other Barrier	______
"Throne" for Counselor	______
Lack of Needed Materials	______
Inappropriate Seating	______

From I. D. Welch & D. M. Gonzalez (1999).

point is awareness. I introduced a nonsensical rule in chapter 1 to teach therapists-in-training how to process nonverbal behavior (all behavior is symbolic; except when it is not). This paradoxical, even nonsensical, sentence is meant to teach two things. First, that we need to be open to the idea that nonverbal messages may carry important information. Second, that we cannot ignore the fact that behavior may be nothing more than what it appears to be. One certainly might "wipe away a dry tear," but one simply might scratch a genuine small itch under his or her eye. Table 8.3 serves as a beginning guide to bring the reader a higher level of awareness of nonverbal behavior and some of its associated common meanings. It is not fact; it is merely a guide.

OPENNESS

Let me tell you a story. It's true. It happened to me. I was driving along a rural road in a farming and ranching community, and I drove past a man walking along the road with a bridle in his hand. I realized quickly that I didn't know if he had found a bridle or lost a horse. And that is the problem with reading

Table 8.3
Nonverbal Clues and Some Possible Meanings

In counseling with clients, nonverbal behavior may carry many clues to vague feelings. The meanings listed below must be taken with caution, since nonverbal language may or may not be symbolic in origin.

Behavior	**Possible Meaning**
Head	Hands on top of head may mean holding something back, keeping the lid on. Hand or fingers to the head may indicate intellectualization, coming from the head.
Hair	Running fingers through hair may mean stringing things along.
Eyes	Wiping fingers under eyes may mean a dry tear, crying without actual tears. Maintaining eye contact may indicate a dominant personality.
Mouth	Fingers stroking mouth may show need for support or nurturance. Hand in front of mouth may mean something is being hidden or that what is being said is unimportant.
Nose	Thumbing the nose may indicate hostility.
Chewing	Chewing may be a way of releasing anxiety or may be a sign of anger.
Throat	Touching throat may be a sign of choking off some feeling. Lump in the throat may represent a need to cry or shout or that something is stuck.
Neck	Stiff neck may be a moralistic sign or may represent control and inhibition, an attempt to keep feelings from moving.
Shoulder	Sore or stiff shoulders may mean carrying a burden. Stiff shoulders may mean inhibiting anger.
Arms	Tension in arms may mean a need to embrace a person, an idea, a value. Crossed arms may mean holding in feelings or hugging self as in a need for comfort.
Hands	Hands represent emotions, may be a source of much information about feelings. Sitting on hands or hand between the legs may mean hidden feelings. Tapping or drumming fingers may mean impatience. "Steeple" may mean intellectualization, coming from the head. Interlocking fingers may mean intertwined ideas, a puzzle, or putting things together. Picking at clothing may mean being picked at by something, or attempting to get rid of something. Holding an object may mean distancing.
Legs	One leg bouncing may mean wanting to kick someone. Two legs bouncing may mean impatience or ambivalence. Rubbing thighs may signal sexual thoughts.

Table 8.3 (continued)

Voice	Soft voice may show lack of confidence. Fluctuating volume may mean that what is said softly is area of insecurity. Whiny voice may mean a need for nurturance, to know people care. Monotone voice may show difficulty making commitments, trying to keep everything on the same level. Laughing or smiling may indicate anger or a need to cry. Talking fast may signal running from something.
Posture	Sitting up and forward may mean eagerness. Slumping may mean defeat, boredom. Head away may mean moving away.

From I. D. Welch & D. M. Gonzalez (1999).

behavior. Behavior has a thousand parents. We have to be guarded in reaching a conclusion about what a nonverbal message is meant to express. Simultaneously, we have to stay open to the possibility that significant and critical information is being presented to us and that it can lead to greater understanding of client's issues and concerns. In supervision, a beginning therapist had a client who, week after week, made the same gesture as he talked about a variety of issues in his life. The client would extend his hand, palm up, and make a slight jabbing motion. It looked to the observers as if he were holding something in the palm of his hand. The therapist was encouraged to explore the gesture with the client but was reluctant to do so. He voiced some doubt that the gesture was anything other than a simple mannerism. After three sessions, the supervisor insisted that the therapist identify and explore the gesture with the client. Finally, in the next session when the client made the gesture, the therapist reluctantly said, "When I look at your hand, it looks like you are carrying something." The client stopped talking, looked at his hand for a moment, and burst into tears. After a few moments, he said, "It's my parents' divorce." Therapy moved more rapidly after that, and the issue was clarified as a central theme in the therapy. This is a dramatic example of the role nonverbal messages can play in counseling and psychotherapy. Not all examples are as dramatic, but all are important. It does illustrate the value of staying open to nonverbal messages.

OBSERVATION

Yogi Berra is reputed to have said once that "you can observe a lot of things just by looking." Yogi was right. It is important to be aware and to be open, but we need to look, to observe. The next step is not as obvious as it might seem. Typically, observation is followed by a conclusion drawn from what we have observed. In the therapeutic relationship, this is exactly what we do *not* want to do without an intervening step. The intervening step might be labeled a "reality check." Meanings are within the client. Whatever we, as counselors and psychotherapists, observe has to be checked against the meanings assigned by the client. The source of these meanings, as we have discussed above, might be cultural or unique. Another note of caution about attempting to read nonverbal messages too concretely is that meanings can shift with context, situations, and time. Some years ago, when values clarification exercises were popular in the classroom, there was a game called "Magic Glasses." The glasses allowed you to change emotions. For example, you could put on "rose-colored glasses," and the world would appear friendly and optimistic. On the other hand, you might put on "suspicion glasses," and the world became dark and laden with misgivings and wariness. The same event viewed through different glasses led the wearers to radically different conclusions. There seem to be two recommendations for finding the meaning of nonverbal messages. The first is to put on "exploration glasses." The second is to take off our glasses, of whatever lens type, and, as openly as possible, permit the client to explain and explore meanings.

A smile may mean friendliness in the United States and surprise in Asia. It may mean deception for a confidence trickster. In pure point of fact, a smile may mean contemplative sadness, reminiscent fondness, suppressed anger, mounting tension, observed stupidity, and a host of other felt and unvocalized thoughts. Thus, we are led again to the caution that has been a theme throughout this chapter—don't interpret. Instead, read, infer, express, explore, stay flexible, adapt, and respect cultural and individual differences within the event, situation, and/or context of the expressed nonverbal message. You are right! It is complicated. And, that is the reason that *not* interpreting is a matter of respect for clients. Counseling is many things. One of them is the willingness of the therapist to take the time to explore meanings so that genuine understanding can come and effective coping strategies can be created.

SUMMARY

Our bodies speak at least as eloquently as the language of words. What we voice may convey only a part of the communication we wish to send. Grounded in a respect for the multicultural world and a profound recognition of the differences among individuals, seeking to understand nonverbal messages is a dynamic path to a trusting and therapeutic relationship. The path begins with the awareness that words alone do not express wholly the meanings and intentions of clients' stories. Centered in an awareness of our own nonverbal messages, we openly and flexibly can explore the meanings of both verbal and nonverbal communication. Listen with an open ear, an open eye, an open heart, and an open mind.

REFERENCES

Egan, G. (1998). *The skilled helper: A problem-management approach to helping* (6th ed.). Pacific Grove, CA: Brooks/Cole.

Ekman, P. (1992). *Telling lies: Clues to deceit in the marketplace, politics, and marriage.* New York: Norton.

Gazda, G. M., Asbury, F. S., Balzer, F. J., Childers, W. C., & Walters, R. P. (1984). *Human relations development: A manual for educators* (3rd ed.). Boston, MA: Allyn and Bacon.

Gazda, G. M., Asbury, F. S., Balzer, F. J., Childers, W. C., & Walters, R. P. (1995). *Human relations development: A manual for educators* (5th ed.). Boston, MA: Allyn and Bacon.

Gendlin, E. T. (1978). *Focusing.* New York: Everest House.

Gorden, L. R. (1992). *Basic interviewing skills.* Itasca, IL: F. E. Peacock.

Grace, M., Kivlighan, D. M., Jr., & Kunce, J. (1995). The effect of nonverbal skills training on counselor trainee nonverbal sensitivity and responsiveness and on session impact and working alliance ratings. *Journal of Counseling and Development, 73*, 547–552.

Highlen, P. S., & Hill, C. E. (1984). Factors affecting client change in counseling. In S. D. Brown & R. W. Lent (Eds.), *Handbook of counseling psychology* (pp. 334–396). New York: Wiley.

Ivey, A. E., & Ivey, M. B. (1999). *Intentional interviewing and counseling: Facilitating client development in a multicultural society* (4th ed.). Pacific Grove, CA: Brooks/Cole.

Lauver, P., & Harvey, D. R. (1997). *The practical counselor: Elements of effective helping.* Pacific Grove, CA: Brooks/Cole.

Long, V. O. (1996). *Communication skills in helping relationships: A framework for facilitating personal growth.* Pacific Grove, CA: Brooks/Cole.

McKay, M., Davis, M., & Fanning, P. (1983). *Messages: The communication book.* Oakland, CA: New Harbinger.

Mehrabian, A. (1971). *Silent messages.* Belmont, CA: Wadsworth.

Russell, J. A. (1995). Facial expressions of emotion: What lies beyond minimal universality? *Psychological Bulletin, 118*, 379–391.

Siegman, A. W., & Feldstein, S. (Eds.). (1987). *Nonverbal behavior and communication* (2nd ed.). Hillsdale, NJ: Erlbaum.

Welch, I. D., & Gonzalez, D. M. (1999). *The process of counseling and psychotherapy: Matters of skill.* Pacific Grove, CA: Brooks/Cole.

Part II

Moral, Ethical, and Social Issues of Counseling and Psychotherapy

Chapter 9

Diversity and Multicultural Concerns

David M. Gonzalez and Ira David Welch

We live in the world of the one and of the many. Our world could be described aptly as multimodal, polyphasic, and multidimensional and by many other adjectives that reflect the complexities inherent in the experience of living within it. Our world is one in which each of us simultaneously lives as an individual born into a cultural sea in which he or she is bathed from the moment of birth with worldviews and traditions. To study and understand all of these diverse cultures seems beyond any single human being. At the same time, neither the stamp of individualism nor the impact of culture can erase our common humanity and the universal experience of being a human being. We *Homo Sapiens* are a single species, identifiable as such, and yet, at the same time, separate from all others. In this multileveled world of experience, the helping professions have worked diligently to find ways to provide effective service to people from various backgrounds.

AMERICA'S CHANGING DEMOGRAPHICS

The changing face of the United States makes it increasingly likely that counselors and psychotherapists, no matter where they practice, will have clients who have backgrounds different from their own. In fact, D'Andrea and Daniels (1997) state:

> it has been predicted that by the year 2010 every major metropolitan area in the United States—with the exception of Milwaukee-Wisconsin—will be composed of a majority of persons who come from non-White, non-European backgrounds. It has been noted further that by 2020, the majority of persons living in the U.S. will come from what have ironically been referred to in the past as minority group backgrounds. This "minority majority" will be primarily composed of persons who are currently clas-

> sified as African-Americans, Asian-Americans, Latino/Latinas, Native Americans, and individuals from diverse Pacific Island groups. (Pp. 291–292)

It has become even more important for therapists to develop multicultural competency skills because of the changes taking place in society. The population numbers reflect a changing population of clients. What is also reflected in the census is that clear definitions and understandings of culture itself are difficult to maintain. A dramatic change in the 2000 census was the option of identifying oneself as multiracial. Figure 9.1 reflects the change in the U.S. population.

The census, which reported six racial categories in 1990, now reports sixty-three categories, most of them combinations of two or more races. There are 126 potential categories if the Hispanic option is included. Hispanics, who can be of any race, generally are considered to be people whose ancestry is from countries where Spanish is the primary language. But many Hispanics say that U.S. racial categories do not make sense to them, and they check "other" instead of "white," "black," or another category.

These demographic facts, of course, bring the matter of culture into focus. As a profession, psychology has had the phenomenon of gender differences between therapists and clients throughout history. We have, in the great span of time, only recently acknowledged that gender differences in understanding and acting in the world can influence our worldview and impact the counseling relationship. We have begun expanding the work of feminist theorists as we also begin to acknowledge the influences of lifestyle and culture as well.

These changes are reflected in the ethical codes that now advise and call for cultural competence (e.g., those of the American Counseling Association, American Psychological Association, National Association of Social Workers, and American Association for Marriage and Family Therapy). Our training programs, which seek to be accredited, are all required to offer courses in diversity issues. These are all profound changes from a decade ago.

UNCONSCIOUS EMPATHIC FAILURES

Counseling and psychotherapy have never been a one-size-fits-all endeavor. We have created a staggering array of helping models with different theoretical orientations and strategies of helping. Even with the variety of counseling theories and strategies open to therapists, it is becoming increasingly clear that so many of these theories are grounded in a North American and European cultural context and may have limited usefulness for clients from other cultures. Indeed, mistakes may be made, often unconsciously. For example, Welch and Gonzalez (1999) relate this story of a therapist and a client:

> A traditional Hispanic mother came to a counselor because she was concerned about her teenaged son who was becoming involved in gang ac-

> tivity, staying out at night and was "out of control." The counselor listened to her story and said that she would like the client to first read a particular book and then return for a follow-up session to begin addressing how to help her son. The recommended book was one that described problems of dependence and codependence, and focused on individual responsibility. It created feelings of depression and guilt in the mother because she now felt as if she was a bad mother. Her culture focused more on interdependence and the importance of family affiliation in which the family came first and the individual second. Feeling overwhelmed, she sought out another counselor. She came to his office clutching the book and told the counselor how much she must be a failure because so many of the practices advocated in the book went against her own parenting. (P. 92)

Welch and Gonzalez (1999) then report the outcome of the client's meeting with the new counselor.

> The therapist, on a hunch, suggested that she throw the book in the trash. With a surprised, wide-eyed look, she paused, then threw the book in the trash and remarked, "You mean I don't have to believe what was written in the book?" She sighed with great relief, "You mean I may not be such a bad mother?" The first therapist had an empathic failure with the client because of a lack of cultural, gender, and lifestyle understanding. That therapist had a book that fit a set of the therapist's beliefs but had little to do with the client's world. Yet the Hispanic woman had consulted an expert and, in her respect for the expert, had blamed herself for not behaving the way the book said she should. Furthermore, she felt like even more of a failure because she could not do what the book said, and interpreted that as personal weakness rather than realizing that the ideas presented in the book simply did not fit her. (P. 92)

One aspect of multicultural counseling competence is the recognition of the need, and the appropriateness, of referring a client to a more culturally similar therapist.

TENSIONS IN APPROACHES

Since we live in a multileveled world, different theorists have focused their efforts at different levels. This new emphasis on specific approaches aimed at gender, culture, and lifestyle differences has not come without tensions. Each theorist, focusing on a particular level, comes to a conclusion that may differ from other theorists' conclusions. Many theories developed in the past, for example, clearly evolved from a Eurocentric point of view. In personality theory classes the theories—sometimes laughingly, sometimes angrily—are referred to as the theories of "dead, white, European males." These theories, as a group,

Figure 9.1

Who lives in the U.S.?

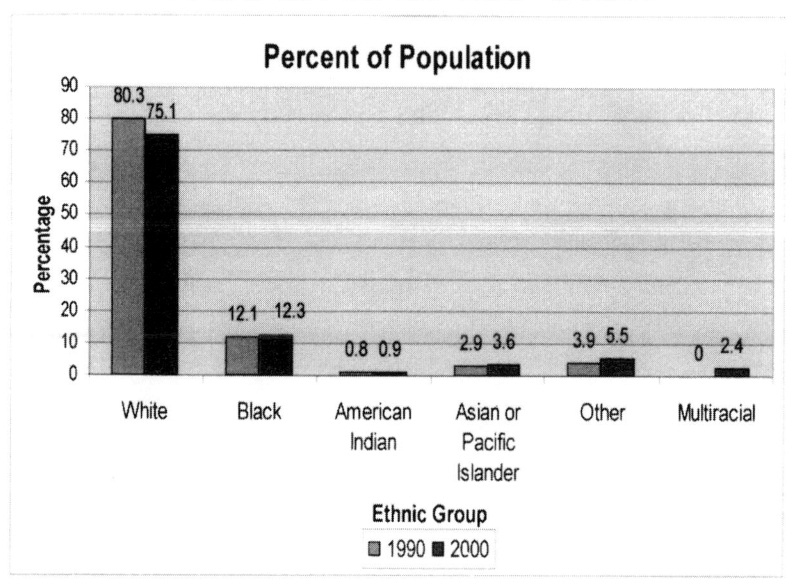

Because Hispanics can be of any race, numbers are not shown here. About 13% of the population identified themselves as being Hispanic.

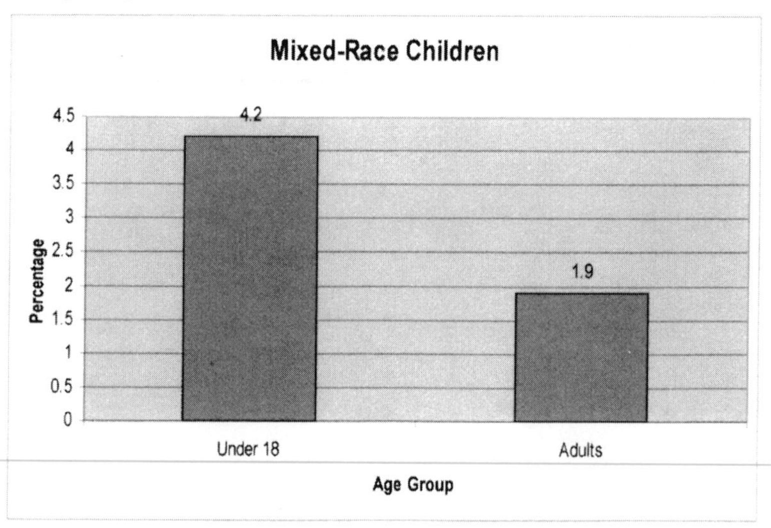

Children are more likely to be listed as being of mixed race due to the increase in the number of interracial marriages.

Adapted from the Washington Post, March 13, 2001, p. 124

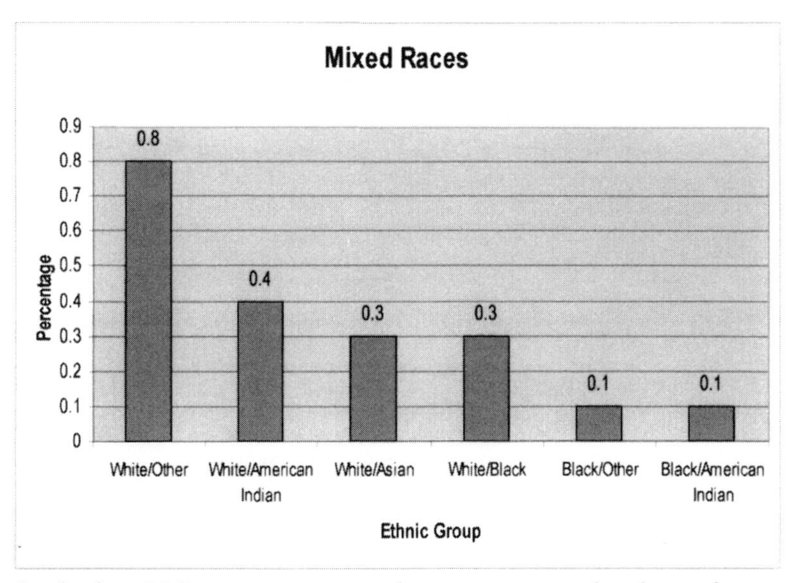

In the last U.S. census, respondents were permitted to select more than one race.

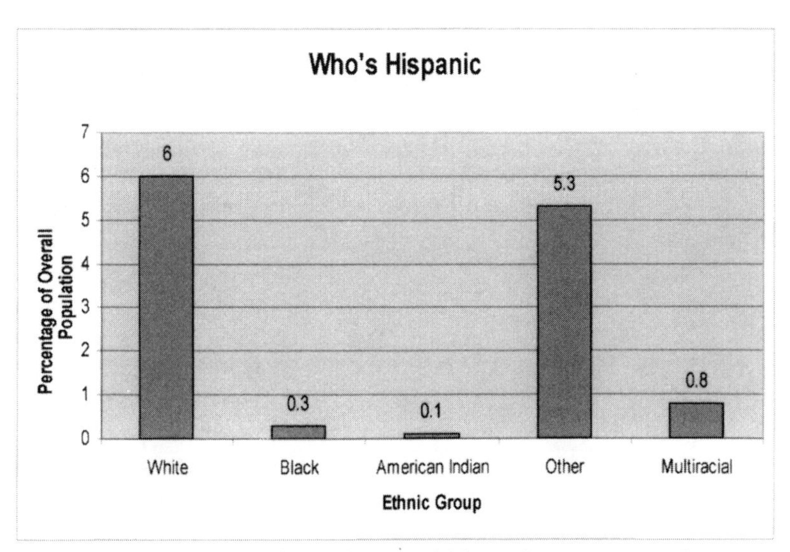

In the U.S. census, Hispanics could be of any race. About 13% of the population identified as being Hispanic.

Graphs Created By Dwight Malcolm, 2002

focused almost exclusively on the forces that determined or influenced the development of an individual's personality. This remains one of the major ways of conceptualizing human beings. Often these theories sought to expand the explanation of how a single individual's personality developed to make the claim that the theory was universal and that it explained the development of all people everywhere. While some might scoff at such a claim, the desire and the perceived need to develop an understanding of people as individuals within a species is a continuing force in psychological science. Later in the twentieth century, theories began to develop that emphasized the forces of culture as a major, perhaps primary, determinant of attitudes, values, beliefs, and behavior. Each of these is discussed in more detail below.

Focus on the Individual

Whatever may be true in the general certainly may be false in the particular. Many counselors and psychotherapists believe that focusing on the individual is the surest path to genuine understanding and to empowering clients. Welch (1998) points to two "paths of diversity." He writes, "The . . . path to diversity is understanding the individual client in all his or her richness and uniqueness. As psychotherapists, we must recognize that regardless of background, the person who sits before us is a unique, self-aware, and conscious being. We must not be so informed about culture and other forms of diversity that we lose sight of the *individual* who has come to us for help" (1998, p. 108). While not denying the importance of cultural influences, the importance of individual understanding remains a central focus. "The path of empathy" is one of two paths Welch recommends in an effort to understand and be of help to clients. The other path is the "path of knowledge" on which we, as counselors and psychotherapists, become informed both about the roles of gender, culture, and lifestyle in our daily lives and about any specific group with which we are called upon to work.

Lauver and Harvey (1997) also follow the theme of the importance of focusing on the individual:

> As counselors, we bring much with us that gets in our way as listeners: our own agendas, expectations, assumptions, experience, habits of categorizing data and people (adults, woman, middle-class, bright, poor self-image, fat, drinker, in denial), our need to appear expert, to be helpful, to be comfortable. It is very difficult to leave these "distractors" behind and to bring what Suzuki (1970) calls "beginner's eyes"—eyes that start at the beginning with this person in this moment, putting aside assuming, interpreting, analyzing, categorizing, labeling, and other processing in favor of openness—to what is here and now. This attitude of intentional naiveté is a powerful asset to counselors. (P. 21)

If we view this statement as including assumptions about our knowledge of culture, then it reads as a caution against making assumptions about individual clients who are identified as coming from a specific culture. For example, if you had just finished studying Hispanic culture and later met someone from that cultural background, there is no guarantee that you would know anything about him or her. He or she might be traditional or nontraditional in terms of culture—somewhere along the continuum of assimilation into the dominant culture. The only way to know is to find out from the person.

One example comes from this account of an awkward interaction: A student who had just completed a course in multiculturalism was introduced to a Hispanic individual and said, "So, you are Hispanic—oops sorry! I just remembered that I am supposed to refer to you as Chicano." All this was a surprise to the Hispanic individual, who had not yet had a chance to speak. It turns out that this particular individual did not relate to the term "Chicano," but rather related to the term "Mexican American." Obviously, the counseling student erred by making assumptions about the other Hispanic individual. The mistake could have been avoided easily by simply asking the individual how he preferred to be referred to in terms of ethnicity. For some, the term "black American" fits best, while others prefer "African American." Some native people prefer "Native American," while others prefer "American Indian." Generally speaking, if we are not sure how to refer to someone, we can ask. Most people are happy to tell us the term that fits best for them. Actually, we sometimes forget that persons in the dominant culture have preferences too. Some do not like to be called "Caucasian" or "white," but rather prefer "Euroamerican" or "Anglo-American" or perhaps some other term.

Client-centered therapy holds a strong influence on counselors and psychotherapists in the United States. While the term "client-centered" has been associated most closely with the work of Rogers (1961), we might also use the term to mean focusing on the individual as a source of primary importance in working with people. In arguing for focusing on the individual, both practitioners and theorists would point to research that indicates that the differences between individuals of the same group are greater than the differences among groups. We are different from one another culturally, they would point out, but the greater differences among us are individual ones. In fact, this point was made strongly in Allport's classic work, *The Nature of Prejudice* (1954).

Focus on Universality

Patterson (1985) argues that effective psychotherapy must be based on an understanding of the universality of human nature and values. According to Patterson, "the assumption that there are no universals in human nature, and no universal values, or no universal goals for counseling or psychotherapy" must be challenged (p. 185). He continues in saying that "the survival of a culture is a necessary but not sufficient condition for the survival and, more important, the development of the individual and his or her potentials. . . . The basic motivation of the human being—a universal motivation—includes but goes beyond survival" (p. 186).

Others argue that the forces of oppression in any culture or society must be recognized, faced, and challenged. West-Olatunji (2001) states:

> . . . counselors promote social responsibility and social action to empower groups of individuals. . . . Behaviors and attitudes which appear dysfunctional may be assessed as healthy coping mechanisms in a dysfunctional environment. Current work in this area suggests that racism, sexism, classism, and other forms of social bias act as insidious contributors to psychological malaise in marginalized communities. Future work in this area can further establish the empirical basis for social action in clinical practice as a cultural competency area for professional counselors. (P. 433)

While West-Olatunji is arguing for social action and social responsibility among therapists, including cultural competence, the argument also advocates a universal understanding of behaviors and attitudes that are appropriate and healthy for human beings.

Within the concept of social justice, there is an assumption that oppression anywhere is oppression everywhere. Such an assumption leads to a valuing of human liberation from oppressive assumptions, values, and behaviors, regardless of the society or culture in which they exist. The strongest tension surrounding the issue of oppression is frequently between an assumption of cultural relativism and the universality of human nature and values.

Focus on Culture

To acknowledge that tension exists among different practitioners and theorists does not detract from the importance of culture in the lives of us all. In fact, it would be wrong to conclude that the tensions discussed above between focusing upon the individual and focusing on universals actually show that culture is not considered an important aspect of the counseling endeavor. Similarly, it would be wrong to conclude that those who argue for a focus on culture do not recognize the importance of individual uniqueness or of our common humanity. Egan (1998) says this forcefully: "valuing diversity is not the same as espousing a splintered, antagonistic society in which one's group membership is more important than one's humanity. . . . Valuing individuality is not the same as espousing a 'society of one' (p. 49). Tensions exist over the primary focus of therapy and the centrality of individuality, humanity, and culture.

Clearly, therapists who ignore the role of gender, culture, and lifestyle do so at the peril of their clients. It seems relatively certain that the overwhelming number of counselors and psychotherapists who agree with Ivey and Ivey (1999) advocate for a concept labeled "cultural intentionality": "The culturally intentional individual [counselor or psychotherapist] can generate alternatives from different vantage points, using a variety of skills and personal qualities within a culturally appropriate framework" (p. 23).

Both informal and formal guidelines have been developed to help counselors and psychotherapists become more culturally competent. Combs and Gonzalez (1994) suggest that

> to begin preparing to live and work in a multicultural society, one must:
>
> 1. Value diversity.
> 2. Stop seeing others as imperfect versions of ourselves.
> 3. Be willing to educate oneself about other cultures.
> 4. Be willing to examine one's own biases and the biases of the majority culture.
> 5. Have contact with different ethnic and cultural groups. (P. 225)

These five suggestions all carry enormous implications in terms of the actual effort required to bring them to fruition.

> King (2001) suggests a different list of elements to aid counselors and psychotherapists in dealing with differences:
>
> 1. We need to do our "homework." We need to learn about the prevalent mores of people with whom we are working.
> 2. We need to ask questions. . . . What should I know about who you are so that I can understand where you are coming from and where you want to be?
> 3. We need to respect our uniqueness as well as theirs. We need to fully recognize and accept that different perceptions and different responses prevail even when different cultural backgrounds are not factors that are involved. (P. 99)

Egan (1998) suggests that counselors:

1. Understand diversity
2. Challenge whatever blind spots you may have
3. Tailor your interventions in a diversity-sensitive way
4. Understand and value the individual

These suggestions from various theorists are all helpful. Challenging ideas regarding cultural competence have come from Sue, Ivey, and Pedersen (1996). They propose a shift away from client-centered theories and practices to a "culture-centered" perspective. They offer a number of assumptions and propositions that challenge the entire field of counseling and psychotherapy to change. Sue, Ivey, and Pedersen (1996) argue that the fundamental practice of counseling and psychotherapy is flawed since it is based so substantially, if not wholly, on North American and European cultural assumptions.

Sue, Ivey, and Pederson (1996) offered a new theory, multicultural counseling and therapy (MCT), based on twenty-one underlying assumptions. Just a few of these assumptions are that

> Current theories of counseling and psychotherapy inadequately describe, explain, predict, and deal with current cultural diversity; diversification is occurring at such a rapid pace that mental-health professionals will increasingly come into contact with clients or client groups who differ from them racially, culturally, and ethically; and, understanding the cultural and social political context of a client's behavior is essential to accurate assessment, interpretation, and treatment. (P. 2)

These assumptions lead to six propositions as the foundation of a theory of multicultural counseling. They are, as Sue, Ivey, and Pederson (1996) define them, the following:

> Proposition 1. MCT theory is a metatheory of counseling and psychotherapy. . . . It offers an organizational framework for understanding the numerous helping approaches that humankind has developed. It recognizes that both theories of counseling and psychotherapy developed in the Western world and those helping models indigenous to non-Western cultures are neither inherently right or wrong, good or bad. Each theory represents a different worldview.
>
> Proposition 2. Both therapist and client identities are formed and embedded in multiple levels of experience (individual, group, universal) and contexts (individual, family and cultural milieu). The totality and interrelationships of experiences and context must be the focus of treatment.
>
> Proposition 3. Cultural identity development is a major determinate of counselor and client attitudes toward the self, others of the same group, others of a different group, and the dominant group. The attitudes, which may be manifested in affective and behavioral dimensions, are strongly influenced not only by cultural variables but also by the dynamics of dominant-subordinate relationships among culturally different groups. The level or stage of racial/cultural identity will both influence how clients and counselors define the problem and dictate what they believe to be appropriate counseling/therapy goals and processes.
>
> Proposition 4. The effectiveness of MCT is most likely enhanced when the counselor uses modalities and defines goals consistent with the life experiences and cultural values of the client. No single approach is equally effective across all populations and life situations. The ultimate goal of multicultural counselor/therapist training is to expand the repertoire of helping responses available to the professional, regardless of theoretical orientation.
>
> Proposition 5. MCT theory stresses the importance of multiple helping roles developed by many culturally different groups and societies. Besides

> the basic one-on-one encounter aimed at remediation in the individual, these roles often involve larger social units, systems intervention, and prevention. That is, the conventional roles of counseling and psychotherapy are only one of many others available to the helping professional.
>
> Proposition 6. The liberation of consciousness is a basic goal of MCT theory. Whereas self-actualization, discovery of the role of the past in the present, or behavior change have been traditional goals of Western psychotherapy and counseling, MCT emphasizes the importance of expanding personal, family, group, and organizational consciousness of the place in self-in-relation, family-in-relation, and organization-in-relation. This results in therapy that is not only ultimately contextual in orientation, but that also draws on traditional methods of healing from many cultures. (Pp. 13–29)

Sue, Ivey, and Pedersen (1996) suggest that MCT is a metatheory that encompasses the major assumptions of many traditional theoretical orientations and adds to them the vital component of cultural awareness. One of the goals of MCT is the increased sensitivity of counselors and psychotherapists that their relationship with clients is a multilayered one. Sue, Ivey, and Pedersen (1996) challenge counselors and psychotherapists to recognize that their personal attitudes about themselves, others, and counseling itself have been influenced by their culture. We are challenged, as well, to embed our interventions in the life experiences and culture of the client rather than from a theoretical or therapist comfort perspective. They suggest that the counseling professional has been too encapsulated by offering services from only specific offices and settings and too limited in permitting nonprofessional, culturally recognized helpers to be involved in the helping process. MCT strongly suggests that the Western focus on the self is inappropriate for many cultures and that we expand our understanding of human development to include an understanding of development of the self in relation to family and group.

Sue, Ivey, and Pedersen (1996) not only have included assumptions and propositions, but also have acknowledged the specific cultural competences developed by Sue, Arredondo, and McDavis (1992) to guide practitioners in developing counseling skills for a multicultural, diverse client population.

Becoming a "fully developed helper" (Egan, 1998) means developing the competences of multicultural counseling. The counseling competences described by Sue, Arredondo, and McDavis (1992) provide guidelines not only for the individual counselor or psychotherapist, but also for training programs as well.

What makes the development of cultural competency challenging for counselors and psychotherapists is that it becomes increasingly difficult to provide specific, culturally appropriate interventions based upon an assumption of identifiable cultural background. The client may seem to come from a specific cultural background only to have come from a racially mixed background in which the assumed cultural influences were missing. This challenges counselors and psychotherapists, particularly in coping with demands to be aware ethically of the client's worldview and to provide culturally appropriate intervention strategies. It does remind us that the goal of multicultural counseling is cultural intentionality in which the intentional therapist is one who can generate a number of alternative responses to clients.

A CAUTION ABOUT CAUTIONS

While reviewing a number of sources regarding multicultural issues, one may notice that it seems common for authors to report anecdotal experiences in which clients have been offended by a dominate-culture counselor or psychotherapist's insensitivity or lack of knowledge. The most frequent example, perhaps, has been the example of 'eye contact.' While eye contact, body language, vocal qualities, and use of language are all involved in multicultural and diversity sensitivity, eye contact seems to be the mistake most often mentioned. Several authors caution counselors and psychotherapists about the differences in assumptions between the North American and European white culture and African Americans, Native Americans, and Asians, for example (Capuzzi & Gross, 2001; Carkhuff & Anthony, 1979; Egan, 1998; Hackney & Cormier, 1994; Ivey & Ivey, 1999; Lauver & Harvey, 1997; Sommers-Flanagan & Sommers-Flanagan, 1993). Euroamericans are described as preferring more direct and sustained eye contact than some other cultures. Counselors and psychotherapists are cautioned about this cultural difference and we believe these cautions are generally beneficial and useful.

Yet, there is a danger in sending an unintended and improper message. While preferences for and meaning of eye contact may differ from culture to culture, it is decidedly not the case that people all over the world do not look at each other! Every culture has ways of noticing nonverbal behavior, and—in order to take note of nonverbal communication, such as facial expression, shoulder shifting, eyebrow movements, giving directions by moving the lips, or any of a variety of bodily signals—we must look at the other person. It is feared that the message being communicated to counselors and psychotherapists, especially young and developing ones, is that eye contact is the same as looking at the client and observing.

Ivey and Ivey (1999) remind us that "attending behavior . . . is a foundation skill of counseling, perhaps, the most important and basic skills of all. We must attend or listen to the client if we are to be of help" (p. 10). They say further, "to make contact with another human being, we need to attend" (p. 42). The point of this caution about a caution is that admonitions against inappropriate eye contact should not lead to a lack of attending behavior for us as counselors and psychotherapists. We need to be able to observe our clients genuinely and respectfully in our relationship with them.

DOMINANT CULTURAL FACTORS

Sometimes persons in the dominant culture ask the questions, "Do you have to be a minority to effectively teach diversity?" or, "Can a white person do effective counseling or psychotherapy with people of color?" The questions are useful because they create a context in which to discuss the problems and the solutions. In order to be a culturally effective helper, as discussed, a variety of things need to be in place. There is an additional crucial factor though: coming to a deep realization that people in the dominant culture have a fundamentally different life experience than people of color, who, at least in the United States, are in minority positions and perhaps even marginalized. People of color usually have to try to understand the dominant culture since it affects them in so many ways on a daily basis. On the other hand, people in the dominant culture do not necessarily have to understand the phenomenology and experiences of people of color, so, unless they are in a particular position that requires it, they are less likely to do so.

For example, a person in the dominant culture may have traveled down a certain road without experiencing any "bumps in the road," and he or she could accurately say there were no bumps in that road. It was smooth driving (at least for him or her). For a person of color, there may have been many nails in that same road. If he or she relates that experience to a person from the dominant culture, who says, What are you talking about, there were no nails in that road—"I just traveled it," then there is a demonstrated lack of understanding on the part of the person from the dominant culture. The culturally effective, white therapist would recognize that there were indeed nails in the road by seeing (and feeling) the world through the eyes of the person of color. It is like developing vision that sees beyond what one has been conditioned to see. The therapist that is unable to see the experience of others communicates that he or she is not cross-culturally effective.

When stepping into the world of diversity, there are multiple complications. Resolving these complications is not just a matter of acquiring new knowledge. There are prejudices, misunderstandings, differing opinions, and issues of social justice. Emotionally charged terms such as "reverse discrimination" cloud the discussion. Also, people often experience the guilt that comes with realizing social privilege and the ramifications of being in the dominant culture. These are powerful motivators for not wanting to face issues. Such realizations can be painful, and it becomes easy to blame the victims (e.g., blame the poor for their poverty) as a way of experiencing relief from any responsibility. So again, a sincere effort to understand various points of view is necessary, even when it is uncomfortable to do so.

SOCIAL PRIVILEGE

One aspect of existence that has particular relevance to a discussion on diversity is that of social privilege (Rothenberg, 2002). With social privilege there is power. Power has numerous dimensions to it (Johnson, 1999). Those in the dominant culture possess the privileges, political power, and economic power and lead a life that is more likely to have paved roads than dirt roads, so to speak. For persons not in the dominant culture, the same is not usually true. To varying degrees, the roads are less likely to be paved, and the opportunities along the way are likely to be fewer, and those opportunities that are there may have barriers, too. The issue is not begrudging the dominant culture for having privileges, the issue is that all should have the same privileges. When a helping professional is unable to realize the difference, it becomes very difficult for him or her to be effective in cross-cultural counseling arenas. One of the hallmarks of effective psychotherapy is the experience of being understood. An obvious question is, "How can a therapist be effective if he or she does not understand that there are important differences in experience?" We invite you to picture how your life might be different if you were forced to live it in the margins, rather than the center of the page. Imagine that your education, career, choice of mates are affected. What kinds of feelings start to emerge? Think of raising children in such an environment. Think of expressing your frustrations and pain to someone in the dominant culture or to those in political power and being told that you just need to work harder and that the real problem is that of individual responsibility. What, then, are your thoughts and feelings?

STRATEGIES FOR INCREASING MULTICULTURAL EFFECTIVENESS

In our view, when we make the decision to enter the helping professions, particularly counseling and psychotherapy, we also have assumed the responsibility of engaging in an introspective process leading to self-awareness in deep and meaningful ways. As is sometimes pointed out in our training programs, how can we facilitate and participate in the growth of others if we do not or cannot do so in our own lives? Like in any high-level skill or capacity, ongoing practice, self-reflection, and refinements are necessary to be culturally competent. In addition to the many useful ideas (cited earlier in this chapter) that others have offered to help us be more culturally competent, we put forth these thoughts and recommendations for counselors and psychotherapists:

1. We should stop seeing others as imperfect versions of ourselves (Ossorio, 1984). As long as we continue to see others as imperfect versions of ourselves, we are destined to want to fix *them*, change *them*, or, in the worst case scenarios found in history, eliminate *them*. For most of us, it takes continual monitoring to keep from slipping back into the trap of

seeing others in comparison to how they are like us or not like us and categorizing or passing judgment accordingly. We need to recognize this tendency in ourselves in order to monitor and transcend it.

2. It is important that we understand the sociopolitical environment that has influenced the lives of minority group members, as people are products of the environment from which they come (Sue, 1997). We wish to add another piece to this equation by emphasizing the importance of understanding how the sociopolitical environment has influenced the lives of those in the dominant culture. A thoughtful look at this dynamic should result in the realization that within the dominant culture, there are inherent privileges like holding the political and economic power. The world is set up to serve those in power, and those relegated to second-class status or the margins typically do not live in the same world and often are left out of the decision-making process. Those who teach courses in multicultural counseling can attest to the common phenomenon that a number of students in the dominant culture struggle with the concept of "white privilege" (Rothenberg, 2002). The discomfort with this concept is understandable as it is often accompanied by feelings of guilt or an urge to explain things away. Yet, without an understanding of privilege and power, the likelihood of empathic failures for counselors and psychotherapists is great. Opportunities and lack there of for education and career as well as how one's reference group is portrayed in books, history, and the media all carry enormous implications for both the dominant group and the minority groups. Our position is that, by choosing the helping professions, we have chosen an obligation to appreciate fully the concept and consequences of social privilege in order to be culturally competent.
3. We should appreciate the importance and psychological impact of historical events. Attitudes such as "Well, that happened a long time ago and had nothing to do with me" or "It's time to get past that" are sure blocks to understanding. In terms of historical sociological change, it has been only a relative blink of the eye since the United States was characterized by such realities as segregation laws, slavery, and overt bigotry. These attitudes have been institutionalized so much that, even today, we continue to discover them in the most subtle of places. Though we are attempting to evolve beyond such limiting attitudes, the effects still linger. In fact, it is important to realize that many people in today's generation were raised and educated by people of generations marked by prejudice.
4. We should realize the fundamental importance of genuine respect for others and ourselves. When words sometimes fail, the ability to convey genuine caring and respect for others builds working bridges at the intuitive level. Our position is that this cannot be feigned. At some im-

portant level, though elusive to science, people usually know when they are respected. The question for us to ask ourselves is, "Do I really respect others?" There is great pressure to give ourselves and others the socially desirable response: "Of course I respect all people!" The recommendation is to recognize that we all have some prejudices and with prejudice comes a lack of respect. To say that we have no prejudice is to say that we have no history. Remember that we were raised in particular environments in which we were taught certain things that have shaped our attitudes and values. Some of those attitudes and values may need to be challenged and unlearned if we are to maximize our ability to be of service to others. Another version of the claim of not having any prejudice is the color-blind notion. That is, some people feel that they have no racial prejudice because they do not notice color. One of the liabilities here is that, by not noticing color, the therapist is denying or not recognizing and appreciating the client's unique ethnic experience. Awareness of a client's ethnicity does not signify prejudice automatically. For those in the helping professions, it means being appreciative of the client in all of his or her richness and uniqueness and being open to hearing about the world in which each particular client lives.

5. We should be be aware of heterogeneity within cultures. Just as we do not want to be uneducated about other cultures, it is important that we not inadvertently make assumptions about someone from a different background because of the misguided notion that all persons from a particular culture are the same. In all cultures there is a great variation between and among persons. As noted by Allport (1954), there is more difference within any one group than there is between any two groups. Again, the client is our avenue to understanding in this regard.
6. We should bring up the cultural differences between ourselves and our clients. The opportunities to do so are natural and frequent and it should be done seamlessly. The idea is not to say, "Next week I am going to bring up my client's cultural background," an approach that would be awkward and unnatural, but rather to demonstrate our awareness that we each have unique experiences. For example, there are unique experiences with all races, with both genders, and with each particular culture. If that unique experience has not been mentioned during the counseling process, there is a good chance that something important is missing and its absence should be regarded as conspicuous.
7. We should be aware of and recognize our clients' spiritual practices. Such practices are sacred to some people's beings and a core part of existence for many. We want to avoid getting caught up in the dogma of who has the "right" religion or is on the "right" spiritual track. Also, this recommendation again implies the importance of being open to hearing and respecting the client's philosophy. This can be tricky, since some

people are taught that there is one right religion and if suffering people found that right religion then their suffering would be over. Such early teachings are like flypaper: It takes more than one vigorous shaking to rid oneself of these beliefs. Pull it off with one hand and it sticks to the other. With perseverance, though, it is possible to get rid of every dogma.

8. We should educate ourselves about cultural identity development models. This includes knowing where we are in terms of our own identity development, not just where our clients might be in terms of their identity development. Knowledge in this arena can enhance greatly the level of understanding between the client and the therapist.
9. We should realize that in some instances we may need to be willing to move beyond the formal therapy setting. For some people, from various backgrounds, therapy and counseling may not work best in the clinician's formal office. There are numerous factors that may prevent clients from coming into our offices. Thinking in terms of outreach, when appropriate, may be increasingly necessary.
10. We should expand our repertoire of possible responses. This may include learning to speak more than one language or having some degree of comfort with different forms of nonverbal behavior. Or it may involve the principle of Cultural Intentionality as proposed by Ivey and Ivey (1999), which includes the notion that we can and should have a variety of possible responses to any client issue.
11. We should regard and utilize the client as an invaluable resource. It would be virtually impossible to know all of the important information about every culture and its unique meaning for any particular client. Of course it is important to educate ourselves as much as possible, but it is unrealistic to think that anyone comprehensively could know all cultures, backgrounds, and related nuances. However, if we are open to it, the client is often a guide and resource of information. He or she can inform us of how he or she thinks and feels, sees the world, as well as the personal and cultural meaning attached to it. A practical example discussed earlier in this chapter is that sometimes therapists are not sure how to refer to the client's racial, ethnic, or cultural background. The solution is simple: Ask the client what term is most comfortable for him or her. The key piece of this recommendation involves a degree of openness to hearing, valuing, and utilizing the information in order to be of effective service. Being open implies that we have cultivated the capacity to set aside our prejudices, assumptions, and other such blocks to our hearing, seeing, and comprehending. We see cultivation as a mindful, intentional process of acquiring self-knowledge as well as knowledge about other cultures.
12. We should expose ourselves to groups and experiences outside what is

familiar and comfortable to us. How far out of our comfort zones we are able to step is largely an individual matter, but the mere experience of moving anywhere near the edge of our routine can heighten our awareness of where we are in our own cultural development and potentially can keep us from being encapsulated culturally.

13. We should maintain a humble attitude about our level of knowledge. An attitude that there is an enormous amount still to learn will keep us seeking to attain more knowledge and understanding. Once we think we know most if not all about a particular domain, the motivation to acquire new knowledge often fades. We want to be able to enjoy the knowledge of what we have learned, yet avoid falling into the delusion that we have completed the process. To paraphrase the German philosopher Schopenhauer, it is the most common of errors to mistake the limits of one's mind for the limits of possibilities.
14. We should incorporate some practice of introspection into our personal lives. This may involve formal meditation or some other mindful practice intended to enhance the process of self-knowledge and continual personal growth. Without self-knowledge, the readiness to work with others is limited. An introspective process creates the opportunity to discover and transcend our biases and other blocks to understanding. We do not become masterful at any endeavor without mindful practice, whether we are talking about becoming an outstanding football player, a master musician, or a masterful clinician.

These recommendations are by no means complete, but the hope is that a careful consideration of these ideas will result in a process of increasing multicultural competency for counselors and psychotherapists.

SUMMARY

We live in a complex world of experience. We live in the world as an individual with unique perceptions which we may or may not share with the people who are most like us—our family and our culture. As dissimilar as we are because of our individuality and the diversity of our cultures, we all share our common humanity. We are a single species, like no other. We have a common biology that makes us recognizable and understandable to one another.

These worlds of experience have led both practitioners and theorists to focus more or less on one of the worlds that seems most important to them and, thus, to emphasize the element of living as primary in the therapeutic relationship. This, which should come as no surprise to anyone, has created tensions among counseling professionals, especially as the importance of gender, lifestyle, and culture have been championed and accepted widely within the profession. It seems clear that cultural issues increasingly will influence the future of counseling and psychotherapy as the face of the United States changes. Language and culture issues promise to become even more important as the demographic picture shifts and the minority representation increases both in the general population and within the profession of counseling and psychotherapy.

Respect lies at the heart of effective counseling. Our attention to diversity issues, gender, lifestyle, and culture, reinforces the importance of respect in effective psychotherapy. One behavioral manifestation of respect is the development of an attitude of cultural intentionality, which defined by Ivey and Ivey (1999),

> is demonstrated when you are able to have many possible responses to any client issue. Though you may have an excellent natural personal style, you are able to build on it by expanding your alternatives for response. In contrast, lack of intentionality may be manifested by inflexibility . . . cultural intentionality requires you to engage in constant growth and change, the learning of new skills, and strategies, and flexibility with ever-changing clients who may come from widely varying cultural contexts. (P. 9)

The United States is a nation and a culture in a state of flux. We live in an ever-changing social environment in which respect for gender, lifestyle, and culture have awakened our profession to the importance of attending to clients with respect for these influences on their perceptions and behaviors.

Making ourselves culturally competent requires a sincere effort to open our hearts and our eyes to the experience of others. It requires an enormous effort to recognize which of our values, beliefs, and attitudes may help and/or hinder the helping process. The process can result in tremendous growth of ourselves as persons and as helpers for all people, not just for those who are like us.

REFERENCES

Allport, G. (1954). *The nature of prejudice*. Reading, MA: Addison-Wesley.

Capuzzi, D., & Gross, D. K. (Eds.). (2001). *Introduction to the counseling profession* (3rd ed.). Boston, MA: Allyn and Bacon.

Carkhuff, R. R., & Anthony, W. A. (1979). *The skills of helping*. Amherst, MA: Human Resource Development Press.

Cohn, D. (2001, March 13). Mixed-race categories: Clarity or confusion? *Washington Post*, A12.

Cohn, D., & Fears, D. (2001, March 13). Multiracial growth seen in census: Numbers sow diversity, complexity of U.S. count. *Washington Post*, A1.

Combs, A. W., & Gonzalez, D. M. (1994). *Helping relationships: Basic concepts for the helping professions* (4th ed.). Boston, MA: Allyn and Bacon.

D'Andrea, M., & Daniels, J. (1997). Multicultural counseling supervision: Central issues, theoretical considerations, and practical strategies. In D. B. Pope-Davis & H.L.K. Coleman (Eds.), *Multicultural counseling competencies: Assessment, educa-*

tion and training, and supervision (pp. 290–309). Thousand Oaks, CA: Sage Publications.

Egan, G. (1998). *The skilled helper: A problem-management approach to helping* (6th ed.). Pacific Grove, CA: Brooks/Cole.

Hackney, H., & Cormier, S. (1994). *Counseling strategies and interventions* (4th ed.). Boston, MA: Allyn and Bacon.

Ivey, A. E., & Ivey, M. B. (1999). *Intentional interviewing and counseling: Facilitating client development in a multicultural society* (4th ed.). Pacific Grove, CA: Brooks/Cole.

Johnson, A. G. (2001). *Privilege, power, and difference*. New York: McGraw-Hill (Mayfield Publishing).

King, A. (2001). *Demystifying the counseling process: A self-help handbook for counselors*. Boston, MA: Allyn and Bacon.

Lauver, P., & Harvey, D. R. (1997). *The practical counselor: Elements of effective helping*. Pacific Grove, CA: Brooks/Cole.

Ossorio, Peter G. (1984). Personal communication.

Patterson, C. H. (1985). *The therapeutic relationship: Foundations for an eclectic psychotherapy*. Monterey, CA: Brooks/Cole.

Rogers, C. R. (1961). *On becoming a person: A therapist's view of psychotherapy*. Boston, MA: Houghton Mifflin.

Rothbaum, F., Weiss, J., Pott, M., Miyake, K., & Morelli, G. (2000). Attachment and culture. *American Psychologist, 55*, 1093–1104.

Rothenberg, P. S. (2002). *White privilege*. New York: Worth Publishers.

Sue, D. W. (1997). The interplay of sociocultural factors on the psychological development of Asians in America. In D. R. Atkinson, G. Morten, & D. W. Sue (Eds.), *Counseling American minorities* (5th ed., pp. 205–213). Boston, MA: McGraw Hill.

Sue, D. W., Arredondo, P., & McDavis, R. J. (1992). Multicultural counseling competences and standards: A call to the profession. *Journal of Counseling and Development, 70*, 484–486.

Sue, D. W., Ivey, A. E., & Pedersen, P. B. (1996). *A theory of multicultural counseling and therapy*. Pacific Grove, CA: Brooks/Cole.

Sommers-Flanagan, J., & Somers-Flanagan, R. (1993). *Foundations of therapeutic interviewing*. Boston, MA: Allyn and Bacon.

Suzuki, S. (1970). *Zen mind, beginner's mind*. New York: Weatherhill.

Welch, I. D. (1998). *The path of psychotherapy: Matters of the heart*. Pacific Grove, CA: Brooks/Cole.

Welch, I. D., & Gonzalez, D. M. (1999). *The process of counseling and psychotherapy: Matters of skill*. Pacific Grove, CA: Brooks/Cole.

West-Olatunji, C. A. (2001). Counseling ethnic minority clients. In D. Capuzzi & D. R. Gross (Eds.), *Introduction to the counseling profession* (3rd ed., pp. 415–434). Boston, MA: Allyn and Bacon.

Worchel, S. (1999). *Written in blood: Ethnic identity and the struggle for human harmony*. New York: Worth Publishers.

Chapter 10

The Ethics of Listening and Responding

Ethics is what we do. It isn't a matter of our intentions, our wishes, our hopes, or even our explanations. It is our behavior. In this sense, ethical behavior is strict and unforgiving. The various organizations to which counselors and psychotherapists belong have codes of ethics and standards of conduct that are demanding and rigorous. These organizations and the dates of their current codes include the American Association for Marriage and Family Therapy (AAMFT), 1991; the American Counseling Association (ACA), 1995; the American Psychological Association (APA), 2002; the Association for Specialists in Group Work (ASGW), 1989; and the National Association of Social Workers (NASW), 1996. Yet, as stringent and exacting as these standards are, they are, paradoxically, simple. The ethics of therapy are based upon fundamental concerns for human rights and make sense not only in the lofty atmosphere of moral philosophy, but also in the common and ordinary understanding of human relationships.

THE GOLDEN RULE

The Josephson Institute of Ethics provides an excellent background for understanding ethics and ethical decision making. The following discussion of the Golden Rule, Immanuel Kant, and utilitarianism are adapted from the institute's *Making Ethical Decisions* (2001). Some might place the foundation of ethics in such philosophical teachings as the Golden Rule as it has been taught throughout history:

- What you do not want done to yourself, do not do to others (Confucius, 500 B.C.)

- We should behave to others as we wish others to behave to us (Aristotle, 325 B.C.)
- Do nothing to thy neighbor which thou wouldst not have him do to thee thereafter (*Mahabharata*, 200 B.C.)
- As ye would that men should do to you, do ye also to them likewise (Jesus, 30 A.D.)

CATEGORICAL IMPERATIVE

Others might suggest Kant's categorical imperatives as the basis for ethics. Kant's absolute moral duties, based upon principle, proposed that ethical duties should be accomplished regardless of the outcome or consequences. Two constructive rules have been teased out of Kant's philosophy:

- The Rule of Universality. We should act as if our actions were not time or culture based. We should act in ways that are appropriate for all people in any time.
- The Rule of Respect. We should respect the individual worth of every person.

Individuals are, in and of themselves, moral ends and should not be treated as mere means to one's own needs or gratification.

The argument against Kant's categorical imperatives is that, while it has the virtue of simplicity, it lacks compassion. Its absolute nature prevents one from acting for the greater good when circumstances call for it. Truth as an absolute, for example, can be used bluntly, harmfully, and dangerously. In therapy, truths often are related to time and psychological strength. What might be useful and bearable later in therapy might be harmful and insufferable earlier. Such judgments are not permitted under Kant's philosophy.

TELEOLOGICAL APPROACHES

The predominate approach to modern ethics takes into consideration the outcomes of our actions. Often referred to as utilitarianism, the prevailing view is that consequences are the best guide for ethical behavior. This view allows practitioners to make judgments about issues that compete with one another in terms of what, in probability, will be the most positive outcome.

Welch (1998) globally has summarized ethical principles in terms of five behaviors that underlie ethical practice: respect, honesty, privacy, competency, and steadfastness. Respect, according to Welch (1998), includes first recognizing the capabilities, skills, and knowledge of clients as they become therapists to themselves. Second, it is the willingness to enter into a relationship in which one of the primary goals is understanding.

Honesty carries at least two meanings in therapy. It means that therapists can be relied upon to be clear, straightforward, and nonevasive, or that they "mean what they say and say what they mean. They don't lie, cheat, or steal from clients" (Welch, 1998, p. 102). The second, more profound meaning of honesty beyond this businesslike approach, is that the therapist is expected to be a real human being in a real relationship. He or she is expected to make him-or herself known to the client. The chapter on self-disclosure, which follows, deals more extensively with this ethical concern. Here, suffice it to say that therapists cannot be phonies, role-players, or actors on a stage and expect to be effective.

A part of an honest relationship is that clients are told early on that privacy is not absolute. While a bedrock condition of effective ethical practice is privacy, it is dishonest to mislead clients into believing that everything that is said is private. This is one of the ethical conflicts with which therapists must cope. The demand for privacy sometimes competes with demands for protection of the client or others. Nevertheless, as Welch (1998) says, "psychotherapists are not gossips. What is said between a client and a psychotherapist is personal, private, and unrevealed. This confidentiality paves the way to trust" (p. 102).

Clients expect competency. Ethically, therapists do not practice in areas in which they are not skilled, trained, practiced, or supervised. This is not so much a matter of specific content issues or even of particular symptomology. It is a matter of being trained and practiced in the fundamental, foundational skills of counseling and psychotherapy with adequate supervision and feedback. No one expects any professional to know specifically every issue, problem, or diagnostic category. The expectations are more global. It is the expectation that therapists are able to enter into a therapeutic relationship and create a therapeutic climate that promotes client movement toward greater coping skills. Aside from the practical listening and responding skills outlined here, two excellent sources for understanding this fundamental level of psychotherapy are Hubble, Duncan, and Miller (1999) and Wampold (2001).

When the going gets tough, the tough go to therapy. I suspect that it would be a more wholesome world if everyone recognized that going to therapy isn't a sign of weakness but, rather, a sign of people doing something to take care of themselves. For our part, as therapists, we are committed to sticking with them when the going gets even tougher than when the client came in for help. This is the quality of steadfastness. In spite of the movement toward brief therapy and the unreasonable demands of the HMOs, successful therapy tends to be a relatively long-term endeavor (Wampold, 2001). As Welch (1998) phrases it, "successful outcomes in psychotherapy often come from staying with the tasks long enough to wear out defenses and push away confusion" (p. 104).

Kitchener (1984) proposes a widely used approach for summarizing ethics and a system upon which many ethical codes are constructed. The five moral principles are autonomy, nonmaleficence, beneficence, justice, and fidelity. Forrester-Miller and Davis (1996) provide a thorough discussion of Kitchener's five moral principles:

- Autonomy—This principle addresses the concept of independence. The essence of this principle is allowing an individual the freedom of choice and action. It addresses the responsibility of the therapist to encourage clients, when appropriate, to make their own decisions and to act on their own values. There are two important considerations in encouraging clients to be autonomous. The first is, helping the clients to understand how their decisions and their values may or may not be received within the context of the society in which they live and how they may impinge on the rights of others. The second consideration is related to the clients' ability to make sound and rational decisions. Persons not capable of making competent choices, such as children, and some individuals with mental handicaps, should not be allowed to act on decisions that could harm themselves or others.
- Nonmaleficence—Often explained as "above all do no harm," this principle is considered by some to be the most critical of all the principles. . . . This principle reflects both the idea of not inflicting intentional harm and not engaging in actions that risk harming others (Forester-Miller & Rubenstein, 1992).
- Beneficence—Simply stated beneficence means to do good, to be proactive, and also to prevent harm when possible (Forester-Miller & Rubenstein, 1992).
- Justice—This principle does not mean treating all individuals the same. Kitchener (1984) points out that the functional meaning of "justice" is "treating equals equally and unequals unequally but in proportion to their relevant differences" (p. 49). If an individual is to be treated differently, the therapist needs to be able to offer a rationale that explains the necessity and appropriateness of treating this individual differently.
- Fidelity—This principle involves the notions of loyalty, faithfulness, and honoring commitments. Clients must be able to trust the therapist and have faith in the therapeutic relationship if growth is to occur. Therefore, the therapist must take care not to threaten the therapeutic relationship nor to leave obligations unfulfilled.

Forester-Miller and Davis (1996) suggest that "by exploring the dilemma in regards to these principles one may come to a better understanding of the conflicting issues one faces in ethical choices" (pp. 1–2).

THE ETHICS OF COUNSELING AND PSYCHOTHERAPY

Welch and Gonzalez (1999) indicate that while "the primary purpose of ethical guidelines is to protect the consumer, such guidelines are also intended to educate practitioners on how to conduct themselves in their work" (p. 114). The issues described later in this chapter highlight principle ethical concerns for counselors and psychotherapists. It is important for each of us to be familiar with the ethical guidelines from our specialty organization, such as the ACA, APA, or NASW. These ethical principles and standards of conduct, while sharing a similar philosophy, are slightly different from one another. If you are a social worker, for example, your ethical guidelines emphasize advocacy for clients more than the guidelines for counselors and psychologists. If a question occurs, you are expected to respond in terms of the ethical guidelines of the particular professional organization to which you belong. It is important, therefore, that you be familiar with that code of ethics. Issues such as client welfare, confidentiality, competence, informed consent, dual relationships, and client rights are central issues in all ethics codes and will be discussed below as an introduction to ethical practice.

Consulting—A Primary Ethical Skill

Early in practice one learns that situations that are not clear cut occur on a regular basis. A client might need a ride home. Does this put one in jeopardy of violating the ethical concerns of a dual relationship? A client brings a gift at the end of therapy. Should one accept or decline? A client might offer a skill or service for your work as a therapist. Is it ethical to agree? These questions are often not answered easily, and it may depend on the circumstances. Even a careful reading of the ethical codes might not provide us with a clear answer. How should we proceed? These are judgments, and this seems an appropriate time to introduce the three principle guidelines to follow when you are undecided about some ethical concern. The first principle is consult. The second principle is consult. The third principle is consult. Anytime one is confused, vague, or undecided is the time to consult with one's colleagues or to call one's professional organization for information and advice. Of course, this is a somewhat flippant way to introduce this concept, and yet the serious side is that it is a central skill in ethical decision making. When you are undecided, unclear, uncertain of the right thing to do, consult. Consulting will be your best friend in the ethical practice of your profession.

Client Welfare

The welfare of clients is considered to be the fundamental and primary obligation of counselors and psychotherapists. The ACA (1995) code of ethics indicates that "the primary responsibility of counselors is to respect the dignity and to promote the welfare of clients." APA (2002) provides a similar principle, stating that psychologists have as a goal the welfare and protection of the persons with whom they work. Robinson Kurpius and Gross (1996) provide suggestions for guarding client welfare:

- Work in harmony with other health care professionals who are assisting your client
- Provide written descriptions of your therapeutic approach, record keeping, fees, testing and reporting strategies, and emergency procedures
- Share your code of ethics with your clients
- Practice within the limits of your competency and use appropriate referral sources
- Ensure that your methods, techniques, and therapeutic approaches are appropriate for the client and that you are trained to use them
- Avoid dual relationships when possible and feasible
- Consider the client's ability to pay your fee and either adjust your fee or assist the client in finding affordable services
- Routinely evaluate client progress and the therapeutic relationship to determine if your services genuinely are assisting the client

The responsibility for client welfare rests primarily with the therapist. Following guidelines such as the ones suggested by Robinson Kurpius and Gross (1996) provides a foundation for protecting that welfare. One essential aspect of client welfare is privacy, which we will consider next.

Confidentiality

Confidentiality and privileged communication are important client rights. Often the word "confidentiality" is used to communicate an ethical obligation, while the term "privileged communication" refers to a legal concept. They have come to be blended in modern times. In its legal use, privileged communication between a therapist and a client is protected in the same way that an attorney and a client relationship is protected. Even a court may not be privy to such information unless specific legal steps are taken to deny the privilege (e.g., a subpoena). While confidentiality does not carry the legal power of a privilege, it is still a professional responsibility and a matter of trust between the therapist and the client.

Confidentiality is not absolute. There is a tension between the client's right to privacy and society's need to know. It is important for clients to understand early in the relationship (not later than the second session) that the limits of confidentiality mean that the therapist will take steps to protect people in harm's way. Commonly recognized limits include

- Protecting the client if he or she is a danger to him-or herself
- Protecting the endangered person(s) if the client is a danger to others (e.g., situations of child abuse)

There are other situations in which confidentiality is limited, including some in states' laws that require reporting danger to incapacitated adults and/or turning unpaid accounts over to a collection agency, which constitutes a break in the agreement for privacy. Robinson Kurpius (2001) states that "other instances where the privilege is typically lost include when a client introduces his or her mental condition as an element in a court case, when the mental stability of either spouse is introduced in a child custody case, when the counselor is working for the court such as in conducting a court-ordered examination, when the client is suing the counselor, and when the counselor believes that the client is in need of immediate hospitalization for a mental disorder" (p. 77). Finally, a continuing controversy in our society includes whether confidentiality should be broken when one has a client with a communicable disease such as AIDS and refuses to inform his or her sexual partner(s) of his or her medical condition. The APA (1991) provides guidelines for therapists who work with clients diagnosed with HIV. These guidelines provide the conditions under which confidentiality would be breached in order to protect others:

1. A legal duty to protect third parties from HIV infection should not be imposed.
2. If, however, specific legislation is considered, then it should permit disclosure only when the provider knows of an identifiable third party who the provider has a compelling reason to believe is at significant risk for infection; the provider has a reasonable belief that the third party has no reason to suspect that he or she is at risk; and the client/patient has been urged to inform the third party and has either refused or is considered unreliable in his/her unwillingness to notify the third party.
3. If such legislation is adopted, it should include immunity from civil and criminal liability for providers who, in good faith, make decisions to disclose or not to disclose information about HIV infection to third parties. (P. 5)

These guidelines boil down to a recommendation that, unless there is an identifiable third party who is specifically at risk, the therapist should not break the agreement for confidentiality.

Therapists must take reasonable precautions to protect client records. This means not only that the office should be locked, but also that client files should be maintained in a locked cabinet or separate room. In modern times, extra precautions must be given to computer records, and safeguards must be installed to protect against an unwanted raid of confidential files stored by computer.

Finally, it should be recognized that the privilege belongs to the client. They may release the therapist, in writing, to communicate with others about the his or her therapy (such as a spouse, another mental health professional, or, commonly, an insurance company about a claim which requires that the client's diagnosis be revealed). Clients are not obligated to keep confidential what goes on in therapy and can talk to anyone, tell anybody, reveal anything that takes place in therapy. The therapist doesn't own the privilege, and, while he or she is obligated to maintain privacy, it is the client's life and he or she can talk about it anytime. It is only the therapist who is responsible for maintaining confidentiality.

Sometimes tension occurs when a client wants to see the therapist's records (e.g., progress notes). As a matter of trust, it is good policy to open the files to the client's inspection. Files are not confidential from clients. It is probably worthwhile to adopt a position that the information in a therapist's files belongs to the client. Legally, it might be the case that the paper belongs to the therapist, but the information belongs to the client.

Competence

Counselors and psychotherapists ethically are instructed to practice only within the limits of their training and experience. Robinson Kurpius and Gross (1996) list five conditions that define competence: "(1) accurate representation of professional qualifications; (2) professional growth through involvement in continuing education; (3) providing only those services for which qualified; (4) maintaining accurate knowledge and expertise in specialized areas; and (5) seeking assistance in solving personal issues which could impede effectiveness or lead to inadequate professional services or harm to a client" (pp. 353–377). Robinson Kurpius (2001) adds the need "to learn basic skills, to integrate academic study with supervised practice, to develop self-understanding, to seek continual evaluation and feedback, and to become intimately familiar with ethical codes of practice . . . and relevant laws influencing our profession" (p. 73).

The competence of the therapist is one of the reasonable expectations of client rights. Clients have a right to assume the person they seek out for assistance has the knowledge, skills, and competency to be of help to them. If the therapist does not, then it is the therapist's responsibility to assist the client in finding an appropriate referral.

Informed Consent

Informed consent has three distinct requirements—the client must be competent to give consent, the client must be given pertinent information, and the consent must be made voluntarily. Each of these is the responsibility of the therapist. While it isn't unreasonable to expect that clients have some responsibility in decisions that directly affect their therapy, they must meet the criteria above in order for their consent to be valid. Let's look at these component parts. First, the client must be competent to make decisions. Children (minors), for example, cannot give consent. They may give *assent* (i.e., they may agree), but they are not considered to be competent to understand the long-term implications of that to which they might agree. Second, the client must be given the information he or she needs, in a language and manner he or she can understand, in order to make an informed decision. Third, the consent must be given freely. The client must not be placed in a position of stress or duress. This raises the issue of whether court-ordered clients, or prisoners, can give consent. The issue of duress or coercion is one that is often delicate when consent is sought from those who may fear some form of retaliation if they do not give it. The APA (2002) code of ethics adds a fourth condition for informed consent and that is that the consent has been appropriately documented.

Dual Relationships

Welch and Gonzalez (1999) tell us that "the most obvious and perhaps most troubling form of a dual relationship is a sexual and/or romantic relationship between a counselor and a client" (p. 119). All codes of ethics stress that sexual contact between therapists and clients is unethical. There is no justification, excuse, or extenuating circumstance that is recognized as an appropriate defense for a therapist involved sexually with a client. The ACA (1995) code of ethics, as an example, reads, "Counselors must not engage in any type of sexual intimacies with current clients and must not engage in sexual intimacies with former clients within a minimum of two years after terminating the counseling relationship. Counselors who engage in such a relationship after two years following termination have the responsibility to thoroughly examine and document that such relations did not have an exploitive nature." The two-year standard is a minimum and remains controversial. Many therapists believe that once a client, always a client, and that the nature of the therapeutic relationship is such that the difference in power and the sometimes unrealistic view of clients toward therapists cannot be overcome and therefore any social, especially romantic, relationship with clients is not possible. This ethical rule applies to persons with whom a therapist might have had a previous romantic relationship as well. In such case, the client should be referred.

Dual relationships are not restricted to sexual intimacies. "Dual relationships occur when there is a professional and a secondary relationship which can be of a financial, social, business, friendship, or intimate nature" (Robinson Kurpius, 2001, p. 72). Therapists are expected to recognize that their helpfulness is restricted when they have a relationship with someone that can impair their openness, thoughtfulness, and/or capacity to suspend judgment. This might include relatives, friends, or business associates. As we have mentioned above, it does include people with whom the therapist had a romantic relationship. It means, for example, that it is wise to refer one's automobile insurance agent if he or she should happen to come to you for counseling. It might extend to a member of your church, temple, or synagogue, depending upon the closeness of the relationship. Certainly, a minister, priest, or rabbi would be inappropriate as a client. If one is a teacher, instructor, or professor, then students in one's program would not be appropriate. This is one of those times to employ the central skill of ethical decision making—consult, consult, consult.

Client Rights

Client rights have been mentioned several times. In fact, there are a variety of client rights that are difficult to summarize. The National Board of Certified Counselors (NBCC, 1987) has developed a summary of client rights. Clients have a right to

- Be informed of the counselor's qualifications, including education, experience, and license(s)
- Be informed of the counselor's fees, billing policies, time commitment, and services offered
- Be informed of confidentiality and the limits imposed by state law
- Be informed of uncommon counseling strategies and techniques
- Be involved in goal setting and evaluating progress
- Be informed of how to contact the counselor in emergencies
- Be informed that they may request a second opinion at any time
- Request copies of records and reports that might be used
- Receive a copy of the code of ethics
- Be informed of the appropriate professional organization for any doubts or complaints of the counselor's conduct
- Terminate the counseling relationship at any time

The NBCC also lists client responsibilities that include keeping appointments, paying fees, planning goals, and following through on goals. What is important to recognize, at least for therapists, is that the burden for maintaining rights rests with the therapist.

MULTICULTURAL AND DIVERSITY CONSIDERATIONS

Throughout this book, I have used Sue, Ivey, and Pedersen (1996) as a resource for discussing diversity and multicultural counseling competences. There are multicultural issues involved in ethical concerns as well. Sue, Ivey, and Pedersen (1996) believe that multicultural counseling competences include attitudes/beliefs, knowledge, and skills. Practicing ethics is a matter of what we do, so it seems most appropriate to examine the skills recommended for multicultural counseling competence as areas of concern for ethics. According to Sue, Ivey, and Pedersen (1996),

- Culturally skilled counselors seek out educational, consultative, and training experience to enhance their understanding and effectiveness in working with culturally different populations. Being able to recognize the limits of their competencies, they (a) seek consultation, (b) seek further training or education, and/or (c) refer out to more qualified individuals or resources. (P. 46)
- Culturally skilled counselors familiarize themselves with relevant research and latest findings regarding mental health and mental disorders of various ethnic/racial groups. (P. 47)
- Culturally skilled counselors take responsibility for interacting in the language requested by the client and, if not feasible, to make appropriate referral. (P. 49)
- Culturally skilled counselors attend to, as well as work to eliminate, biases, prejudices, and discriminatory practices. (P. 49)
- Culturally skilled counselors take responsibility in educating their clients to the processes of psychological intervention, such as goals, expectations, legal rights, and the counselor's orientation. (P. 49)

As you can see, multicultural counseling competence reflects the ethical issues of competence, informed consent, and client rights.

West-Olatunji (2001) provides a sound discussion of ethical considerations in counseling with ethnic minority clients and raises several important questions that will require answers in the near future:

- Should counselors without multicultural counseling training be cited by certification and licensing boards for working with ethnically diverse populations (or is it just "bad practice")?
- Can clients lodge complaints against counselors who lack cross-cultural competence when it affects therapeutic outcomes? (P. 428)

West-Olatunji's questions go to the heart of competence. Ethically, will we insist that multicultural counseling competences be equated with fundamental training in counseling and psychotherapy? These questions are unanswered at the moment, but the issues are pressing and we will be forced to deal with them soon. What position will you take?

SUMMARY

Ethical is a matter of what we do. This chapter has provided a broad-brush background on the basis upon which ethical codes are written and provided an overview of principle ethical concerns for counselors and psychotherapists.

The ethical codes of our professional associations are founded on five basic principles: autonomy, justice, beneficence, nonmaleficence, and fidelity. Autonomy is the client's right to make decisions freely and take responsibility for their acts; justice is a concept that strives for fairness; beneficence asks us to do good, nonmaleficence asks us to do no harm, and fidelity speaks to trust. These concepts form the basis for the minimum principles and standards for which counselors and psychotherapists are held responsible and accountable.

The various codes speak especially to such concerns as client welfare, therapist competence, confidentiality, informed consent, dual relationships, and client rights. Therapists are expected to practice only in those areas in which they are trained, have experience, and are skilled. It is expected that, except in unusual circumstances such as harm to self or others, the relationship between a therapist and a client is private. Clients have a right to make decisions about their therapy, and these decisions need to be informed. It is the therapist's responsibility to provide the information necessary for a client to make informed decisions and give consent. Therapists are expected to provide services only to those with whom they do not have a prior relationship that could be considered romantic, social, or financial. Sexual intimacies are forbidden, and there is no acceptable reason for entering or maintaining a sexual relationship with a client. Finally, clients have rights that include an active and involved decision-making role in their therapy, including access to records, timely information, routine progress reports, and the right to end therapy whenever they like.

Multicultural counseling competences are playing an increasing role in the ethical practice of counseling and psychotherapy. These competences are most apparent in the skills therapists are expected to have and practice. The most noticeable are practicing in one's area of competence—including training in diversity and multicultural knowledge and procedures—sensitivity to both cultural and language issues, informed consent, and client rights.

As beginning counselors and psychotherapists, each of you is responsible for being familiar with the ethical code of your particular training program, whether it is counseling, psychology, or social work. The reference section provides the website for each of these professional organizations where you can download the ethical code. It is recommended that you do that and spend the time necessary to become familiar with your particular ethical principles and standards.

REFERENCES

American Counseling Association (ACA). (1995). *Ethical standards.* Alexandria, VA: Author. <www.counseling.org>.

American Psychological Association (APA). (1991). Resolutions related to HIV/AIDS. Washington, DC: American Psychological Association. <www.apa.org/pi/hivres.html>.

American Psychological Association (APA). (2002). Ethical principles of psychologists and code of conduct. *American Psychologist, 57*, 1060–1073. <www.apa.org>.

Forester-Miller, H., & Davis, T. (1996). A practitioner's guide to ethical decision making.

Online resource catalog. Alexandria, VA: American Counseling Association. <www.counseling.org>.

Forester-Miller, H., & Rubenstein, R. L. (1992). Group counseling: Ethics and professional issues. In D. Capuzzi & D. R. Gross (Eds.), *Introduction to group counseling*. Denver, CO: Love Publishing.

Hubble, M. A., Duncan, B. L., & Miller, S. D. (Eds.). (1999). *The heart and soul of change: What works in therapy*. Washington, DC: American Psychological Association.

Josephson Institute of Ethics. (2001). *Making ethical decisions*. <www.josephson institute.org>.

Kitchener, K. S. (1984). Intuition, critical evaluation and ethical principles: The foundation for ethical decisions in counseling psychology. *Counseling Psychology, 12*, 43–55.

National Association for Social Workers (NASW). <www.naswdc.org>.

National Board for Certified Counselors. (1987). Client rights. Alexandria, VA: American Counseling Association. <www.nbcc.org/admin/clientrights.htm>.

Robinson Kurpius, S. E. (2001). Ethical and legal considerations in counseling: What beginning counselors should know. In D. Capuzzi & D. R. Gross (Eds.), *Introduction to the counseling profession* (3rd ed., pp. 69–84). Boston, MA: Allyn and Bacon.

Robinson Kurpius, S. E., & Gross, D. R. (1996). Professional ethics and the mental health counselor. In W. J. Weikel & A. J. Palmo (Eds.), *Foundations of mental health counseling*, pp. 353–377. Springfield, IL: Charles C. Thomas.

Sue, D. W., Ivey, A. E., & Pedersen, P. B. (1996). *A theory of multicultural counseling and therapy*. Pacific Grove, CA: Brooks/Cole.

Wampold, B. E. (2001). *The great psychotherapy debate: Models, methods, and findings*. New York: Lawrence Erlbaum.

Welch, I. D. (1998). *The path of psychotherapy: Matters of the heart*. Pacific Grove, CA: Brooks/Cole.

Welch, I. D., & Gonzalez, D. M. (1999). *The process of counseling and psychotherapy: Matters of skill*. Pacific Grove, CA: Brooks/Cole.

West-Olatunji, C. A. (2001). Counseling ethnic minority clients. In D. Capuzzi & D. R. Gross (Eds.), *Introduction to the counseling profession* (3rd ed., pp. 415–434). Boston, MA: Allyn and Bacon.

Part III

Responding Skills

Chapter 11

The Role of Responding in Counseling and Psychotherapy

Clients come to therapy not only to be heard and understood, but also to be acknowledged. The twin of effective listening is effective responding. "The function of the therapist, at least in the beginning of therapy (and, essentially, throughout the process), is to respond to the client. Interviews in which the client is responding to the therapist are not therapy interviews but interrogations" (Patterson, 1985, p. 106). Martin (1983) describes this process clearly: "There are two steps in responding: first you must hear the message, and then you must find the words to articulate what was intended. . . . Your job is to find the words that will exactly capture your client's meaning and evoke (arouse, stimulate) the feelings your client is moving toward. You are to bring to life what is only being talked about" (pp. 31–32).

PRINCIPLES OF RESPONDING

There seem to be straightforward principles of responding to clients. First, the therapist should be responding to the client rather than the other way around. Second, how the therapist responds makes a difference. One obvious practical skill to master in responding is limiting questions. Such a question-and-answer approach makes it clear who is responding to whom and places the therapist in the lead, a position against which effective therapy argues. So, asking questions, especially closed questions, puts the therapist in the lead (see chapter 20 for a full discussion of questions). Moralizing shuts the client down. Early problem-solving responses lead to intellectualizing. As we shall see in subsequent chapters, responses that encourage exploration, clarification, understanding, and, ultimately, focused action are the goal of attending and purposeful listening. Third, *responding will lead somewhere*. In responding, the therapist is involved in an active and energetic relationship with the client. The effective therapist listens with purpose and responds with purpose. Responding has as its goals the

Table 11.1
Guidelines for Responding

Positive	**Negative**
Direct	Circuitous
Immediate	Delayed
Clear	Vague
Genuine	False
Supportive	Obstructive
Brief	Prolonged
Frequent	Rare

exploration of client concerns, understanding of the source of those concerns, and focused actions necessary and possible for dealing with them. Finally, *the client will correct inaccurate and vague responses*, if permitted. There is a pattern to responding. Listening precedes responses; listening follows responses. Clients will correct our responses, and, by listening to the verbal and nonverbal clues clients give us, we can further clarify and understand the client's intended meanings.

GUIDELINES FOR RESPONDING

McKay, Davis, and Fanning (1983) discuss guidelines for effective expression. They are adapted and expanded here as guidelines for effective responding in counseling and psychotherapy (see Table 11.1). Effective responding is direct, immediate, clear, genuine, supportive, brief, and frequent. When something needs to be said, say it. That is the purpose of being direct. Effective therapists are not vague, roundabout, or devious. Clients come to therapy in part because they often are not receiving accurate feedback from their environment. Being direct provides the client with accurate feedback, so that he or she is able to make more effective decisions. The role of timing in responding is important, and directness is, as is true for any principle in therapy, modified and adapted so that its expressions have a reasonable chance of being therapeutic.

There is an old saying, "Strike while the iron is hot." The metal is malleable, susceptible, and ready. A response that is immediate is one that seizes the psychological moment to provide the client with feedback on what has been communicated to another person. Often, in that moment, clarity and the seeds of understanding can be planted and nourished. Immediate does not mean instantly necessarily. It is not so much a matter of linear time as it is a matter of psychological or emotional time. It is immediate in the sense that the client's meanings are responded to without evasion.

Clients are not helped by theoretical jargon. Responses need to be clear and as precise as they can be made in the moment. The purpose is to clarify and illuminate what might be vague and shadowed for the client. Part of being clear is focusing on one thing at time or on separating parts of messages into understandable chunks. The listening skill of focusing on intensity or frequency helps here. If a client has emphasized one part of a long list of concerns, then being clear is identifying what has been emphasized and exploring that with the client.

Genuineness is one of the core conditions necessary for effective therapy. Your responses need to be genuine. If therapists send double messages, then the therapy is confused and confounded. In a practical sense, genuineness buys a lot of goodwill. Even when you entirely miss the meanings a client is trying to communicate, a genuine miss still teaches the client that you are trying to understand, and he or she will be forgiving and, perhaps, try harder themselves to be clearer so that you can understand. In those times when you are accurate, the genuine quality of the response adds power and substance to your response for the client.

Being supportive means that your response is given in such a way that the client recognizes that the purpose and intent of the feedback is to clarify and explore the issues and concerns that he or she has verbalized, hinted at, or in some nonverbal way suggested. Support in this sense means that responses are not judgmental, moralistic, or condemning.

Responses should be brief. Effective therapists respond in words, phrases, and short, declarative sentences. You should not respond in paragraphs or lectures. In therapy, interventions are short and have the intention of stimulating client talk. Stimulating client talk allows the therapist to respond to the client. It is helpful to think in terms of the Rule of Two-Thirds. Two-thirds of talk in therapy should be client talk. Two-thirds of client talk should be meaningful (dealing with issues and concerns and not small talk). And, as an important reminder, it is likely that roughly two-thirds of communication will be nonverbal.

Finally, responses should be frequent. "The therapist needs to respond frequently because his or her function is partly to be the vehicle for self-confrontation by the client. Frequent responding keeps therapy going by giving feedback, by making the client feel understood, by preventing aimless circling, and by making mutual exploring the overall focus of therapy" (Martin, 1983, p. 39). The danger of overresponding is that the therapist seizes the lead, dominates, and teaches the client that the therapist will do the work. Egan (1998) invites the therapists to imagine a continuum with "directing client lives" at one end and "leaving clients completely to their own devices" at the other. Between these two extremes will be "helping clients make their own decisions and act on them" (p. 52).

Effective responses in counseling and psychotherapy are direct, immediate, clear, genuine, supportive, brief, and frequent. Imagine, if you will, responses that are described as circuitous, delayed, vague, false, obstructive, prolonged, and rare as descriptive of a relationship with a therapist. This list is hardly a recommendation for effective communication. In this sense, even though there isn't a handy mnemonic device, these guidelines for effective responding do hang together and make sense both logically and clinically. They facilitate clarification, exploration, and understanding and pave the way for effective action by the client.

CAUTIONS

There is a danger when beginning counselors and psychotherapists view both listening and responding skills as easy. They might view themselves as "sensitive" or "gifted" or even as compassionate people who believe their caring will be sufficient to create a healing environment. Such beliefs can seduce beginning therapists into ignoring the hard work that is necessary to learn attending, listening, and responding skills so that they become second nature, natural, and genuine. Egan (1998) describes three dimensions of responding skills necessary to become "fluid" in their use. First is *perceptiveness* (knowledge). "Your responding skills are only as good as the accuracy of the perceptions on which they are based. . . . The kind of perceptiveness needed to be a good helper comes from basic intelligence, social intelligence, effective attending, and careful listening. It does not come automatically with experience" (pp. 81–82). This takes us back to the importance of listening skills. There is a direct link between effective listening and effective responding.

Second, once therapists are aware of which response is needed, they need the skills to respond effectively. Egan labels this *know-how*. In supervision, for example, beginning therapists often comment, "what I was thinking and wanted to say was . . ."—to which, I am certain, many supervisors have responded, "Don't say it to me, say it to the client!" It doesn't do clients any good for therapists to have insights, understandings, ideas, or even hunches if they are not communicated to the clients as tentative feedback.

In this vein, sound perceptions and even solid know-how are of little usefulness if therapists don't act when necessary. This quality of *assertiveness* (courage) is the third needed dimension of effective responding. Obviously, it takes courage to act on perceptions and to use one's skills. This is the Giraffe principle: You have to stick your neck out from time to time to be a good servant. Sometimes the responses and feedback needed by clients can be hard to hear. Even responding to content alone can be an act of courage when the topic is death, abuse, violence, or any of the painful events of human life. Of course, clients don't come to therapy to share good news, and their expectation of therapists is that they will have the perceptiveness, skill, and courage to help them cope with the issues, concerns, problems, and dilemmas that have prevented them from living their lives effectively and well.

Another caution has to do with falling into a pattern of responding. Hackney and Cormier (1994) warn therapists against becoming too reliant on either cognitive or affective responding. If one responds only in a cognitive way, there are dangers for the therapy. First, the therapist may reinforce intellectualizing and the denial of feelings. Second, responding only in a cognitive way may interfere and even prevent the client from sharing feelings in a nonjudgmental climate. Third, there is the danger that such cognitive responses may repeat a pattern in the client's life in which he or she has been unable to express feelings.

There are dangers in responding only to feelings as well. First, such a pattern of responding is unrealistic and doesn't reflect the larger society in which the client lives. It may reduce the probability of being able to generalize and use what has been learned in therapy in a larger context. Second is the danger that focusing only on feelings "fosters only an internal focus to the exclusion of the world around the client" (Hackney & Cormier, 1994, p. 115). Third, focusing only on feelings "induces catharsis—the ventilation of pent-up feelings and concerns. For some clients this may be all that is necessary. For other clients this is not a sufficient goal. With catharsis there is a greater possibility of reinforcing 'sick talk'; that is, the therapist's responses to feelings may only generate more client negative self-referent statements" (p. 115). What is called for in effective responding is a balance between cognitive and affective concerns, so that clients are able to both reflect and confront the feelings and meanings they give to experiences and to generalize their understandings to their daily lives.

TYPES OF RESPONSES

There are essentially two types of therapeutic responses. First, therapists can respond to content. Second, therapists can respond to feelings, or meanings. Of course, effective responding integrates these, but experienced counselors and psychotherapists know that if therapists recognize and acknowledge the clients' feelings/meanings, then the clients will assume the therapists understand the content. The reverse, however, is not assumed. That is, if the therapist recognizes and responds only to content, then the client will not assume that the therapist understands feelings/meanings.

A BRIEF HISTORY OF RESPONDING SKILLS

Miars and Halverson (2001) provide a short and excellent history of responding skills developed through time:

> Rogers (1958) identified four conditions that he believed all counselors should provide in the context of a helping relationship. These necessary, but not necessarily sufficient, core conditions were: (1) unconditional positive regard for the individual, (2) genuineness, (3) congruence, and (4) empathy. Later, Carkhuff and Berenson (1967) added two additional traits or skills to the list: respect and concreteness. Thirteen years later Ivey and Simek-Downing (1980) labeled these traits "communications skills," and added warmth, immediacy, and confrontation to the list. (P. 52)

This list of research-derived responding skills drives the remainder of this book. The following chapters—which include ineffective responses, empathy, warmth and respect, genuineness, immediacy, self-disclosure, focusing (concreteness), confrontation, questions, and nonverbal messages—provide a thorough, though not exhaustive, training in responding skills. The practice of these skills, along with those discussed earlier for attending and listening, greatly increases the probability of establishing an effective therapeutic relationship and predicting a successful outcome for psychotherapy.

MULTICULTURAL AND DIVERSITY CONCERNS

I have used Sue, Ivey, and Pedersen (1996) throughout this book to highlight multicultural and diversity concerns. Their listing of multicultural counseling competences seems to me to be the most thorough and understandable approach to developing listening and responding skills that are used sensitively with clients who are from a culture and background different from our own. Those competences that apply to responding in general deal with attitudes/beliefs, knowledge, and skills. Sue, Ivey, and Pedersen (1996) include the following competences, which seem most necessary as a therapist considers the multicultural and diversity issues of the therapeutic relationship:

- Culturally skilled counselors have moved from being culturally unaware to being aware and sensitive to his/her own cultural heritage and to valuing and respecting differences.(P. 46)
- Culturally skilled counselors are aware of how their own cultural background/experiences, attitudes, values, and biases influence psychological processes. (P. 46)
- Culturally skilled counselors are able to recognize the limits of their competencies and expertise. (P. 46)
- Culturally skilled counselors possess knowledge about their social impact upon others. They are knowledgeable about communication style differences, how their style may clash or facilitate the counseling process with minority clients, and how to anticipate the impact it may have on others. (P. 46)
- Culturally skilled counselors seek out educational, consultative, and training experience to enhance their understanding and effectiveness in working with culturally different populations. Being able to recognize the limits of their competencies, they (a) seek consultation, (b) seek further training or education, and/or (c) refer out to more qualified individuals or resources. (P. 46)
- Culturally skilled counselors value bilingualism and do not view another

language as an impediment to counseling (monolingualism may be the culprit). (P. 48)

- Culturally skilled counselors have a clear and explicit knowledge and understanding of the generic characteristics of counseling/therapy (culture-bound, class-bound, and monolingual) and how they may clash with the cultural values of various minority groups. (P. 48)
- Culturally skilled counselors are able to engage in a variety of verbal/nonverbal helping responses. They are able to send and receive both verbal and nonverbal messages accurately and appropriately. They are not tied down to only one method or approach to helping, but recognize that helping styles and approaches may be culture-bound. When they sense that their helping style is limited and potentially inappropriate, they can anticipate and ameliorate its negative impact. (PP. 48–49)
- Culturally skilled counselors take responsibility for interacting in the language requested by the client and, if not feasible, to make appropriate referral. A serious problem arises when the linguistic skills of a therapist do not match the language of the client. If not possible, therapists should (a) seek a translator with cultural knowledge and appropriate professional background, and (b) refer to a knowledgeable and competent bilingual counselor. (P. 49)

These multicultural competences include not only attitudinal assumptions, but also the willingness to obtain specific knowledge and seek consultants' help in working with clients whose culture and background are different from that of the therapist. They provide guidelines for beginning and experienced therapists as they seek to enhance their skills and knowledge in the diverse demographic world of today.

SUMMARY

The skills of listening and responding are not easy and require practice. There are pitfalls for both the beginning and the practiced therapist. This introductory chapter provides principles, guidelines, and cautions for counselors and psychotherapists.

Effective responding is grounded in effective attending and listening. An effective therapist is one who has developed perceptiveness, skill, and the courage to provide important feedback assertively to clients when it is needed and how it is needed. Guidelines for effective responding include recommendations that responses be direct, immediate, clear, genuine, supportive, brief, and frequent.

Responding makes a difference in the counseling relationship. It demonstrates that the therapist is present, focused, and attentive. While it is true, to a degree, that the therapist's responses focus the therapy, it should be clear that the client guides the content and pace of therapy and that the therapist is responding to the client. In this response pattern, it is clear that the client is leading, not the therapist.

The counselor/psychotherapist in the modern world is one who is aware of the wide-ranging cultural, ethnic, national, and linguistic possible clients who might seek his or her services. While it is not possible to be familiar with, much less master, the knowledge and skills necessary for working with *all* possible clients, it is possible to be sensitive to and aware of strategies for working with a diverse population.

REFERENCES

Carkhuff, R. R., & Berenson, B. (1967). *Beyond counseling and therapy*. New York: Holt, Rinehart & Winston.

Egan, G. (1998). *The skilled helper: A problem-management approach to helping* (6th ed.). Pacific Grove, CA: Brooks/Cole.

Hackney, H., & Cormier, S. (1994). *Counseling strategies and interventions* (4th ed.). Boston, MA: Allyn and Bacon.

Ivey, A. E., & Simek-Downing, L. (1980). *Counseling and psychotherapy*. Englewood Cliffs, NJ: Prentice-Hall.

Martin, D. G. (1983). *Counseling and therapy skills*. Prospect Heights, IL: Waveland Press.

McKay, M., Davis, M., & Fanning, P. (1983). *Messages: The communication book*. Oakland, CA: New Harbinger.

Miars, R. D., & Halverson, S. E. (2001). The helping relationship. In D. Capuzzi & D. R. Gross (Eds.), *Introduction to the counseling profession* (3rd ed., pp. 50–68). Boston, MA: Allyn and Bacon.

Patterson, C. H. (1985). *The therapeutic relationship: Foundations for an eclectic psychotherapy*. Pacific Grove, CA: Brooks/Cole.

Rogers, C. R. (1958). The characteristics of a helping relationship. *Personnel and Guidance Journal, 37*, 6–16.

Sue, D. W., Ivey, A. E., & Pedersen, P. B. (1996). *A theory of multicultural counseling and therapy*. Pacific Grove, CA: Brooks/Cole.

Chapter 12

The Inadequate Response

What we say matters. It is not enough to simply respond to clients; we must respond appropriately and effectively. As King (2001) states "There are counseling techniques and, then again, there are counseling techniques" (p. 69). Our obligation to clients, and our ethical responsibility as we have seen in chapter 10, is to practice competently. There is more to it, of course, than merely meeting an obligation. Counselors and psychotherapists come to the discipline for a host of reasons, not the least of which is a healthy dose of compassion. So, we care about practicing in wholesome and effective ways.

In spite of our compassion and our motivations to do good, we sometimes—perhaps even *often* early on—"tend to ask questions, offer opinions, and make speeches" (Martin, 1983, p. 31). It is worth our time to look over some common mistakes in responding in order to avoid them.

INEFFECTIVE RESPONDING

When clients have been slow to respond to their own internally felt issues and concerns in therapy, we as a discipline have been quick to identify "resistance and the processes of defense" as causes. Yet, "we have been unwilling to use the same explanations for ourselves when we mask ourselves" (Welch, 1998, p. 87). Ineffective responding may have its roots not only in our lack of skill, but also in our fears and defenses. It follows, therefore, that an early step in effective responding is tending to our own house. Welch (1998) addressed some "false roles" that ineffective therapists sometimes adopt and metaphorically labeled these "masks." First, there is the Mask of the Pundit. "What do pundits do? . . . they do what pundits do. They analyze. They conclude. They offer opinions" (p. 88). Second, there is the Mask of the Wizard. "Wizards heal by magic. They see themselves as possessing unique qualities or knowledge that produce amazing and astounding cures that baffle the professional community" (p. 89).

Third, some ineffective therapists adopt the Mask of the Priest. The priest, used in its metaphoric and disparaging form, "is one who moralizes or makes sermons about some *a priori*, pre-supposed good. This person pontificates on the way it is supposed to be" (p. 90). Finally, there is the Mask of the Clerk. "A clerk is one who takes information, keeps records, tabulates, writes reports, and so on. . . . Such behavior is the pretense of care and the accomplishment of nothing" (p. 92). Welch labels these as "false roles," and the metaphor of the mask is used to make clear that they are ways of hiding the therapist from the client (see chapter 15 for a longer discussion of these false roles). This need to hide is not a matter of skill; it is more likely that it is a matter of defensiveness. Defensiveness can lead to what Lauver and Harvey (1997) call "bailing out" or "shifting the focus from a painful or awkward moment to some other topic" (p. 85). We have to deal with our own "unfinished business" so that we can attend to the business of clients. That said, this chapter focuses on ineffective responses in therapy.

A number of authors have discussed this "blocking" dimension of therapy and have identified common ineffective responses (Egan, 1998; Gordon, 1974; Hackney & Cormier, 1994; King, 2001; Long, 1996; Martin, 1983; Sommers-Flanagan & Sommers-Flanagan, 1993; Welch & Gonzalez, 1999). Blocking "refers to the counselor's reaction to client feelings in ways that reduce or restrict his or her helpfulness" (Hackney & Cormier, 1994, p. 103).

Egan (1998), for example, lists a number of "possibilities to be avoided," including no response, distracting questions, clichés, interpretations, advice, parroting, and sympathy and agreement (which he calls "forms of collusion with the client") (p. 96–97). Let's look at how these ineffective responses might come across to a client. Gina is an attractive woman in her midthirties who teaches at the college level. She holds a master's degree and is considering studying for her doctorate. She comes to therapy because, as you will see, she has "self-concept" issues and wants to deal with them. Her short introduction begins with a description of what she wants from therapy:

> Cl: I'm spending more time worrying about myself. I want to go back for my doctorate but I'm not sure I can. Because of time and money and . . . well, I'm just feeling insecure about myself. I don't want to spend any more than four sessions on my self-concept and then make a decision.

How should the therapist respond? Chapters 13–21 discuss effective responses including empathy, warmth and respect, genuineness, immediacy, self-disclosure, concreteness (focusing), confrontation, appropriate questions, and nonverbal facilitation. For the moment, however, let's deal with some ineffective responses:

> *No Response*: Consider the effect on yourself if you came to a therapist and said what Gina said and then the therapist didn't respond. You are sitting

just waiting and the therapist does nothing. No response means no nonverbal gesture to encourage you to continue talking and no verbal acknowledgement. Silence, of course, has different meanings in different cultures, but early in therapy it should be used cautiously. Sue, Ivey, and Pedersen (1996) warn that "interviewers who begin their sessions with silence and continue using silence liberally, without explaining the purpose of their silence to their clients, run the risk of scaring clients away" (p. 71). The better alternative is to respond either verbally or nonverbally, acknowledging that you have heard them, and encourage them to continue.

Distracting questions: Suppose now that the therapist does respond. He or she asks, "What do you want to study for your doctorate?" or "Have you been teaching at the university long?" Such questions are at best irrelevant and more likely distracting for the client. They ignore what the client has said and provide no recognition of any feelings that may be present in her statements. Chapter 20 provides a discussion of questions in therapy, but again, for the moment consider the advice that questioning in therapy ought to be limited, nondirective, justifiably needed, and, when used, generally open-ended.

Clichés: A therapist might say, "As one considers a big step like a doctorate it's normal to have self doubts." Such a response again ignores the client's concerns and, in fact, dismisses her as if to say her concerns are unwarranted and unimportant. It is labeled a "cliché" because it tends to be a common response in ordinary, daily exchanges.

Interpretations: "Women in our society are often concerned with intellectual issues. That is one of the outcomes of our oppressive culture. I'm thinking that the problem isn't self-concept so much as it is society's oppression." However true it may be that our society is gender oppressive, this is the therapist's agenda and again fails to acknowledge what the client has said, replacing it instead with an interpretation based upon the therapist's worldview.

Advice: "Take two aspirin and see me next week." Just kidding! Still, most advice is nearly as irrelevant. The therapist, for example, might advise, "I'm certain it would be worthwhile to talk to one of the senior professors in your field about going on for your doctorate." Such responses ignore what the client has said (let me know when I've said this enough) and ignore the fact that the client is likely to have explored the common solutions to her perceived issues before she came to therapy. Frankly, giving advice early in therapy is disrespectful and treats the client as if she is stupid.

Parroting: "Parroting is a parody of empathy. . . . Mere repetition carries no sense of real understanding of, no sense of being with, the client" (Egan, 1998, p. 96). "You're worrying about yourself and want to go back for your doctorate, but you're just not sure you can because of time and money and

Table 12.1
Ineffective Responses

Possibilities to be Avoided*	Common Response Styles**
1. No Response	1. One-Upper
2. Distracting Questions	2. Discounter
3. Clichés	3. Expert
4. Interpretations	4. Advice-Giver
5. Advice	5. Cross-Examiner
6. Parroting	6. "Canned" Counselor
7. Sympathy and Agreement	7. Problem Solver

*Adapted from Egan (1998).

**Adapted from V. O. Long (1996).

insecurities about yourself." This response does have the virtue of being accurate, but that is all. Simply repeating back to a person what they have said provides little, if any, clarification or understanding. Empathy adds something for the client. Something on which she can build. Parroting will lead to irritation and resentment.

Sympathy and Agreement: As you will see in chapter 13, empathy and sympathy are not the same. "Oh, I'm so sorry that things aren't working out for you." Empathy gives the client your understanding of her feelings and meanings, whereas sympathy conveys feelings of compassion or even pity. It is, of course, human to share the feelings of others, especially those close to us, but it is not an especially helpful counseling response. As I noted above, empathy adds something for the client. It communicates the therapist's understanding and, in its best application, provides a step toward greater clarification of issues and concerns. (See Table 12.1.)

Long (1996) provides a slightly different discussion of eight "common response styles," only one of which can be considered helpful. These colloquial styles are the one-upper, the discounter, the expert, the advice giver, the cross-examiner, the "canned" counselor (judgmental), the problem solver, and the empathizer, which, as the only facilitative style, will be examined in chapter 13. Long (1996) focuses on the outcomes of the response and the underlying motives of the responder. The following response styles represent Long's clever understanding of ineffective responses in therapy:

One-Upper: It doesn't matter what the client says, the one-upper has something to top it in her experience. This can reflect one of the dangers of self-disclosure in therapy. The therapist might say to Gina, "I had to put off my doctorate for ten years before I was able to feel financially comfortable doing it." As Long writes, "[O]ne-uppers generally reflect *control* rather than an acknowledgement of *rights*" (p. 158).

Discounter: Similar to Egan's (1998) cliché responses, Long's (1996) discounters "discredit your feelings, thoughts, behaviors, or experience" (p. 158). "I wouldn't worry too much. These are ordinary concerns as we think about changes in our lives." Statements such as this one dismiss the client's concerns by seeking to reassure or diminish the issue. "Discounters reflect *judgment* rather than *respect*" (p. 158).

Expert: The experts suggest "directly or indirectly that they have the answer and your job is to do what they say" (p. 158). "Gina, I see what's going on here and I know how to deal with this. I have therapeutic exercises that I am going to have you go through to deal with these issues." With this response the therapist has taken control of the session and set the direction. "Experts can communicate *control, judgment*, and *rescuing*" (p. 159).

Advice Giver: For Long, the key word for advice giver is "should" "Gina, you should talk to others in your situations to see what they did." Advice givers "set themselves up to assume responsibility for their client's (rescuing) and then to be blamed when their advice doesn't work. Advice-givers can reflect *control*, *judgment*, and *rescuing*" (p. 159).

Cross-Examiner: This is a style that relies heavily on questioning. "The underlying message with cross-examiners is that if they can get enough information, they can do something" (p. 159). Typically, the questions are closed. "Gina, who have you talked to? What did they tell you to do? How long have you been concerned about this?" These questions appear to be seeking information, but they are largely irrelevant and merely give the appearance of counseling effectiveness. The focus is on the therapist, and the therapist determines the direction. "Cross-examiners can demonstrate *control, judgment, rescuing*, and/or *blaming*" (p. 159).

'Canned' Counselor: Long uses this term to identify a somewhat deceptive therapist who appears to be interested in client concerns but is attending only to content and not the client meanings. "So you are insecure about pursuing a doctorate? And money plays some role in this?" These questions reflect surface client concerns but provide no understanding of client meanings, and, as Long suggests, the true focus is on the therapist and his or her viewpoint. Once the therapist has a grasp of the client's surface issues, then he or she will evaluate or analyze the client. " 'Canned' counselors can reflect *judgment* rather than *respect*" (p. 159).

Problem-Solver: The problem solver takes charge of the problem and communicates, "I know what your problem is. . . . The hidden message is that you don't, or can't. The trouble with this response style is that clients never get a chance to figure things out for themselves" (p. 160). A therapist might say, "Gina, this is an issue of assertiveness and I can help you with that."

Long indicates that problem solvers might use a questioning style and give advice as they "reflect *control*, *judgment*, and *rescuing*" (p. 160).

Gordon (1974), some years ago, provided a most helpful discussion of unhelpful responses, labeled "communication roadblocks." Please see Table 12.2 for a description of Gordon's blocks to effective responding, which include solution, judgment, and denial messages. Solutions include ordering, warning, moralizing, advising, and arguing. Judgment messages are such responses as criticizing, praising, shaming, sympathizing, questioning, and interpretating. Denial has to do with distracting the person from problems by making jokes, for example. I invite you to look over the information in Table 12.2 and consider how you might respond if the "dirty dozen" weren't available.

A final caution: Look at the lists above and take note that each mentions advising as a response to be avoided. "Giving advice is very much interviewer-centered; it clearly casts interviewers in the role of expert. Giving advice is easy, and as the old saying goes, advice is cheap" (Sommers-Flanagan & Sommers-Flanagan, 1993, p. 101). The difficulty is, paradoxically, that clients might take your advice. If they do, then the therapist has robbed them of the achievement. Martin (1983) is cautious: "Your solutions might be all right for you, but a lot of humility about what the Good Life is like is called for in a therapist" (p. 28). Giving advice is a dangerous counseling practice and, justifiably, is mentioned frequently as a practice to be avoided.

Probing, distracting, and irrelevant questions share an equally dismal reputation as effective methods of therapeutic help for clients. The problem with questioning is that it creates conditions in therapy that may be harmful in the long run. These include the client's passivity, as he or she learns to wait until asked a question before offering anything and even then will answer only what is asked; sense of dependency on the therapist; and helplessness, he or she waits for the therapist to solve the problem.

CHECKING YOUR RESPONSES

Table 12.3 provides a Therapist Observation Form that can be useful for either direct observation by a supervisor or peer or self-assessment in reviewing audio- or videotapes as you seek to develop more effective ways of responding to clients. This process provides the therapist with concrete feedback so that bad habits or ineffective responses can be identified and eliminated, and positive, effective responses can be increased, which can enhance the counseling relationship. The form includes both facilitating and blocking dimensions. The facilitative dimensions are discussed in later chapters devoted to empathy, warmth and respect, genuineness, immediacy, self-disclosure, concreteness (focus), confrontation, questions, and nonverbal facilitation.

Table 12.2
Communication Roadblocks

Often when a person seeks help, friends or colleagues commonly respond by giving advice or asking questions. However, as the following twelve descriptions indicate, these common responses tend to block helping rather than to facilitate it.

It should be noted that in daily life where there is no problem many of the "roadblocks" (e.g., asking questions, giving directions and advice) are both appropriate and helpful. Expressions that "put down" and demean, of course, are to be avoided both in our daily lives and in counseling and psychotherapy.

Solution Messages

These roadblocks take responsibility away from people and tend to make them more susceptible to external control. Solution messages communicate, "You're too dumb to figure out the problem, so I'll have to do it for you."

1. Ordering, Directing, Commanding. Telling the other person to do something; giving an order or command.
2. Warning, Admonishing, Threatening. Alluding to the use of your power by telling the other person what consequences will occur.
3. Moralizing, Preaching, Obliging. Telling the other person what should or ought to be correct behavior.
4. Advising, Giving Suggestions or Solutions. Telling the oher person how to solve his or her problems.
5. Persuading with Logic, Arguing, Instructing, Lecturing. Trying to influence the other person with facts, counterarguments, logic, information, or your own opinions.

Judgment Messages

These roadblocks diminish the worth and dignity of people. They communicate, "There is something wrong (bad) about you that needs to be fixed."

6. Judging, Criticizing, Disagreeing, Blaming. Making negative comments or judgments of the other person.
7. Praising, Agreeing, Evaluating Positively. Flatter the other person, implying reward.
8. Name Calling, Ridiculing, Shaming, Stereotyping. Characterizing the other person as foolish or in other negative ways.
9. Interpreting, Analyzing, Diagnosing. Evaluating motives and behavior, suggesting that you have the other person "diagnosed" or figured out.
10. Reassuring, Consoling, Sympathizing, Supporting. Trying to comfort, reduce strong feelings, or make the person feel better.
11. Probing, Questioning, Interrogating. Searching for reasons, motives, causes to solve the problem.

Denial Messages

These roadblocks seek to avoid dealing with a problem by withdrawing, joking, or distracting the person saying, in effect, "You are overreacting to this, and it isn't really a problem."

12. Withdrawing, Distracting, Humoring. Trying to keep the other person from focusing on the problem; withdrawing from the person; trying to distract the person by making a joke; ignoring the problem.

Adapted from T. E. Gordon (1974).

Table 12.3
Therapist Observation Form

Observer ______________________ Date & Time ______________

Therapist ____________________ Client ____________________

Observations

Facilitating Dimensions		Blocking Dimensions	
Content Paraphrase (Content Understanding)	_____	Content Parroting (Mere Repeating)	_____
Affect/Feeling/Meaning (Emotional Understanding)	_____	Using Power (Leading)	_____
Genuineness	_____	Moralizing/Judging	_____
Warmth/Respect	_____	Giving Advice	_____
Concreteness (Focusing)	_____	Interrupting	_____
Appropriate Metaphor	_____	Lecturing (Logic) Arguing	_____
Appropriate Confrontation	_____	Inappropriate Confrontation	_____
Immediacy	_____	Evaluative Praise/Approval	_____
Open-Ended Statement/Question	_____	Closed/Probing Question	_____
Clarification (Question or Statement)	_____	Labeling	_____
Appropriate Self-Disclosure	_____	Explaining/Interpreting	_____
Productive Silence	_____	Unproductive Silence	_____
Appropriate Physical Contact	_____	Inappropriate Physical Contact	_____
Appropriate Positive Reframing	_____	Humoring/Withdrawing	_____
Nonverbal Facilitation	_____	Nonverbal Blocking	_____
Attending Posture	_____	Sympathy	_____
Appropriate Summary	_____	Minimizing/Maximizing	_____

Adapted from I. D. Welch & D. M. Gonzalez (1999).

SUMMARY

Clients come to therapy with hopes that their issues, problems, and concerns can be understood and that solutions or resolutions can be identified. What and how we respond matters. Both research and experience have informed us about what is effective and ineffective as we respond to client concerns.

This chapter has provided an overview of ineffective responses as an introduction to the chapters that follow, which give you more effective ways to respond to client problems and issues. Two therapist responses that seem to be identified most frequently as ineffective are advice giving and probing closed-ended questions. A sure step to becoming an effective therapist means eliminating these responses from your style.

There is no secret to mastering effective responding skills. There is an old joke that involves a tourist asking a native New Yorker, "How do I get to Carnegie Hall?" The reply, of course, is, "Practice!" How does one become an effective, therapeutic responder in therapy? Practice.

REFERENCES

Egan, G. (1998). *The skilled helper: A problem-management approach to helping* (6th ed.). Pacific Grove, CA: Brooks/Cole.

Gordon, T. E. (1974). *T. E. T.: Teacher effectiveness training*. New York: P. H. Wyden.

Hackney, H., & Cormier, S. (1994). *Counseling strategies and interventions* (4th ed.). Boston, MA: Allyn and Bacon.

Ivey, A. E., & Ivey, M. B. (1999). *Intentional interviewing and counseling: Facilitating client development in a multicultural society* (4th ed.). Pacific Grove, CA: Brooks/Cole.

King, A. (2001). *Demystifying the counseling process: A self-help handbook for counselors*. Boston, MA: Allyn and Bacon.

Lauver, P., & Harvey, D. R. (1997). *The practical counselor: Elements of effective helping*. Pacific Grove, CA: Brooks/Cole.

Long, V. O. (1996). *Communication skills in helping relationships: A framework for facilitating personal growth*. Pacific Grove, CA: Brooks/Cole.

Martin, D. G. (1983). *Counseling and therapy skills*. Prospect Heights, IL: Waveland Press.

Patterson, C. H. (1985). *The therapeutic relationship: Foundations for an eclectic psychotherapy*. Pacific Grove, CA: Brooks/Cole.

Sommers-Flanagan, J., & Sommers-Flanagan, R. (1993). *Foundations of therapeutic interviewing*. Boston, MA: Allyn and Bacon.

Sue, D. W., Ivey, A. E., & Pedersen, P. B. (1996). *A theory of multicultural counseling and therapy*. Pacific Grove, CA: Brooks/Cole.

Welch, I. D. (1998). *The path of psychotherapy: Matters of the heart*. Pacific Grove, CA: Brooks/Cole.

Welch, I. D., & Gonzalez, D. M. (1999). *The process of counseling and psychotherapy: Matters of skill*. Pacific Grove, CA: Brooks/Cole.

Chapter 13

Responding with Empathy

The cracker-barrel philosopher says, "Even a blind squirrel may find an acorn every now and then." Such a trial-and-error approach to counseling and psychotherapy, however, is accidentally helpful at best and harmful at worst. Empathy is the cornerstone of counseling and psychotherapy. It is the acid test of an effective therapist. Any therapeutic intervention that is not based in empathy is predictably ineffective and inefficient.

DEFINITIONS OF EMPATHY

Empathy is a central, core condition of counseling and psychotherapy. Many have provided definitions in the attempt to capture its meaning, substance, and nuances. For example:

- Empathy is "an accurate, empathic understanding of the client's world as seen from the inside. To sense the client's private world as if it were your own, but without losing the 'as if' quality—this is empathy" (Rogers, 1961, p. 4).
- Empathy is "the ability to tune into the client's feeling and to be able to see the client's world as it truly seems to the client" (Long, 1996, p. 186).
- Empathy is when "[y]ou can feel with the client yet you do not take on the client's feelings and actually feel them yourself" (Hackney & Cormier, 1994, p. 15).
- "Empathy means understanding—not only the words another speaks, but the personal meanings attached to those words. It means understanding intellectually and emotionally" (Welch, 1998, p. 6).
- Empathy is "the ability to put oneself in the place of another and to see things . . . as he or she sees them" (Patterson, 1985, p. 6).

- Empathy is when "you grasp the facts, the feelings, and the significance of another person's story; more important, empathy involves the ability to convey your accurate perceptions to the other person" (Young, 2001, p. 50).
- Empathy is "an active, immediate, continuous process of living another's feelings, their intensity, and their meaning instead of simply observing them" (McWhirter, McWhirter, & Townsend, 2001, p. 137).
- Empathy can be seen as an intellectual process that involves understanding correctly another person's emotional state and point of view. . . . Empathy can also refer to empathic emotions experienced by the helper. . . . It is important that helpers understand the feelings and emotions of their clients and their meaning for the clients even though they might not 'feel along with' the clients (Egan, 1998, p. 73).

Empathy is a skill. It is an ability that can be learned, practiced, developed, and, as stated above, forms the bedrock foundation of effective counseling and psychotherapy. While empathy seems to have come to be associated with the humanistic or Rogerian theories, its role is acknowledged by other theories as well.

ACKNOWLEDGMENT OF EMPATHY

Psychoanalytic, behavioral, family systems, existential, cognitive-developmental, and humanistic therapy all recognize the importance of empathy in the therapeutic relationship.

- Psychoanalytic: "Empathy is the operation that defines the field of psychoanalysis. No psychology of complex mental states is conceivable without the employment of empathy" (Kohut, 1984, pp. 174–175).
- Psychoanalytic: "Frequently underestimated is the degree to which the therapist's presence and empathic listening constitute the most powerful source of help and support one human being can provide another" (Strupp & Binder, 1984, p. 41).
- Behavioral: "The truly skillful behavior therapist is one who can both conceptualize problems behaviorally and make the necessary translations so that he [or she] interacts in a warm and empathic manner with his [or her] client" (Goldfried & Davidson, 1976, p. 56).
- Family: "A major design of the treatment is to enable each spouse to receive empathic understanding when he or she communicates with the therapist, and for the task of the spouse who is listening to be defined as an attempt to put aside his or her complaints and empathically enter the world of the other" (Lansky, 1986, p. 562).
- Existential: "Empathy is a basic necessity for all forms of 'genuine interpersonal encounter,' including counseling" (May, 1989, p. 61).

- Cognitive-Developmental: "The importance of empathy in counseling and psychotherapy is unmistakable" (Welch & Gonzalez, 1999, p. 31).
- Humanistic: "[T]he helper needs accurate conceptions of the ways his or her clients are thinking, feeling, and perceiving themselves in their worlds" (Combs & Gonzalez, 1994, p. 167).

While each of these approaches may differ in its theory and style, each recognizes the central role of empathy in the process.

THE EFFECT OF EMPATHY

"Things are connected. An attitude of respect leads to empathic responding; empathic responding leads to trust. Trust leads to energetic exploration; exploration leads to personal understanding. And understanding leads to personal, optimal solutions, if they exist" (Welch, 1998, p. 4). This is the underlying reason for establishing an empathic relationship with clients. It isn't just that it is nice. It isn't simply that it is warm and feels good. It is that it is effective, helpful, and therapeutic. Martin (1983) captures this sense: "[A]s your client learns that even when you are ahead, even when you miss the point, even when the material is painful, your intent is consistently that of facilitating his or her thinking and feeling, an expectation of trust builds" (p. 40). As therapists, we are looking for a direct path to trust, and empathy is our best friend. It is probably important to point out here that it isn't necessary for counselors and psychotherapists to be accurate 100 percent of the time. As Young (2001) points out, "[I]t is important that our clients recognize that we are struggling to understand, that we care enough to try" (p. 51). In fact, in this attitude of empathic understanding even when we are wrong, clients will value our struggle and provide the correction necessary.

I was leading a group in a correctional facility when one of the group members said, "The only people I trust are Andy, Tom, and George." I responded with the mild, empathic paraphrase (I thought), "So you've learned in here not to risk anything personal with anyone except your friends." Well, the group just exploded into laughter! I was taken aback and dumbfounded. As the members on either side of me slapped my back, the member finally explained, "I only trust Andrew Jackson, Thomas Jefferson, and George Washington." He was talking about money. I was somewhere else, of course. Still, it was a light and funny moment, and the group enjoyed getting one over on the "shrink." I was able to laugh at my naiveté, and the member let me off the hook by saying something like, "Well, that part about friends is true, too." Even though I was wrong, I was sincere, and so the members helped me.

There are predictable outcomes of therapeutic empathy. First, as discussed above, empathy leads to trust (Hackney & Cormier, 1994; Sommers-Flanagan & Sommers-Flanagan, 1993; Welch, 1998). Second, empathy helps create a

Table 13.1
The Outcomes of Empathy in Therapy

Empathy leads to:
Trust
Free Exploration
Deep Exploration
Climate of Warmth
Client Self-Acceptance

climate in which the client can explore freely (Sommers-Flanagan & Sommers-Flanagan, 1993). Third, empathy permits the client to explore deeply (Sommers-Flanagan & Sommers-Flanagan, 1993). Fourth, empathy helps establish a climate of warmth (Hackney & Cormier, 1994; Sommers-Flanagan & Sommers-Flanagan, 1993; Welch, 1998). Finally, empathy can aid clients' movement toward self-acceptance as they experience understanding from the therapist. Table 13.1 summarizes these outcomes. In a climate of therapeutic empathy clients can recognize that their confusions, thinking, feelings, and behaviors can be acknowledged and understood, which leads to a greater acceptance of themselves and a greater willingness to acknowledge needed changes in their lives.

BARRIERS TO EMPATHIC RESPONDING

Given that empathy is recognized as a central, core aspect of counseling and psychotherapy, why does it takes such an effort to train therapists in its reliable and effective use? First, "the counselor does not know what would be appropriate ways of responding" (Hackney & Cormier, 1994, p. 102). The therapist simply doesn't have the words or doesn't understand. Second, "the counselor 'blocks' upon recognizing the client's feelings (Hackney & Cormier, 1994, p. 102). This can be a matter of fear of or a misguided concern with not hurting the client. Additionally, we have to recognize that empathy is an uncommon experience in our daily lives. Much of the frustration we have as ordinary citizens stems from a common lack of being understood. Perhaps you have experienced taking your car to the mechanic, returning defective merchandise, or trying to convince the telephone company to believe that you don't know anybody in Mishawaka, Indiana, and therefore couldn't have made a long-distance phone call to them. We won't even go into our lack of understanding of other drivers on the road. Even in our more intimate relationships, frustrations occur as we try to explain our feelings and behaviors to one another—sometimes with little success. Suffice it to say that understanding one another tends to be unstated and assumed. These two approaches are harmful in therapy.

Barriers to our understanding can come in a variety of ways. Our values, beliefs, attitudes, traditions, culture, language, fears, and background can all interfere with understanding another person. Some have argued that empathy, as it is used in psychotherapy, is mere projection (Pietrofesa, Hoffman, & Splete, 1984). In order to counteract such criticism, therapeutic empathy needs to be verified by the client. In order to provide accurate empathy responses to clients, therapists have to be able to both use their personal experiences and their knowledge of human behavior to understand the unique client. This is a matter of risk, a matter of courage. Time to be a giraffe (see p. 118).

Sometimes these barriers can lie outside our personal awareness and require the observation and feedback of others to help us see what can be seen only through the eyes of others.

Lauver and Harvey (1997) believe there are "two powerful forces that interfere with accurate, perceptive listening" (p. 83). These are habits and needs. We may tend to be "defensive listeners, alert and responsive to potential threats to our self-esteem and to opportunities for self-enhancement" (Lauver & Harvey, 1997, p. 83). When we listen from a perspective of our personal needs, we are not able to attend to the inner meanings of the client. Lauver and Harvey (1997) list ten examples of problematic habits:

1. Questioning
2. Judgment
3. One-upping the client. "If you think that's something, let me tell you . . ."
4. Identification. "That same thing happened to me."
5. Denial of client's issues. "You're okay."
6. Silence or no response
7. Acting as an expert
8. Routine responses. "You feel . . . You feel . . . You feel . . ."
9. Stone face—passive or flat responding
10. Word factory—over talking the client. (Pp. 83–84)

Such lists are helpful as we try to learn and master what *not* to do in therapy. While paraphrasing isn't empathy, it is sometimes useful. So, to paraphrase a wise philosopher from another planet, ALF (from the television program of the same name and meaning Alternative Life Form), find out what doesn't work and don't do it. Here is what empathy is not:

- "Empathy is not sympathy. Sympathy means feeling, experiencing what another person feels. . . . Sympathy and identification are not helpful in psychotherapy precisely because they provide no additional clarity for the person seeking help" (Welch, 1998, pp. 6, 8).

- "Empathy is not the same as agreeing, condoning, or encouraging" (Long, 1996, p. 186). These responses do not help clarify or provide any information or insight for the client.
- Pseudo-empathy is not empathy. "I know what you mean," "I hear that," "I know where you are coming from," "I've been there, done that," "I got that!"—While each of these alludes to understanding it does not provide the client with any real evidence that you do understand. Empathy is a clear statement of understanding of the client's issues, problems, or concerns and the thoughts, feelings, and meanings the client attributes to them.
- Empathy is not interpretation. "An interpretation is given from the therapist's frame of reference to point out to the client relationships and insights that the more perceptive therapist understands better than the client. . . . The empathic therapist's intent, however, is not to cleverly guide the client toward the truth but to bring the client's experiencing to life, so the client will deal with it and find his or her own truth—will accurately know his or her own experience" (Martin, 1983, p. 7).

RESPONDING WITH EMPATHY

"Empathy is a complex affective-cognitive-experiential concept" (Sommers-Flanagan & Sommers-Flanagan, 1993, p. 121). This somewhat intimidating statement reveals a truth. Empathy is complex. It isn't so complex, however, that it cannot be learned and mastered. Empathy is a process that involves several steps. Some of these steps are attitudinal, some are intellectual, some behavioral. The word "empathy" stems from the German word *einfuhlung*, meaning something like "feeling oneself into" or "feeling into" (Brammer, 1988; Young, 2001). May (1989) traces the root somewhat differently by indicating that the word has two components. The first, *em*, means 'in.' The second, *pathos*, means 'a strong and deep feeling.' He arrives at the same definition, however, which is 'feeling into.' Empathy begins with an attitude of willingness, the willingness to listen. This is a particular type of listening in which one is attempting to feel into the world of the client. As the therapist feels into the meanings of the client, he or she begins to formulate words and short phrases that can convey that meaning. Finally, the therapist communicate his or her understanding to the client. This is the five-step process from willingness to communication (see Table 13.2). (Just a note: Phrases like "feel into the meaning of a client" might put off some practical-minded people who suspect it of being psychobabble without conveying any real meaning. To those, I would say to read it as struggling to understand what the other really means.)

Above, I have given you a complete step-by-step walk-through of the empathy process. It might be simpler, however, to think of it as a two-step process: (1) Listen for understanding and, when you think you have it, (2) verbally share it with the client to ensure its accuracy.

Table 13.2
The Process of Empathy

Step 1 - Willingness to Listen
Step 2 - Listen (using listening skills such as the I/F and DAMS principles)
Step 3 - "Feel into" the client's feelings/meaning
Step 4 - Formulate words and phrases to communicate your understanding
Step 5 - Communicate your response

Table 13.3
Some Possible Communication Leads

I hear you saying . . .
It seems like . . .
I'm getting a couple of things . . .
It seems clear that . . .
I'm not sure . . . is it something like . . .
It looks like it might be . . .
I'm feeling . . .
My sense of what you are saying is . . .
This part is clear: . . . And this part I'm only vaguely sensing: . . .
I feel . . .
Right now, it's . . .
One way to look at it is . . . , and another way would be . . .
You used to feel . . . , and now you are feeling . . .
My picture is . . .
One part of me says . . . and another part says . . .

Sometimes it is difficult to think of words to describe clients' feelings. A good source for building an affective vocabulary is Welch and Gonzalez' (1999) *The Process of Counseling and Psychotherapy: Matters of Skill.* It provides an extensive list of "feeling words." It may be helpful too to develop a list of practiced "leads" in order to avoid becoming too reliant on a single approach ("I hear you saying . . . I hear you saying . . . I hear you saying . . ."). Some examples of effective communication leads are provided in Table 13.3. These leads do two important things. First, they buy us a little time to help us formulate the words or phrase we want to use. Second, they are tentative enough to allow the client to take them in and respond to them without the need to over defend.

BASIC AND ADVANCED EMPATHY

Authors have tried to explain the concept that empathy can be a layered process by defining it further as "basic" (introductory) and "advanced" (additive) empathy. Following are some examples of different definitions used to explain the movement from superficial to deep responses that therapists might use at different stages of therapy.

Martin (1983) suggests three levels of empathy. First, there is the *superficial* level, to which a client might respond with some irritation, "Well, of course, that's what I just said." Second, there is an *effective empathic response*, to which the client might say, "Yes, that's it. I didn't think anyone could really understand what I was talking about." Third, there is *exceptionally effective empathy*, in which the therapist catches the subtle and even vague meanings on the edge of what the client says. The client might pause for a moment of reflection and then say, "I hadn't really thought of it that way. I'm not sure, but I do have some of those feelings."

Young (2001) describes two types of empathy. First is *emotional empathy* in which the therapist is responding to the feelings of the client. Second, Young (2001) describes as *cognitive empathy*, in which the therapist takes the time to describe an understanding of the client's motives, intentions, values, and thinking.

Miars and Halverson (2001) describe primary and advanced empathy. Primary empathy "sees the world from the client's frame of reference and communicates that it has been understood. The goal is to move the client toward identifying and exploring crucial topics and feelings" (p. 63). Advanced empathy involves getting at "feelings and meanings that are hidden or beyond the immediate reach of the client" (p. 63).

Long (1996) provides a model in which empathy is described as explicit and implicit. Explicit empathy provides a communication of understanding of what the client plainly and unambiguously has said. Implicit empathy is "understanding your clients' perspectives before they do. Keep in mind, however, that implicit empathy is focusing on what the client is confusedly saying, but *is* saying or implying, however, vaguely. It is not the helper's interpretation of what the client is saying" (p. 220).

Egan (1998) uses basic and advanced empathy as his model for describing this early and later use of empathy in therapy. Basic empathy can be learned by using a formula that, at first, may seem stilted and artificial. Its purpose is to ensure that both content and feelings/meanings are included in the response. When a client has talked about his or her issues and concerns, a basic empathy response would include:

You feel . . . (name the correct emotion expressed by the client)

When . . . (describe the events, situations or people involved)

Egan (1998) warns that "the formula is a beginner's tool to get used to the concept of empathy. . . . Ignore how stylized it sounds—for practice purposes" (p. 84).

Advanced empathy identifies "the message behind the message" and helps the client make the implied explicit, identify themes in the story, and make connections that might have been missed. A final aspect of advanced empathy for Egan (1998) is that this is the time to share one's hunches with clients. Advanced empathy is using one's whole body, one's overall felt sense, one's intellect as well as intuition as a way of helping the client identify the vague and undifferentiated thoughts and feelings and bring them out into the open.

Often, a guide for helping beginning counselors and psychotherapists identify client's vague or even hidden thoughts and feelings is Carkhuff's (1987) "empathy question." This is a matter of listening to the client and, at the appropriate time, asking yourself, "How would I have to feel to be saying what the client is saying?" This is asked silently of yourself. The internal answer you hear is what you verbally communicate to the client. A client might be talking about his boss at work and say, "I just don't know. I think I'm competent and I even think I'm doing a good job, but he's after me all the time. Nothing I seem to do seems right." Read this passage and ask yourself the empathy question: "How would I have to feel if I had a boss like that?" Think of a response and phrase it as, "You feel ___(your response)___ when the boss talks to you that way."

My response was, "You feel angry and confused when the boss talks to you that way." Remember, this is a basic empathy response in which you are giving the client what seems to be explicit in their communication.

To help you form your response, here are some guidelines to follow. First, take some time. One of the reasons for using communication leads like the ones above is to buy a little time before you talk. President Reagan was famous for using the word "well" before nearly every answer he gave to reporters' questions. A reporter would ask a question and the president would say, "Well," and then pause briefly. Counselors and psychotherapists use the same strategy. This small amount of time is often enough to allow you to organize your response. Second, use short and frequent responses. Remember, it is more important that the client talk than it is that the therapist talk. Short, frequent responses allow you to stay on track and make sure you understand and have the effect of reinforcing the client's talk. Third, use the listening skills described in the first section (especially I/F and DAMS principles) and respond in the client's style (visual, auditory, kinesthetic senses) without sacrificing too much of your personal style.

Here are some suggestions that can help as you work to improve your skill in responding. First, use empathy at every stage of the counseling process. Anytime you, as a therapist, are in trouble, lost, confused, or uncertain, empathy is your best friend. Second, respond selectively to client messages. Use the listening skills from the beginning chapters of this book, such as the I/F and DAMS principles. Third, respond to the whole message, including verbal and nonverbal as well as developmental and situational clues. Fourth, use advanced empathy to move the therapy forward. Fifth, just as above, when you have misstated, misread, or simply misunderstood a client, use empathy to recover. Sixth, use empathy to bridge multicultural and other diversity gaps. Finally, do not try to fake understanding. This, obviously, violates the principle of genuineness and has the potential of damaging the therapeutic relationship. When you are lost, return to basic empathy and, even if you are an experienced therapist, return to the basic empathy formula: "You feel . . . when. . . ." This will get you back on track, and it reassures the client that you genuinely are trying to understand.

DIVERSITY AND MULTICULTURAL CONCERNS

Young (2001) challenges us to take a courageous step. He argues that "empathy is a first step in getting us off our ethnocentric narcissism and signals to clients that we are trying to 'feel ourselves into' their world, rather than attempting to convert them to our perspective" (p. 51). In order to "get off our ethnocentric narcissism," we must know that we have it and what it entails. "The path of empathy often begins in self-examination, and by extension, in an examination of our own background and cultural beliefs" (Welch, 1998, p. 109). Perhaps what often is neglected in the study of differences is the importance of starting with ourselves and our own cultural traditions and backgrounds. All cultures contain much that is valuable and, arguably, aspects that are objectionable. Someone once said that, if we were to pile up all that a culture thought was good and honorable then take away what another culture thought was bad and dishonorable, nothing would be left. Sometimes, of course, we simply have to agree to disagree with one another and be tolerant of that with which we disagree. For all of us, and especially for counselors and psychotherapists, a careful examination of our attitudes, beliefs, and values as well as the general assumptions of our backgrounds, traditions, and cultures not only informs us, but also allows us to accept graciously the challenges that cultures impose on one another.

As far as the therapeutic relationship is concerned, "empathy is a crucial skill in overcoming cultural, gender, and other differences between client and helper. Empathy means taking a 'tutorial stance' rather than an authoritarian position when we are confronted with a person's life experience that clashes with our own. A tutorial stance means the helper becomes a learner, seeking to understand the client—recognizing that the helper must learn from the client what it is like to be that person" (Young, 2001, p. 51).

What remains constant for many is the idea that we are all one people. Biologically, we are human, different from all other species. Gazda and his colleagues (1984) teach that "feelings are universal—they are the same among all people throughout the world—even though the things that cause us to experience a particular emotion may be quite different from one culture to another. It is possible, therefore, to communicate empathy without having had the particular life experience of the [client]" (p. 86). Wohl (1981), on the other hand, says "that despite this universality, it is possible, even probable, that the constituents of the 'good human relationship' are different in one culture than they are in another. . . . The question needs to be raised as to the extent to which our American conception of the good therapeutic relationship is universally valid" (pp. 192–193). These are important and controversial questions. Patterson (1985), for example, challenges this criticism on empirical grounds:

> It is certainly justifiable to raise the question, but [none of those] who do so have presented any evidence to support differences. The evidence from studies involving a wide variety of clients with a wide variety of problems in various groups in Western society supports their universality, though admittedly studies in quite different cultures have not yet been done. Given the basic similarities of human nature, it is not likely that the conditions [empathy, respect, genuineness] would not be necessary in other cultures. (P. 189)

Welch (1998) follows this argument somewhat. "The . . . path to diversity is understanding the client in all his or her richness and uniqueness. . . . We must recognize that regardless of background, the person who sits before us is a unique, self-aware, and conscious being. We must not be so informed about culture and other forms of diversity that we lose sight of the individual who has come to us for help" (p. 108). As counselors and psychotherapists, we are faced with a multileveled approach to multiculturalism. We have to inform ourselves, about our own culture, about ourselves and about the cultures of others with whom it is likely we will come into contact. We also must stay open to the use of empathy as a sure way to come to know and understand the unique person who is our client.

SUMMARY

Welch (1998) has written that "all psychotherapy begins in empathy. Any psychotherapy that does not have this origin is, at best, predictably unhelpful and, at worst, harmful" (p. 6). This is the premise of this chapter. Whatever other skills we develop, whatever techniques we learn, whatever theory we follow, empathy must be present in the relationship if it is going to be therapeutic and helpful. Empathy begins in the willingness to listen to others with the specific desire to understand and to communicate our understanding. Various authors define empathy as the ability to understand the issues, problems, and dilemmas presented by clients from their point of view both intellectually and emotionally. Empathy is presented as a skill that can be learned and mastered. It is not some special talent given to some and denied to others.

The necessity of an empathic relationship is recognized widely among competing theories and has come to be seen as something of a metatheoretical *sine qua non* of effective psychotherapy. It is viewed as one of the most effective ways of establishing trust in a therapeutic relationship as well as encouraging and permitting effective exploration with clients.

Basic empathy is the recognition of explicitly stated or surface thoughts, feelings, and meanings. Advanced empathy is a concept of recognizing feelings that lie beneath the surface or have greater depth.

Whether one takes the stance that people are much the same all over the world or tends to emphasize differences among people, empathy remains a central, core aspect of multicultural counseling.

REFERENCES

Brammer, L. M. (1988). *The helping relationship: Process and skills* (4th ed.). Englewood Cliffs, NJ: Prentice-Hall.

Capuzzi, D., & Gross, D. R. (Eds.). (2001). *Introduction to the counseling profession* (3rd ed.). Boston, MA: Allyn and Bacon.

Carkhuff, R. R. (1987). *The art of helping* (6th ed.). Amherst, MA: Human Resource Development Press.

Combs, A. W., Gonzalez, D. M. (1994). *Helping relationships: Basic concepts for the helping professions* (4th ed.). Boston, MA: Allyn and Bacon.

Egan, G. (1998). *The skilled helper: A problem-management approach to helping* (6th ed.). Pacific Grove, CA: Brooks/Cole.

Gazda, G. M., Asbury, F. S., Balzer, F. J., Childers, W. C., & Walters, R. P. (1984). *Human relations development: A manual for educators* (3rd ed.). Boston, MA: Allyn and Bacon.

Goldfried, M., & Davidson, G. (1976). *Clinical behavior therapy*. New York: Hold, Rinehart & Winston.

Hackney, H., & Cormier, S. (1994). *Counseling strategies and interventions* (4th ed.). Boston, MA: Allyn and Bacon.

Ivey, A. E., & Ivey, M. B. (1999). *Intentional interviewing and counseling: Facilitating client development in a multicultural society* (4th ed.). Pacific Grove, CA: Brooks/Cole.

King, A. (2001). *Demystifying the counseling process: A self-help handbook for counselors*. Boston, MA: Allyn and Bacon.

Kohut, H. (1984). *How does analysis cure?* London: University of Chicago Press.

Lansky, M. R. (1986). Marital therapy for narcissistic disorders. In N. S. Jacobson & A. S. Gurman (Eds.), *Clinical handbook of marital therapy*. New York: Guilford.

Lauver, P., & Harvey, D. R. (1997). *The practical counselor: Elements of effective helping*. Pacific Grove, CA: Brooks/Cole.

Long, V. O. (1996). *Communication skills in helping relationships: A framework for facilitating personal growth*. Pacific Grove, CA: Brooks/Cole.

Martin, D. G. (1983). *Counseling and therapy skills*. Prospect Heights, IL: Waveland Press.

May, R. (1989). *The art of counseling* (rev. ed.). New York: Gardner.

McWhirter, B. T., McWhirter, J. J., & Townsend, K. C. (2001). Individual counseling: Traditional approaches. In D. Capuzzi & D. R. Gross (Eds.), *Introduction to the counseling profession* (3rd ed., pp. 123–138). Boston, MA: Allyn and Bacon.

Miars, R. D., & Halverson, S. E. (2001). The helping relationship. In D. Capuzzi & D. R. Gross (Eds.), *Introduction to the counseling profession* (3rd ed., pp. 50–68). Boston, MA: Allyn and Bacon.

Okun, B. F. (2002). *Effective helping: Interviewing and counseling techniques* (6th ed.). Pacific Grove, CA: Brooks/Cole.

Patterson, C. H. (1985). *The therapeutic relationship: Foundations for an eclectic psychotherapy*. Pacific Grove, CA: Brooks/Cole.

Pietrofesa, J. J., Hoffman, A., & Splete, H. H. (1984). *Counseling: An introduction* (2nd ed.). Boston, MA: Houghton Mifflin.

Rogers, C. R. (1961). *On becoming a person*. Boston, MA: Houghton Mifflin.

Sommers-Flanagan, J., & Sommers-Flanagan, R. (1993). *Foundations of therapeutic interviewing*. Boston, MA: Allyn and Bacon.

Strupp, H. H., & Binder, J. L. (1984). *Psychotherapy in a new key*. New York: Basic Books.

Sue, D. W., Ivey, A. E., & Pedersen, P. B. (1996). *A theory of multicultural counseling and therapy*. Pacific Grove, CA: Brooks/Cole.

Welch, I. D. (1998). *The path of psychotherapy: Matters of the heart*. Pacific Grove, CA: Brooks/Cole.

Welch, I. D., & Gonzalez, D. M. (1999). *The process of counseling and psychotherapy: Matters of skill*. Pacific Grove, CA: Brooks/Cole.

Wohl, J. (1981). Intercultural psychotherapy: Issues, questions, and reflections. In P. B. Pederson, J. G. Draguns, W. J. Lonner, & J. E. Trimble (Eds.), *Counseling across cultures* (2nd ed., pp. 133–159). Honolulu: University of Hawaii.

Young, M. E. (2001). *Learning the art of helping: Building blocks and techniques*. Upper Saddle River, NJ: Merrill/Prentice-Hall.

Chapter 14

Responding with Warmth and Respect

There are two kinds of respect. One of them is therapeutic and the other isn't. Often the word "respect" is used in statements like, "We need to respect our enemies" or "I respect our opponents today. They are a dangerous team." This use might better be labeled "prudence," "watchfulness," "caution," or, perhaps, even "fear." Such attitudes or concerns do not advance psychotherapy.

THERAPEUTIC RESPECT

Therapeutic respect is something quite different. It has a long history of recognition of centrality in psychotherapy, but many recognize Rogers' (1957) "The Necessary and Sufficient Conditions for Therapeutic Personality Change" as the first point in history when the "core conditions" of effective psychotherapy were reported as a data-based phenomenon. Rogers labeled one of the core conditions "unconditional positive regard" and, because of confusions with this term, many have used the term "respect" to capture this aspect of therapeutic responding. Respect is a core, fundamental concept in psychotherapy and yet its precise definition remains intangible. Here are a few ideas:

> Respect . . . demonstrates a belief in the client's ability to deal with his or her problems in the presence of a facilitative person. . . . Respectful counselors use communication skills to actualize the power, ability, and skills already possessed by the client. In other words, the counselor believes in the problem-solving ability of the client. (Miars & Halverson, 2001, p. 61)

> We cannot help people if we have not faith in their ability to solve their own problems. Respect develops as we learn about the uniqueness and the capabilities of helpees. (Gazda, Asbury, Balzer, Childers, & Walters, 1984, p. 15)

> Respect lies at the heart of psychotherapy. Respect is demonstrated in two distinct ways. First, it is revealed in how we act toward the people who come for help. . . . There is more to respect than competence. The second way to demonstrate respect is by a willingness to understand the client's point of view. (Welch, 1998, pp. 100–101)

> The necessary components of a facilitative response are: . . . respect—communicating acceptance of the helpee as a person of worth. (Gazda, Asbury, Balzer, Childers, & Walters, 1984, p. 130)

> Respect refers to the therapist's belief in the client. It is crucial that the helper believe in the capacity of the client to find healthy answers to his or her dilemmas. (Welch & Gonzalez, 1999, p. 46)

> Respect is reflected in the dependable acceptance the therapist gives the client—a nonjudgmental openness to let the client think, feel and say whatever he [or she] is experiencing without losing the sense that the therapist accepts him [or her] as a person with worth. (Martin, 1983, p. 12)

> [Respect is] [A]cknowledgment that our clients are inherently unique and worthy individuals, with the capability and capacity to problem solve, to develop their abilities, and to do what they need to do to be who they are and to live their own lives. (Long, 1996, p. 184)

What emerges from these definitions is an agreement that therapeutic respect includes both the recognition and acceptance of clients as persons of worth and honoring their capabilities for learning to cope with their personally felt issues, problems, and dilemmas.

RESPECT AND WARMTH

Respect and warmth are siblings, even twins. They are like twins in that they are often impossible to differentiate from one another, and yet they are individuals. While we have defined respect above, warmth is the outward, often nonverbal, communication of "friendliness, approachability, and interpersonal openness" (Welch & Gonzalez, 1999, p. 184). I have combined them here because, in truth, in responding it is difficult to distinguish between a response of warmth and one of respect. They are indeed therapeutic twins.

STRUGGLING WITH RESPECT AND WARMTH

Honoring clients as persons of worth and respecting their capacity to solve their own problems is thorny and easier said than done. Clients may come to therapy with many behaviors, attitudes, and beliefs that are unwholesome, cruel, and/or violent. How are we to deal with persons and behaviors that violate our own sense of values and morality?

The Problem of Judgmentalness

This leads us, naturally, to the problem of judgmentalness. Long (1996) labels judgmentalness "the antithesis of respect" (p. 131). "Judgmentalness is the tendency to form critical opinions about another based on the imposition of *your* beliefs and values" (Long, 1996, p. 125). There is also a recognition that imperfections, failures, foibles, and mistakes are a part of the human condition and that these can be accepted without any fundamental rejection of personally felt values. Yet we are left with crimes against persons. As therapists, we are sometimes called upon to work with people who are rapists, child abusers, batterers, racists, and even murderers. Most of us, as counselors and psychotherapists, do not face these extremes of human behavior, but many do. So it is necessary and important to come to grips with the problem of judgmentalness and its opposite, respect and warmth.

There appears to be two underlying assumptions necessary to adopting a position of therapeutic respect and warmth. First, we have to believe that there is a fundamental difference between *who* the person is and *what* they have done. That is, we have to be able to separate in our minds the client as a person and the client's behavior. When we consider the extremes of human behavior, this seems an improbable separation. When we consider, however, our lives and our daily interactions, it is something we do every day. Parents practice this separation of who and what with their children whenever they have to discipline them for some misbehavior. All effective parents have mastered the ability to correct misbehavior and at the same time communicate their love for their children. It may be a flawed analogy for psychotherapy, but it can be instructive as well. Welch and Gonzalez (1999) have addressed this problem of judgmentalness eloquently:

> Respect in therapeutic terms is for the person, not the behavior. Sometimes it is necessary to engage in a form of "age regression" to recognize that every bigot was once a person free of prejudice. Even the most disgusting clients were once innocent and malleable children whose life experience and, perhaps, personal decisions have contributed to their present state. Somehow, effective counselors find a way to view clients as persons of worth in spite of their socially destructive actions. (P. 14)

There is a second assumption that is crucial as we counselors and psychotherapists seek to find a firm ground from which to be therapeutic for clients whose behavior and actions can be offensive and opposite from our personal values and beliefs. We can strive to separate behavior from the person, of course. Welch (1998) addresses this second assumption.

> To be respectful, to respond nonjudgmentally, and to strive for understanding do not represent approval or agreement. In their private lives, psychotherapists hold a wide variety of personal values. . . . They may hold deeply rooted values, and have personally strict moral codes. Professionally, however, they have agreed to suspend their personal views, no matter how deeply felt, in favor of a professional value system that emphasizes understanding and respect. (P. 101)

What has to be recognized, understood, and integrated into the lives and behaviors of therapists is that psychotherapy is not a value-free endeavor. Counselors and psychotherapists, for all the talk about gifted therapists and the art of psychotherapy, work in the framework of science and informed practice. The necessity of nonjudgmental respect and warmth is not a mere sentiment but research phenomenon (Wampold, 2001). The acceptance and use of respect and warmth represents a foundational value of effective psychotherapeutic practice. Hadley and Strupp (1976) found, for example, that such qualities as therapeutic coldness, hostility, an overemphasis on change, and a need to analyze client behaviors actually contributed to a harmful outcome in psychotherapy. Thus, when a therapist suspends judgmentalness and responds with respect and warmth, he or she is not acting in an ethically neutral or value-free way, but is responding out of the recognition and acceptance of the value of researched practice.

These two understandings—that the person and behavior are separate and that suspension of judgment is a researched therapeutic value—appear to be the solution for the problem of judgmentalness or the urge to impose personal values on clients.

Long (1996) also recognizes a third clarification for the therapist's struggle with the issue of judgment. "Professional judgment" is a necessary and time-honored practice of therapists. Long (1996) suggests that professional judgment "means assessing circumstances, behaviors, thoughts, feelings, events, and context, and making decisions regarding client growth. Professional judgment is not judgmental. Professional judgment works in tandem with respect for the client as a person, regardless of circumstance or behavior" (p. 131). Long is making the point that assessment, evaluation, and therapeutic decisions should not be confused with personal values, political views, or moral positions and that such therapeutic decisions have an important role in the successful outcome of therapy.

THE SKILL OF RESPONDING WITH RESPECT AND WARMTH

There is danger in responding with warmth and respect. Brammer (1988) describes the skill of warmth and respect as learning "how to convey this feeling of closeness, affection, and caring concern to the [client] without emotional entanglements, offensive forwardness, or threat of seduction" (p. 38).

It seems clear that respect and warmth tend to be communicated nonverbally. Gazda, Asbury, Balzar, Childers, and Walters (1984) indicate that "warmth is communicated primarily through a wide variety of behaviors such as gestures, posture, tone of voice, touch, or facial expression" (p. 107). Ivey and Ivey (1999) echo this nonverbal emphasis: "You show respect and warmth by your open posture, your smile, and your vocal qualities. Your ability to keep your comments congruent with your body language and your willingness to touch (in appropriate situations) are indicators of respect and warmth" (p. 161). Such nonverbal responses do carry the danger of being misinterpreted and should be used with sensitivity and appropriate caution.

Welch and Gonzalez (1999) provide a table of nonverbal communication of therapist attitudes that includes warmth and respect. Their table provides a listing of counseling dimensions, nonverbal behaviors likely to be associated with ineffectiveness. Those associated with ineffectiveness for respect and warmth include: mumbling, using a patronizing tone of voice, engaging in doodling or paperwork, lack of appropriate eye contact, insincere effusiveness, and signs of wanting to leave. Nonverbal behaviors likely to be associated with effectiveness include: being fully attentive, using appropriate physical contact, and extending nonjudgmental empathy. As you can see, the suggestions above are not concrete verbal or behavioral suggestions. The quality of respect and warmth tends to be more attitudinal and nonverbal. These nonverbal responses include the acknowledgment of the client's right to individual uniqueness, positive regard, suspension of judgment, and acknowledgment of the client's individual capability for self-responsibility (Long, 1996).

MULTICULTURAL AND DIVERSITY CONCERNS

Inherent in any discussion of respect is the recognition of clients' backgrounds, traditions, and cultures. Okun (2002) defines respect as "stating positive opinions for the [client] and openly and honestly acknowledging, appreciating, and tolerating difference" (p. 42). Long (1996) is even more explicit, indicting that respect "is an acknowledgement and honoring of individuals' cultural, ethnic, spiritual, racial, gender-role, individual, and familial perspective" (p. 102). Sue, Ivey, and Pedersen (1996) provide a list of multicultural counseling competencies that includes respect for "clients' religious and/or spiritual beliefs and values, including attributions and taboos, since they affect worldview, psychosocial functioning, and expressions of distress" (p. 48). These important considerations of culture and background should not, however, cloud our understanding that humans share the same nature and, "given the basic similarities of human nature, it is not likely that the conditions (the core conditions of empathy, genuineness, and respect) would not be necessary in other cultures" (Patterson, 1985, p. 189). While the expression of respect and warmth might be different, the need for a therapeutic climate characterized by these qualities seems apparent for all people. Nevertheless, nonverbals such as gestures, proximity, eye contact, and appropriate touch can differ significantly among both cultures and individuals, requiring both study and an openness to learn from clients in order to avoid therapeutic mistakes.

GUIDELINES FOR RESPECT AND WARMTH

Egan (1998) has provided a list of guidelines that seek to transform attitudes into behaviors that reflect respect and warmth.

1. Do no harm. Just as with the Hippocratic oath, it is a core assumption for counselors and psychotherapists that a minimum standard of practice is that clients should leave us with at least the same level of coping skills that they came with.
2. "There is no place for the 'caring incompetent' in the helping professions" (Egan, 1998, p. 44). Become competent and committed. There are a variety of helping models, methods, and theories. There is no firm evidence that one theory, model, or single approach fits all or can demonstrate it is clearly superior to others (Wampold, 2001). What we can draw from this, therefore, is the importance of finding a way of working that fits for you, getting good at it, and practicing it.
3. Make it clear that your are "for" the client. This means striving to understand the client's point of view and respecting it. Respect can be both "tough and tender" (Welch, 1998) "gracious and tough minded" (Egan, 1998) and it may involve challenging clients to push themselves to learn new, more effective ways of coping.
4. Assume the client's goodwill. Clients can be frightened, suspicious, or wary. Often, in the past, we have characterized such behavior as resistance. However we characterize it, it is important to remember that such behavior isn't necessarily ill will. The competent and respectful therapist will enter the world of the client in order to understand and work through apparent resistance.
5. Do not rush to judgment. "You are not there to judge clients, . . . you are there to help them identify, explore, and review and challenge the consequences of the values they have adopted" (Egan, 1998, p. 45).
6. Keep the client's agenda in focus. Even when we think we know better, respect and warmth are best demonstrated by allowing the client to set the content and pace of therapy. The task is to help clients deal with their goals and not to impose our own.

These guidelines for moving from attitude to behavior are important and useful. They hinge, however, on one's attitude toward clients. When respectful behavior is joined with genuineness and empathy, what is communicated to clients is sincere understanding.

SUMMARY

Respect lies at the heart of therapy; it is a core condition of effectiveness. What lies at the heart of respect is the willingness to suspend judgmentalness at least long enough for the client's point of view to be understood genuinely. What is at issue here is therapeutic respect in which the suspension of judgment is an experientially or clinically learned and research-demonstrated central condition of effective psychotherapy. It is not maudlin sentiment or mere speculation.

In this chapter, respect and warmth have been discussed as a single phenomenon. While they are, of course, separate, they are simultaneously so closely related that the advice for one becomes advice for the other. Respect has to do with the belief in the client's capacity to learn and change. Warmth is the outward manifestation of friendliness and approachability.

The skill of responding with respect and warmth includes not only the willingness to suspend judgmentalness, but also a foundational belief in the capacity of people to be the primary agents in their own lives. The path away from judgmentalness appears to be the understanding that the worth of persons is not tied directly to their behavior. That is to say that, while we may disapprove of the acts or behavior of a client, we are able to respect their fundamental dignity as a human, a unique individual of worth. It is important as well to base that belief in the firm ground of science. Suspension of judgment is a therapeutic necessity.

Respect is another bedrock assumption of multicultural and diversity competence. One simply cannot be a functioning and effective psychotherapist without an appreciation for the differences reflected, for example, by culture, ethnicity, language, gender, and sexual orientation. Each of these affects us as individuals and as members of social groups both large and small. The appreciation of one's own background and experience can become the place from which we seek to understand and appreciate the background and experience of others.

REFERENCES

Brammer, L. M. (1988). *The helping relationship: Process and skills* (4th ed.). Englewood Cliffs, NJ: Prentice-Hall.

Egan, G. (1998). *The skilled helper: A problem-management approach to helping* (6th ed.). Pacific Grove, CA: Brooks/Cole.

Gazda, G. M., Asbury, F. S., Balzer, F. J., Childers, W. C., & Walters, R. P. (1984). *Human relations development: A manual for educators* (3rd ed.). Boston, MA: Allyn and Bacon.

Hadley, J., & Strupp, H. (1976). Contemporary views of negative effects in psychotherapy. *Archives of General Psychiatry, 33*, 1291–1294.

Ivey, A. E., & Ivey, M. B. (1999). *Intentional interviewing and counseling: Facilitating client development in a multicultural society* (4th ed.). Pacific Grove, CA: Brooks/Cole.

Long, V. O. (1996). *Communication skills in helping relationships: A framework for facilitating personal growth.* Pacific Grove, CA: Brooks/Cole.

Martin, D. G. (1983). *Counseling and therapy skills.* Prospect Heights, IL: Waveland Press.

Miars, R. D., & Halverson, S. E. (2001). The helping relationship. In D. Capuzzi & D. R. Gross (Eds.), *Introduction to the counseling profession* (3rd ed., pp. 50–68). Boston, MA: Allyn and Bacon.

Okun, B. F. (2002). *Effective helping: Interviewing and counseling techniques* (6th ed.). Pacific Grove, CA: Brooks/Cole.

Patterson, C. H. (1985). *The therapeutic relationship: Foundations for an eclectic psychotherapy.* Pacific Grove, CA: Brooks/Cole.

Rogers, C. R. (1957). The necessary and sufficient conditions of therapeutic personality change. *Journal of Consulting Psychology, 21*, 95–103.

Sue, D. W., Ivey, A. E., & Pedersen, P. B. (1996). *A theory of multicultural counseling and therapy.* Pacific Grove, CA: Brooks/Cole.

Wampold, B. E. (2001). *The great psychotherapy debate: Models, methods, and findings.* Mahwah, NJ: Lawrence Erlbaum.

Welch, I. D. (1998). *The path of psychotherapy: Matters of the heart.* Pacific Grove, CA: Brooks/Cole.

Welch, I. D., & Gonzalez, D. M. (1999). *The process of counseling and psychotherapy: Matters of skill.* Pacific Grove, CA: Brooks/Cole.

Chapter 15

Responding with Genuineness

Why is it so difficult to be naturally and simply who we are? Some years ago in a doctoral-level supervision class, this became the principal focus of the group. Each of us in the class was struggling with the awkward, stiff, and, in some cases, aloof and distancing behaviors of our relationships with clients. In a word, we were struggling with genuineness.

Genuineness is a difficult concept to pin down—a bit like nailing mercury to the wall. Yet, in personal experiences and in research over the years, therapists have affirmed repeatedly the concept of genuineness as an important dynamic of effective psychotherapy (Patterson, 1985; Truax & Mitchell, 1971; Welch, 1998). Bluntly put, an effective counselor or psychotherapist is not a phony.

DEFINITIONS OF GENUINENESS

Rogers is often mentioned as one of the pioneers of introducing the concept of genuineness into the therapeutic relationship. His (1957) seminal article "The Necessary and Sufficient Conditions of Therapeutic Personality Change" formed the foundation for the metaconditions of effective psychotherapy, empathy, therapeutic genuineness, and positive regard or respect. Rogers (1961) defines genuineness in this way: "By this we mean that the feelings that the counselor is experiencing are available to [his or her] awareness, that [he or she] is able to live with these feelings, be them in the relationship, and able to communicate them if appropriate. . . . It means that [he or she] is being [him- or herself], not denying [his-or herself]" (Rogers, 1961, p. 417). Ivey and Ivey (1999) believe that genuineness means working "in an egalitarian fashion with your client rather than 'working on' your client. If you are a genuine person and discuss issues openly in the session, your client will most likely be open with you" (p. 87). Therapists who are genuine "are involved in the relationship and not simply mirrors, sounding boards, or blank screens. . . . They are freely and deeply themselves, without facades, not phony. They are not thinking and feeling one thing and saying something different" (Patterson, 1985, p. 63). McWhirter, McWhirter, and Townsend (2001) conclude that "genuineness is used to denote honesty, directness, and sincerity, and an absence of a professional façade" (p. 136). It must be clear that genuineness, sincerity, honesty, and directness are qualities that one does not put on and take off willy-nilly. Egan (1998) argues that, for counselors and psychotherapists, such qualities "are part of their lifestyle, not a role they put on. . . . [It] is far away from being patronizing and condescending" (p. 50).

THE PROBLEM OF FACADES

Doing therapy is not acting. We have no real faith in the actor on television who tells us, "I'm not a real doctor, but I play one on television." It is satire and sarcasm. Yet there appear to be common roles some psychotherapists adopt in working with clients. "Being a counselor is not just a role played by the individual. Instead, it is the appropriate revelation of one's own feelings, thoughts, and being in the counseling relationship" (Miars & Halverson, 2001, p. 61).

Welch (1998) provides a description of four ineffective roles. The first is what is labeled the "pundit." This is the role of the expert who distances him- or herself from the client by remaining aloof. They do not make themselves known and they do not enter into a genuine relationship.

The second role is the "wizard." These faux psychotherapists see themselves as gifted with special talents, insights, or qualities that give them unique abilities to "heal," "cure," or teach others. Welch (1998) summarizes their approach to psychotherapy as charlatarian. "Charlatans throughout history have made their larcenous way by healing the unsick. They assign mysterious explanations to ordinary human experience. They take credit for the natural power of the body and of the mind and, in so doing, insult and demean people" (p. 90).

The third role is labeled the "priest." This term is used in its disparaging form and is meant to mean one who moralizes and sermonizes about their understanding of proper and right attitudes and behavior. It is founded on the opposite of an empathic relationship. The "priest" therapist already knows what is right and proper, and what the client thinks, feels, or believes must only be countered and replaced with the "truth."

Fourth, there is the "clerk." The clerk assembles and records information. Clerks might give tests and conduct clinical interviews and even arrive at a diagnosis but "are uninvolved in the lives and understandings of the people they have sworn to serve" (p. 93).

Each of these roles is created to shield the therapist from a genuine encounter with the client. Why is it so difficult to be simply and naturally who we are? What is the proper role of the therapist? In concluding a discussion of roles, Welch (1998) says that "when psychotherapists mask themselves, they prevent a genuine relationship from forming. The role of the psychotherapist is to have no role. . . . It means not presenting yourself as an *image* of a psychotherapist. It means presenting *who you are* as a psychotherapist" (p. 93).

SOME PROBLEMS WITH GENUINENESS

There are two main problems with the concept of genuineness. The first is the overemphasis of genuineness. The second is the underemphasis of genuineness. This problem of too much or too little plagues beginning therapists as they labor to understand the concept and translate their understanding into effective behavior. As we have seen above, some experienced therapists have not mastered genuineness and instead have developed roles to mask their genuine thoughts and feelings.

Overemphasizing Genuineness

Genuineness may not always be therapeutic. Patterson (1985) makes the point that "genuineness does not require that therapists always express all their feelings; it only requires that whatever they do express is real and genuine and not incongruent" (p. 64). It is obvious, of course, that not all thoughts and feelings are therapeutic. The concept of genuineness is not meant to be "license" to say anything or be impulsive, thoughtless, or even careless in what and how we respond to clients. In therapeutic genuineness, "one is not brutally frank in one's relations with others," and it does not "involve expressing hurtful or threatening thoughts and feelings" (Patterson, 1985, p. 7). Thus, the concept of genuineness has to be separated from the concept of therapeutic genuineness. What the research reveals is interesting: It is not necessarily true that genuineness is necessarily therapeutic. What appears more likely is that it is the absence of defensiveness, of guile, and of phoniness that correlates more with successful outcome. Truax and Mitchell (1971) did pioneering work on this idea, which might have been lost over the years. They found that "what is effective is an absence of defensiveness and phoniness—a lack of evidence that the therapist is not genuine. . . . [It] is not the positive end of the genuineness scale that contributes to the therapeutic outcome. Instead, it is a lack of genuineness that mitigates against positive client change" (p. 316). This leads us to the second problem of genuineness.

Underemphasizing Genuineness

Beginning therapists wrestle with genuineness for a number of reasons. The primary reason is the problem of "everyday dishonesty," which describes our tendency not to be genuine with one another in our daily contacts. Instead, we are courteous, mannerly, social, protective, defensive, and concealing for what are probably good social reasons. Our private lives are not open to the inspection of strangers, and so we have developed socially acceptable ways of dealing with unsettling thoughts and feelings without offending or angering others. The problem comes when, as therapists, we are asked to be transparent, genuine, and honest in our relationships with clients. We are asked to use our feelings as *instruments* to be of service to the client. The problem is one of "having to cope with not trusting one's cultural instincts while being taught that therapists must act upon their hunches, guesses, and inner stirrings" (Welch & Gonzalez, 1999, p. 184). It is a "double bind" for many beginning therapists. First, they are not acting on their impulses, stirrings, or hunches that challenge their genuineness. Second, their impulses, stirrings, or hunches that stem from the teaching of the dominant culture are probably not trustworthy because the teaching of the culture is to avoid unpleasantness (the MUM effect), and acting on them also would be nontherapeutic. (As noted previously, the MUM effect is the tendency identified by Egan [1998] to withhold bad news even when it is in the client's best interest to hear it.) So the awkwardness of early training is recognized, expected, and considered a natural part of unlearning cultural teachings and learning therapeutic responses in place of the culturally learned responses to discomfort. The knack to be mastered is threefold. First, is learning to replace nontherapeutic responses with therapeutic ones. Second, is learning to respond nondefensively when challenged. Egan (1998), for example, in describing genuine therapists, suggests that "when clients express negative attitudes toward them, they examine the behavior that might cause the clients to think negatively, try to understand the clients' points of view, and continue to work with them" (p. 50). Third, is that the learned therapeutic responses become second nature and are so integrated into one's lifestyle that they are natural, immediate, and congruent. In this case, hunches and impulses can be trusted to be both genuine and therapeutic.

MULTICULTURAL AND DIVERSITY CONCERNS

Sue, Ivey, and Pedersen's (1996) discussion of multicultural counseling competences (MCCs) has relevance for genuineness in counseling and psychotherapy. They have divided MCCs into attitudes/beliefs, knowledges, and skills. These categories seem to have special importance in the responding skill of genuineness. Attitudes and beliefs have to do with awareness of differences and the acknowledgement of how those differences can affect the counseling process. For example, an important MCC reflecting the awareness of one's own cultural values and biases is, "Culturally skilled counselors are comfortable with differences that exist between themselves and clients in terms of race, ethnicity, culture, and beliefs" (Sue, Ivey, & Pederson, 1996, p. 46). This comfortableness seems likely to enable the therapist to respond naturally and genuinely with clients who are culturally different from the therapist. A therapeutic degree of comfort with differences is an active pursuit of multiculturally competence therapists. "Culturally skilled counselors seek out educational, consultative, and training experience to enhance their understanding and effectiveness in working with culturally different populations" (Sue, Ivey & Pedersen, 1996, p. 46). The combination of attitudes, knowledge, and skills that reflect an awareness of how cultural background can affect the therapeutic relationship enables the therapist to interact with clients in genuine and therapeutically helpful ways that are not hampered by awkwardness, second guessing, and indecisiveness.

USING GENUINENESS EFFECTIVELY

Gazda, Asbury, Balzer, Childers, and Walters (1984) have developed a scale to measure the genuineness of a therapist's responses. The scale ranges from punitive, defensive, and deceitful to spontaneous and fully congruent.

1	2	3	4
Punitive; Defensive; Deceitful	Role-Bound	Faciliative	Spontaneous; Fully Congruent

Level 1

Cl: I'm not feeling like what we are doing is helping. I'm . . . still . . . where I was when I came in . . . I mean, you know what I mean?

Th: I've been doing this for quite a long time and I can reassure you these things take time.

A punitive or defensive response is one in which the therapist "uses his or her feelings to punish the [client], or a response in which the helper's communications are clearly unrelated. . . . There is considerable incongruence between the helper's feelings and his or her verbal and/or nonverbal expressions. The helper may be defensive (unaware of his or her feelings), or quite false and deceitful" (Gazda, Asbury, Balzer, Childers, & Walters, 1984, p. 157).

Level 2

Cl: No one understands! I'm not who people think I am! I'm . . . I'm fooling them at work and . . . I know . . . sooner or later they will find out I can't do the job.

Th: [shrugs and gestures outward with hand] All of us have doubts.

We have discussed the flaws of role-playing above. The role-player is not responding genuinely, but out of some idea of how a therapist should respond. Thus, this is a "response in which the helper's communications are slightly unrelated . . . [and] there is incongruence between the helper's feelings and his or her verbal and/or nonverbal expressions. The helper responds according to some preconceived role" (p. 157).

Level 3

Cl: Who knows what is going on with me. I'm . . . feeling nutty . . . my girlfriend is angry with me and . . . and I'm . . . I'm . . . what?

Th: You're feeling at loose ends and hoping somebody can figure you out, like "I sure can't!"

A faciliative response is considered the minimal level helpful response. This is the level expected of students at the end of their training. It is a response in which the therapist is clearly not behaving hurtfully or defensively. The therapist is striving to demonstrate "no incongruence between expressions and feelings. The helper gives a controlled expression of feelings which facilitates the relationship, refraining from expressing feelings which could impede the relationship" (p. 157). The controlled aspect of the response can be considered the therapist's attempt to respond therapeutically rather than impulsively or hurtfully.

Level 4

Cl: My parents are getting a divorce and I'm caught in the middle. They are both expecting me to do something. I don't know what. I love them both but . . . I'm [gesturing with both hands in front of his chest in a circle] in the middle.

Th: [making a gesture that mirrors the client's] Just a mix of feelings: love . . . perhaps anger . . . um, I'm not certain, . . . guilt? and that sense of being in the middle—almost as if they want you to play a role like a therapist . . .

When a therapist has integrated effective listening and responding skills to the extent that they are second nature, spontaneous responses are considered both genuine and therapeutic. At this level, "the helper is spontaneous and dependably real. The helper's verbal and nonverbal messages, whether positive or negative, are congruent with how he or she feels. In the event of negative responses, the helper communicates these constructively, in an effort to open up new areas of inquiry" (p. 157). This open, immediate, and facilitative manner is one in which clients can come to trust the therapist and move forward in bringing important personal issues to the therapy. It's nondefensiveness invites clients to feel at ease in bringing up even feelings of stress related to the therapy itself as well as the pain and vulnerability in their lives.

This scale provides you with a guideline as you seek to bring genuineness into your responses to clients. As you encounter exchanges in observing therapist sessions and even television and movies, take some time to view the exchanges in terms of how genuine they seem to you. It is fun, even instructive, to speculate how scenes might be changed if the characters would have responded with genuineness. While watching television and movies is an entertainment, it is an essential part of your training as you review your own and your peers' sessions.

In addition, there seem to me to be three attitudinal and behavioral skills that can increase your facilitative genuineness. First, study and master the listening and responding skills. While therapeutic responding is to some degree different and strange in the dominant culture of the United States, in the specific culture of counseling and psychotherapy it has been demonstrated to be effective by both experience and research. Listening and responding therapeutically is more than a matter of faith. It is a matter of skill. Beginning therapists' early awkwardness with uncomfortable topics, with tested language, and with unaccustomed directness gives way with experience and supervision.

Second, the way to move toward an integrated genuineness is to take risks (the Giraffe principle). As a therapist you are expected, even by clients themselves, to help explore unknown and frightening aspects of their lives. Often these explorations might frighten you. It is taking mild risks, based on sound listening and responding skills, that helps push experience.

Third, coupled with taking risks, is the ability to respond nondefensively when challenged. If you can learn simply to acknowledge a mistake and then move on without becoming overly apologetic, then you will be able both to take risks and to continue in spite of occasional gaffs. Even a mistake, offered genuinely, can be appreciated by clients who, recognizing the authentic spirit of the intervention, simply correct it and can move on. Mastering skills, taking risks, and responding nondefensively provide the foundation for making genuine, spontaneous therapeutic responses a natural part of your counseling and psychotherapy.

SUMMARY

Effective psychotherapists are not phonies. Research has affirmed the role of genuineness in therapy again and again. The concepts of honesty, sincerity, and directness along with the therapist's ability to convey these to clients form the basis for the elusive definition of genuineness. Perhaps, one of the most revealing aspects of the research is that it is not the presence of genuineness in the therapy that seems most important, but rather the absence of phoniness. When clients see their therapists as withholding, institutional, aloof, or phony, then therapeutic effectiveness is threatened.

This problem of roles may stem from defensiveness on the part of the therapist. Some common roles therapists adopt that interfere with a genuine presence in therapy may include the role of the "expert," in which the therapist is aloof and distant; the "wizard," who heals by magic or rituals that create expectations of forces that lie outside the client's control; the "pundit," in which the therapist analyzes and predicts; and the "clerk," who collects information. Each of these common roles masks the person of the therapist, constitutes a threat to the therapeutic relationship, and imposes false assumptions on the nature of the therapeutic process. This seems nowhere more important than in the critical role of MCC, where comfortableness with differences is essential to working with clients from a variety of backgrounds, cultures, and lifestyles. The masks of roles interfere with the flexibility needed to adapt nondefensively to different client styles.

Genuineness can be measured along a scale from hurtful to spontaneously therapeutic. Studying this scale and formulating responses is one way to increase your ability to respond genuinely to clients. Attitudinal and behavioral skills that can also lead to more genuine responding include mastering listening and responding skills, taking risks, and learning to respond nondefensively.

REFERENCES

Egan, G. (1998). *The skilled helper: A problem-management approach to helping* (6th ed.). Pacific Grove, CA: Brooks/Cole.

Gazda, G. M., Asbury, F. S., Balzer, F. J., Childers, W. C., & Walters, R. P. (1984). *Human relations development: A manual for educators* (3rd ed.). Boston, MA: Allyn and Bacon.

Ivey, A. E., & Ivey, M. B. (1999). *Intentional interviewing and counseling: Facilitating client development in a multicultural society* (4th ed.). Pacific Grove, CA: Brooks/Cole.

McWhirter, B. T., McWhirter, J. J., & Townsend, K. C. (2001). Individual counseling: Traditional approaches. In D. Capuzzi & D. R. Gross (Eds.), *Introduction to the counseling profession* (3rd ed., pp. 123–138). Boston, MA: Allyn and Bacon.

Miars, R. D., & Halverson, S. E. (2001). The helping relationship. In D. Capuzzi & D. R. Gross (eds.), *Introduction to the counseling profession* (3rd ed., pp. 50–68). Boston, MA: Allyn and Bacon.

Patterson, C. H. (1985). *The therapeutic relationship: Foundations for an eclectic psychotherapy*. Pacific Grove, CA: Brooks/Cole.

Rogers, C. R. (1957). The necessary and sufficient conditions of therapeutic personality change. *Journal of Consulting Psychology, 21*, 95–103.

Rogers, C. R. (1961). *On becoming a person*. Boston, MA: Houghton Mifflin.

Sue, D. W., Ivey, A. E., & Pedersen, P. B. (1996). *A theory of multicultural counseling and therapy*. Pacific Grove, CA: Brooks/Cole.

Truax, C. B., & Mitchell, K. M. (1971). Research on certain therapist interpersonal skills in relation to process and outcome. In A. E. Begin & S. L. Garfield (Eds.), *Handbook of psychotherapy and behavior change: An empirical analysis* (pp. 299–344). New York: Wiley.

Welch, I. D. (1998). *The path of psychotherapy: Matters of the heart*. Pacific Grove, CA: Brooks/Cole.

Welch, I. D., & Gonzalez, D. M. (1999). *The process of counseling and psychotherapy: Matters of skill*. Pacific Grove, CA: Brooks/Cole.

Chapter 16

Responding with Immediacy

Our temporal world consists of three periods—the past, the present, and the future. Part of the myth surrounding psychotherapy is that much of the time spent in therapy is in reexamining the past. Both modern psychotherapy and modern personality theory, however, have abandoned the drive reduction theories of the early twentieth century toward more relationship-based and goal-directed theories that lend themselves to more present-focused interventions. Whether one adopts a cognitive-behavioral, humanistic, constructivist, object relations, or systems theory, the "here and now" occupies significantly more emphasis than the "there and then." Ivey and Ivey (1999) crystallize this emphasis in pointing out the importance of immediacy: "You will find that as interviews move more to present tense immediacy, your presence in the interview will become more powerful and important" (p. 162).

IMMEDIACY

"Immediacy" is a term used to describe several different present-focused issues that can emerge in therapy. It can refer to time itself; that is, the therapy is more focused on present thoughts, feelings, and behavior. It is also used to describe an intervention in which the therapist openly discusses the relationship between the therapist and the client. It can also refer to nontherapy-related issues that are affecting the therapy. Let's discuss each of these in turn.

The Present

There are two ways in which immediacy is used to make therapy more present focused. First is the recognition of obvious feelings in the room (Ivey & Ivey, 1999; Long, 1996; Welch & Gonzalez, 1999), and the second is bringing past events into the present (Long, 1996).

Obvious Feelings. As we discussed previously, nonverbal messages play an important role in understanding clients' feelings and meanings. Below is an example of a client talking about one thing and her nonverbal messages indicating a present feeling. Immediacy is a skill that can acknowledge present feelings.

Cl: I got the promotion I was talking about and I'm happy about that [she fidgets in the chair].

Th: Happy and relieved.

Cl: Yes, I was worried about it [she wraps her scarf tightly around her fingers].

Th: I know you are happy and relieved and I'm feeling something like anxiety in the room. Anxiety or . . .

The therapist has acknowledged both the stated feelings and the nonverbal behavior and has expressed it tentatively as anxiety. This tentativeness is an important part of using immediacy skills.

Bringing the Past into the Present. Clients come to therapy for personally felt reasons. Often those reasons have to do with past events and/or relationships. The client may talk about those events in the past tense. Yet, even though the event occurred in the past, the feelings they are expressing are not past feelings (their behaviors are not past behaviors, their relationships are not in the past); they are felt presently, and effective therapy deals with present thoughts, feelings, and behaviors. This form of immediacy is to bring past events into the present (Ivey & Ivey, 1999; Long, 1996). A client, for example, might have unresolved issues with a parent. Larry is a 43-year-old man who came to therapy because of his "midlife crisis" and in the third session has started talking about his deceased father:

Cl: I know I'm not supposed to talk about my father this way, but he was a tyrant. He was oppressive and dominating and I'm remembering how much I . . . resented him and . . . uh, rebelled.

Th: Feeling like it isn't proper to "speak ill of the dead" and yet remembering the way you felt controlled, . . . and it seems that there might be guilt and even anger, not just in the past but right now.

The therapist has paraphrased the client's content and, again tentatively, explored whether the feelings of guilt and anger are current and immediately felt. This is a point where it is important to bring up the delicate nature of immediacy. The therapist isn't leading the client or even suggesting that guilt and anger are present. The intent is to explore whether the therapist's personal understanding of the client's feelings being in the present is accurate. In this way, as is the case in many therapeutic interventions, empathy is a crucial skill.

Table 16.1
General/Specific and Positive/Negative Aspects of Relationship

	Positive	Negative
General	"I believe our relationship is growing in trust"	"I'm feeling some tension in our relationship"
Specific	"The risk you just took has helped our relationship so much"	"I think you have been pulling away in this session and I'm worrying about what that means for our relationship"

The Relationship

The meaning of immediacy has to do with the quality of the relationship between the therapist and the client (Egan, 1998; Ivey & Ivey, 1999; Long, 1996; Martin, 1983; Patterson, 1985; Welch & Gonzalez, 1999). This aspect of immediacy is akin to transference and countertransference in psychoanalytic theory, although without the therapeutic centrality of that form of therapy. Like time, immediacy issues in the relationship may be divided into two relatively different issues: general relationship issues and some specific event in therapy that affects the relationship. Either of these issues may be positive or negative (see Table 16.1).

General. There are times in therapy, both good and bad, when the overall relationship can benefit from a direct dialogue. It can become of such importance that to ignore what is going on between the therapist and the client becomes a real obstacle for future development. Whether the issue is positive or negative, neglecting to give it proper attention can stall the therapy.

A hardworking, contentious client can be acknowledged without evaluating them and creating dependency, and that is the skill of immediacy. A counselor or psychotherapist who fails to acknowledge the positive qualities of a building relationship is ignoring a major contributor to successful outcome. A therapist might say, for example, "It seems to me that we have formed a good, solid and trusting relationship quickly. It's evident to me by how hard your are working in sessions." Such a statement can build the relationship even further and lay a stronger foundation for more difficult work to come.

It seems obvious that the negative side of a relationship has to be addressed in therapy as well. A deteriorating relationship, or one that fails to be established, signals a negative outcome for the therapy. A client may continue to come to therapy but never get much beyond surface issues and talk in a droning and matter-of-fact way about superficial life issues. In such a situation, the therapy is not making progress and there is no apparent gain for the client. It is essential for a therapist to bring this therapeutic issue into the present. Immediacy is best when it is tentative and clear that the therapist is talking about his or her concerns. It avoids blaming, evaluating, or judging the client for the concerns the therapist introduces into the session. In the example above, in which the client seems not to get beyond surface issues, a therapist might raise this issue in the following way:

> Th: This might be a good place to stop and look at what you are getting from therapy. We seem to be stuck on the same issues, and I'm not sure we have a level of trust that can help move us forward. How is it for you?

The therapist has alluded to the issues and brought the issue of trust into the session. The open-ended question allows the client to respond in an undirected way to the therapist's concerns. There are risks in introducing an immediate negative concern. These can range for denial of the therapist's feelings to anger to leaving the therapy. It is a judgment that the psychotherapist has to make in recognizing the importance of the therapeutic relationship. If, in the judgment of the therapist, something is awry in the relationship, then some intervention is necessary.

Specific. In the context of an overall relationship, specific events may occur that call for an immediacy response. A client may begin to arrive to sessions consistently late or begin to miss sessions. Another might become sarcastic, become flirtatious, wear revealing clothing, or challenge the use of some counseling technique. Such behavior can signal a deteriorating relationship, or it may be "parallel to other relationships in the client's life. . . . [T]he helping relationship provides a powerful opportunity to address general relationship dynamics with the client" (Long, 1996, p. 228). Whatever the case, individual events may need to be brought into the present in order to ensure the long-range successful outcome of the therapy. Welch and Gonzalez (1999, p. 189) provide an example drawn from a direct-supervision session in which a female therapist was working with a male client. When the session ended, the male client said goodbye by saying, "See you next week, Babe." The therapist reacted by saying, "Bill, come back for a minute. When you said 'Babe,' it sounded as if you were seeing me as an eligible female, someone you might date. I need to be clear with you and let you know that I don't think I can be of help to you if you see me that way. I am your therapist and not an eligible woman."

This therapist-in-training responded immediately and effectively, if somewhat bluntly. If she had not, the therapy might have taken on underlying dynamics which would have continued to interfere with the relationship and been much more difficult to address later. In this case, the client responded appropriately and the therapy continued.

It is equally important to respond to positive events in therapy that can contribute to successful outcome. Clients work hard, gain insights, change behaviors, take risks, and express sentiments that signal their own perception of the positive nature of the relationship. These thoughts and behaviors can be acknowledged therapeutically with immediacy. Clients' transition from past to present feelings in therapy marks a change in their internal understanding of what it will take for them to learn to cope effectively with the issues and concerns of their lives. Such a moment calls for an immediate response.

> Cl: I keep talking about how I didn't tell my children I loved them when they were little and I'm just now realizing I'm not telling them I love them right now.
>
> Th: and I'm aware that you aren't talking about the past—you are talking about the present. That feeling of love is with you right now.

By acknowledging the specific feelings of the moment, the therapist is not only addressing this specific moment, but also building a firmer foundation for the overall relationship.

Extraneous Events

One other variable that calls for the skill of immediacy is something that affects the therapy but is not related directly to the therapy (Welch & Gonzalez, 1999). A client might have a friend who accompanies him or her to therapy and who creates a scene in the waiting room. Another might wear a perfume or an aftershave to which the therapist is allergic (it happens!), and another might offer gifts during holiday seasons. A simple example of how extraneous events can affect the therapy was illustrated when the city was making road repairs next to the therapist's office. While several clients during the day had not responded to the construction, one clearly was distracted.

> Th: I'm thinking that the noises outside are bothering you . . . hurting your concentration?

This is an example of a quick immediacy response that brings an event into the present and, through its acknowledgment, permits the client to deal with it and move on. This is an important principle of immediacy. Distractions interfere with therapy. Immediacy is a skill that is meant to keep the therapy on track and forward moving.

THE NEED FOR IMMEDIACY

There are, as we have seen above, several types of immediacy that may be called for in therapy. It is the same for those situations or events that call for the skill of immediacy. Egan (1998) has provided the following list of situations that call for immediacy:

Lack of Direction. Sometimes therapy wanders and immediacy may be needed to address relationship concerns such as trust or dependence that may be blocking movement and depth.

Tension. Sometimes misunderstandings, miscommunications, or miscues can create pressure and strains in the therapy that have to be addressed before you can move on.

Trust. Trust is central to the therapeutic alliance and without mutual trust little beyond surface concerns will be addressed.

Diversity. Multicultural counseling skills are vital to any therapy in which the client and the therapist come from different cultural traditions.

Dependency. If clients see the therapist as a person in authority, then they will not take the lead and instead wait for instructions. Immediacy is one skill that can be used to bring this issue into the therapy.

Counterdependency. Therapists are not immune to liking clients, enjoying clients, and wanting to be liked by them in turn. Such feelings can seriously interfere with moving into more painful aspects of the client's issues, problems, and concerns. Immediacy around these issues, as delicate as they are, is necessary.

Attraction. Clients, understandably, can become attracted to a person who is interested in listening to them, gives them their full attention, and is nonjudgmental. Clients have often viewed their therapists in unrealistic and unhelpful ways. Therapists can experience the same feeling of attraction as well. If they interfere with therapy, then they have to be dealt with and immediacy is a helpful skill in doing this. (Pp. 183–184)

POTENTIAL PROBLEMS

The problems of immediacy are of two sorts. First, there are problems of responding inappropriately (Long, 1996; Patterson, 1985). Patterson (1985) states that "it is not always appropriate to respond . . . [B]efore the therapist knows and understands the client, he or she cannot be too certain of his or her experience of the client. . . . Therefore, the therapist's expression of immediacy is tentative" (p. 86). Discretion might be the better part of valor. We have discussed, however, the MUM effect in which therapists are reluctant to bring up unpleasant events or topics. In fact, that is the second potential problem—*ignoring* important thoughts, feelings, or behaviors and relationship factors that call for immediate attention.

The Problem of Intervening

There appear to be three problems with using immediacy in counseling (Long, 1996; Sue, Ivey, & Pedersen, 1996):

1. The problem of judgmentalness. One of the reasons immediacy is a delicate skill is that wording, inflection, timing, and topic are all important considerations. The purpose of immediacy is, of course, to strengthen the relationship and advance the therapy. What is delicate is that this has to be done in such a way that the client clearly recognizes that it is the therapist who is presenting this issue in therapy out of therapist's feelings and perceptions. The therapist is not blaming the client for the perceived issue, but bringing it into the present to explore. If this nuanced understanding is not achieved, then the therapy can be harmed.
2. The problem of interpreting and drawing conclusions. Another danger is that the therapist can describe the event or situation and then explain what it means for the client. This act of interpretation is, of course, disrespectful, and the need to come to a conclusion has more to do with the therapist than it does with the event or situation.

   Th: I'm aware of the tension in the room now, and you're probably angry at being pushed today, but it is necessary if we are going to make progress.

   The therapist has described his or her feelings and then gone on to explain why those tensions are in the room and why the client is feeling them. Such therapist behavior is unhelpful and likely to cause a worsened relationship.
3. Multicultural concerns. Sue, Ivey, and Pedersen (1996) indicate that "culturally skilled counselors possess knowledge about their social impact upon others. They are knowledgeable about communication style differences, how their style may clash or facilitate the counseling process with minority clients, and how to anticipate the impact it may have on others" (p. 46). They add that "culturally skilled counselors are aware of their negative emotional reactions toward other racial/ethnic groups which may prove detrimental to their clients in counseling. They are willing to contrast their own beliefs and attitudes with those of their culturally different clients in a nonjudgmental fashion" (p. 47). These principles of multicultural counseling and psychotherapy remind us that we have to be aware of our own values and to be careful in responding immediately without a good understanding of the origins of our urges to intervene. A multicultural awareness is a demanding and essential aspect of the skill of immediacy.

The Problem of Not Intervening

If we do not acknowledge the factors that affect relationships in therapy, then we run the risk of not establishing or even damaging the therapeutic alliance (Long, 1996; Patterson, 1985; Welch & Gonzalez, 1999). Ignoring relationship dynamics can come from two sources. First, the therapist may not be aware of them. We cannot respond to things we don't see or feel. The solution for such lack of perception is training. This is especially true for multicultural training in which we may learn not only about cultural differences, but also about how interventions are perceived and facilitated for particular populations.

The second type of failing can be more serious. A therapist may be aware of the need but choose to ignore it. This is a failure of nerve, perhaps. The MUM effect has been mentioned above as one force that prevents therapists from bringing up unpleasant thoughts, feelings, events, or behaviors. This neglect of the painful does a real and substantial disservice to clients. It does not provide them with feedback that can increase their chances of learning more effective coping strategies for their issues and concerns. The strategy for dealing with immediacy issues involves supervision by an experienced psychotherapist who can teach both the importance of and the skill of immediacy. Egan (1998) recognizes that "immediacy is a difficult, demanding skill" (p. 184) and offers these three suggestions for its practice: First, the "helper needs to be aware of what is happening in the relationship without becoming self-preoccupied and without 'psyching out' the client" (p. 184). Second, Egan insists that "immediacy demands both social intelligence and social competence in all the communication skills" (p. 184). Third, the therapist has to transcend the MUM effect and "challenge the client even though he or she is reluctant to do so" (p. 184).

The use of immediacy demands three sometimes elusive prerequisites. It requires that the therapist have experience (Egan, 1998). This is life experience as well as counseling experience. Immediacy calls for both skill and timing. Skill can be practiced and even mastered relatively quickly, but timing seems to come with experience. Therapists need wisdom. Making the decision of when and how to intervene in the eternally gray world of psychotherapy requires a good understanding of human behavior, a better knowledge of the individual clients, and a profound knowledge of the self in order to ensure that our motivation is good and our judgment clear. Immediacy is a skill that should be used in moderation. It is not a primary tool of counseling and psychotherapy; it is a skill that is called out by client behavior and not one that is used without an invitation.

SUMMARY

Temporal perspective can be an issue in counseling and psychotherapy. Clients can focus too much on past concerns and avoid the coping skills they need in the present. Others might fantasize about the future, putting off making decisions and developing skills needed for their own imagined future. Effective therapists bring the present into therapy and focus on the thoughts, feelings, and behaviors of clients both within the session and in their daily lives.

Clients may need the help of the therapist not only to talk about their life concerns in the present tense, but also to bring their living struggles into therapy. Paramount among the uses of immediacy is building, maintaining, and strengthening the therapeutic relationship. Both positive and negative long-and short-term events can influence the relationship between the therapist and the client. Immediacy is a useful skill in dealing with those times when, for good or ill, relationship factors seem likely to influence the course of therapy.

MCCs are important considerations in developing immediacy skills. It is important to be aware of one's own attitudes, values, and behaviors that can influence clients and how one's own cultural values impact clients from different cultural backgrounds. Other concerns influencing immediacy include cautions about judgmentalness and interpretation.

Immediacy is a delicate, demanding, and difficult skill that requires not only training and understanding, but also experience, social competence, and tact. The best advice is to introduce immediacy issues into the therapy tentatively. The skill involves being able to do this tentatively but not apologetically. It involves the ownership of one's feelings while, at the same time, using empathically understood cues from the client as the vehicle for exploring the issues that concern you. It is this blending and balancing that calls for experience and judgment. Immediacy is a skill that is invited by a client. It is an important skill to develop and will enhance your counseling effectiveness.

REFERENCES

Egan, G. (1998). *The skilled helper: A problem-management approach to helping* (6th ed.). Pacific Grove, CA: Brooks/Cole.

Ivey, A. E., & Ivey, M. B. (1999). *Intentional interviewing and counseling: Facilitating client development in a multicultural society* (4th ed.). Pacific Grove, CA: Brooks/Cole.

Long, V. O. (1996). *Communication skills in helping relationships: A framework for facilitating personal growth.* Pacific Grove, CA: Brooks/Cole.

Martin, D. G. (1983). *Counseling and therapy skills.* Prospect Heights, IL: Waveland Press.

Okun, B. F. (2002). *Effective helping: Interviewing and counseling techniques* (6th ed.). Pacific Grove, CA: Brooks/Cole.

Patterson, C. H. (1985). *The therapeutic relationship: Foundations for an eclectic psychotherapy.* Pacific Grove, CA: Brooks/Cole.

Sue, D. W., Ivey, A. E., & Pedersen, P. B. (1996). *A theory of multicultural counseling and therapy.* Pacific Grove, CA: Brooks/Cole.

Welch, I. D., & Gonzalez, D. M. (1999). *The process of counseling and psychotherapy: Matters of skill.* Pacific Grove, CA: Brooks/Cole.

Chapter 17

Responding with Self-Disclosure

Self-disclosure is a concept pioneered by Jourard (1958, 1959, 1964). It is a concept that recognizes the importance of being known by, at least, the close and significant people in our lives. Sometimes, clients are people who do not have people in their lives by whom they are deeply known. We expect and encourage clients to reveal their hurts, vulnerabilities, and inner turmoil. Yet, when it comes to therapist's disclosure, the issue is far more complex. "We expect [clients] to share themselves, and we need to experience and understand that same process of sharing and relating. The underlying principle here is that we do not ask others to do what we cannot or would not" (Okun, 2002, p. 288). It seems straightforward and simple. It is, however, a controversial issue (Egan, 1998; Hackney & Cormier, 1994; Ivey & Ivey, 1999; Martin, 1983; Patterson, 1985; Welch & Gonzalez, 1999).

Ivey and Ivey (1999) believe that self-disclosure "can encourage client talk, create additional trust between counselor and client, and establish a more equal relationship in the interview" (p. 289). Okun (2002), while recognizing the controversial nature of therapist self-disclosure, indicates that "many helpers believe that judicious self-disclosure can enhance the helping relationship and aid in problem solving" (p. 287). Martin (1983) approaches therapist self-disclosure tentatively: "You and the client are in an important human encounter, but one with an unusual one-way structure. You are there to serve the client's personal growth. In some cases, your disclosure of how you feel will serve that growth" (p. 99). Miars and Halverson (2001) share Martin's reservation even when they recognize that self-disclosure "can be a powerful intervention for making contact with clients, but it should not be an indiscriminate sharing of personal problems with clients" (p. 64). This sentiment on the cautious and reserved use of therapist disclosure is echoed by King (2001): Self-disclosure "would best serve the client if it was limited to acknowledging resulting feelings rather than indicating shared events" (p. 72). Martin (1983) states the case more strongly, indicating that it is possible that self-disclosure "hampers therapy by taking responsibility away from the client and by turning therapy to meet the therapist's needs" (p. 99).

Others, however, argue more strongly in favor of therapist self-disclosure. Okun (2002), for example, insists "it is important that helpers have the capacity to share themselves intimately with other people" (p. 288). Hackney and Cormier (1994) believe that "self expression and disclosure are important ways of letting the client know that you are a person and not just a role" (p. 24). Gazda, Asbury, Balzer, Childers, and Walters (1984) state clearly that clients "need to know who the helpers really are so that they can relate to them fully" (p. 166). They added that "effective helpers do not meet their [client's] with a mask; they are willing to be known as unique human beings and are easy to get to know" (p. 168).

Frankly, there is little mystery about the varying opinions regarding therapist self-disclosure. The research is vague and often contradictory. This was a conclusion drawn in 1973 (Cozby, 1973), affirmed in 1985 (Patterson, 1985), and reached again as recently as 1998 (Egan, 1998). Since the research does not provide clear guidelines, this is one of those situations where we have to rely upon reasonableness and guidelines provided by experienced practitioners. "Self-disclosure is appropriate when it is the intention of the psychotherapist that the disclosure help the client explore, understand, or move toward action" (Welch & Gonzalez, 1999, pp. 190–191).

THE NATURE OF THERAPEUTIC SELF-DISCLOSURE

What should the therapist disclose? Therapists may find it helpful to disclose their own experience as a way of modeling and as a way to explore blind spots (Egan, 1998). Long (1996) thought that "self-disclosure provides a nonthreatening invitation to the client to consider another perspective." Hackney and Cormier (1984) indicate that therapists might disclose their own problems, facts about their role, reactions to the client (feedback), or reactions to the relationship (p. 24). They believe that reactions to the client and to the relationship are more effective and productive forms of therapist disclosure. Gazda, Asbury, Balzer, Childers, and Walters (1984) provide a thorough list of what therapists might disclose:

> Where they have been
>
> What they have been through and how they got through it
>
> Why they behaved as they did; why they behave as they do
>
> What attitudes they used to hold and those they hold now
>
> What they used to value and what they value now
>
> What goals they used to have for themselves
>
> What goals they have for themselves now, (pp. 166, 168)

Whether such lists of specific areas of therapist disclosure are helpful or not, it is important to recognize that as counselors and psychotherapists we are in a significant human relationship characterized by empathy, genuineness, and respect. A part of therapeutic responding surely includes the appropriate use of the therapist's background and experience that can model, inform, normalize, and reassure clients. While research of therapist disclosure is not as firm as research on the therapeutic outcomes of demonstrated empathy, for example, there is support for its use. Sometimes this is a straightforward statement of a shared experience. Some years ago, during a supervision session, the client was talking about his Vietnam War experience. His therapist was also a veteran of that war, but had not revealed his past experience to the client. After the first and second sessions, the therapist had been encouraged to disclose his background to the client, but he was reluctant to do so. Finally, after the third session, the therapist was strongly encouraged to reveal his own background as a veteran. The effect was remarkable. The client physically reacted, sat back in his chair and said, "Man, am I glad you told me that. I have things I want to talk about, but I didn't want to do it with somebody who wouldn't understand. You know what I mean? Now that I know you were in 'Nam, I don't have to hold back." (This example also can be used to make a point about genuineness and immediacy for a therapist who does not share a background or is culturally different from a client. In that situation, it is better, more therapeutic, to discuss openly the differences and lack of experience the client is bringing into therapy. While you do not share the client's background or experience, you can make yourself open to hearing and struggling with the client to understand his or her experience. Further, there might be situations where it is more reasonable to refer a particular client to another therapist who is more culturally or experientially similar to the client and therefore might be able to respond more sensitively to the client's issues).

ADVANTAGES AND DISADVANTAGES

Appropriate and well-intended self-disclosure can have positive and lasting effects in therapy. Therapist self-disclosure "can generate a more open, facilitative counseling atmosphere, encourage client talk and additional trust, and create a more equal relationship" (Miars & Halverson, 2001, p. 64). The positive outcomes of therapist self-disclosure include: (1) effective role modeling; (2) validation or universality of feelings; and (3) permission giving (Long, 1996, p. 226).

Clients might come to therapy without any clear idea of how to talk about their experiences. A therapist can model not only how a person reveals content, but also how the meanings, emotions, or feelings about that content can be verbalized. This role modeling is an important use of self-disclosure.

Clients often come to therapy troubled by feelings and behaviors that are normal and expected in the client's situation. Therapist disclosure can validate the client's feelings and provide some sense that such feelings are normal and widespread.

Welch (1998) discusses the concept of *die Gedanken sind frei* (literally, 'the thoughts are free'—based on a song popular with allied prisoners of war during World War II). The concept is used to mean that our feelings are what we feel and that we do not have to justify them or necessarily to experience guilt or shame for them. A part of therapist disclosure may be giving permission to clients to feel what they feel. Then it is more likely that they will be able to bring their feelings into therapy to explore and understand the role their feelings play in their lives.

There appears to be a level or degree of therapist disclosure that is optimally effective. There is a danger of revealing too much. There is a corresponding danger of revealing too little. Therapists who disclose very little hazard being seen as distant, aloof, and role-conscious (Egan, 1998). Therapists who disclose too much can be seen as untrustworthy (Levin & Gergen, 1969), preoccupied (Cozby, 1973), or in need of personal help (Capuzzi & Gross, 2001).

Therapist disclosure is a skill that involves challenges. It is a form of intimacy that may intimidate some clients (Egan, 1998). It may place expectations on the client. "Helper revelations, even when they deal with past failures, usually deal with problem situations that have been overcome" (Egan, 1998, p. 178). These considerations are nested in the skills of therapeutic goals, genuineness, timing, and appropriateness (Capuzzi & Gross, 2001; Ivey & Ivey, 1999).

Without a sensitivity to these challenges, the outcomes of therapist disclosure can be negative. First, the outcome can be distracting or even overwhelming for a client. Second, the client may see the disclosure as irrelevant and unconnected to his or her concerns. Third, there is the danger of the disclosure being perceived as one-upping or as if the therapist is saying, "Well, if you think that is something, wait until I tell you this!" Fourth, there is a danger of role reversal in which the client feels sympathy for the therapist's problems and is deflected from his or her own (Long, 1996).

GUIDELINES

In order to optimize the advantages and minimize the disadvantages, a number of authors have provided guidelines for the use of therapist disclosure. Hackney and Cormier (1994) recommend a core and fundamental guideline: Each therapist disclosure is preceded by the internal question, "Whose needs am I meeting when I disclose this idea or feeling—the client's or mine?" (p. 224). If the internal answer is "the client's," then disclosure seems appropriate, and the therapist is faced with choices in using self-disclosure. What should be disclosed and how much? See Table 17.1 for guidelines that can be helpful in deciding when and how to use therapist self-disclosure. If the intention of the disclosure genuinely is meant to be therapeutic, then these guidelines help turn intention into behavior. Grounded in empathy, judged for appropriateness, kept, and

Table 17.1
Guidelines for Using Self-Disclosure in Therapy

Study these guidelines as you consider when and how to introduce self-disclosure into your counseling practice. The principle guideline is to ensure that what is being disclosed is needed and serves some therapeutic purpose.

1. When in doubt, do not disclose (Long, 1996)
2. Early in the relationship let the client know that therapist disclosure is a part of the counseling experience (Egan, 1998)
3. Ground disclosure in empathy and the immediate relationship (Ivey & Ivey, 1999; Welch & Gonzalez, 1999)
4. Ensure that the relationship is strong enough to support the disclosure (Welch & Gonzalez, 1999)
5. Ensure that the disclosure is appropriate and relevant (Egan, 1998; Ivey & Ivey, 1999; Welch & Gonzalez, 1999)
6. The disclosure should be selective, focused, and brief (Egan, 1998: Ivey & Ivey, 1999; Long, 1996; Welch & Gonzalez, 1999)
7. Do not burden or overwhelm the client with an overly intense or frightening disclosure (Egan, 1998; Welch & Gonzalez, 1999)
8. The disclosure should be true (Welch & Gonzalez, 1999)
9. After the disclosure, refocus attention back on the client (Ivey & Ivey, 1999; Long, 1996)
10. Observe client reaction and check (verbally and nonverbally) the effects of the disclosure on the client (Long, 1996; Welch & Gonzalez, 1999)

checked for its effect on the client, the use of therapist disclosure can become another skill in effective responding.

SUMMARY

Therapist self-disclosure is not a core condition of effective psychotherapy, and, as we have seen, there is some controversy regarding its use in therapy. Still, many therapists agree with Carkhuff (1969) who years ago wrote that "spontaneous sharing on the part of both parties is the essence of a genuine relationship" (p. 209). It is the sense of psychotherapy as a genuine relationship that leads many therapists to use self-disclosure as one more skill of effective responding. Miars and Halverson (2001) have continued this sense of need for disclosure into the therapeutic relationship as they recognize the vulnerability and obligation of therapist disclosure: "You become vulnerable when you share you own experiences, feelings, and reactions, yet can you expect your clients to become vulnerable in front of you if you rarely show them anything of yourself?" (p. 65).

Therapist disclosure must be grounded in empathy, genuineness, and respect. Built upon this foundation of core conditions, disclosure can be an effective tool in counseling and psychotherapy. Advantages for therapist disclosure include role modeling, validation or normalizing client feelings, and permission to bring sensitive material into the therapy. Disadvantages may include overwhelming clients, distracting the therapy, irrelevancy, competitiveness with clients, and role reversal in which the client feels protective for the therapist.

The use of therapist disclosure can be aided by using a set of guidelines that include internally ensuring that the disclosure is meant to be therapeutic and can be grounded in empathy, immediacy, brevity, and effectiveness.

REFERENCES

Capuzzi, D., & Gross, D. R. (Eds.). (2001). *Introduction to the counseling profession* (3rd ed.). Boston, MA: Allyn and Bacon.

Carkhuff, R. R. (1969). *Helping and human relations* (Vol. 1). New York: Holt, Rinehart and Winston.

Cozby, P. C. (1973). Self-disclosure: A literature review. *Psychological Bulletin, 79*, 73–91.

Egan, G. (1998). *The skilled helper: A problem-management approach to helping* (6th ed.). Pacific Grove, CA: Brooks/Cole.

Gazda, G. M., Asbury, F. S., Balzer, F. J., Childers, W. C., & Walters, R. P. (1984). *Human relations development: A manual for educators* (3rd ed.). Boston, MA: Allyn and Bacon.

Hackney, H., & Cormier, S. (1994). *Counseling strategies and interventions* (4th ed.). Boston, MA: Allyn and Bacon.

Ivey, A. E., & Ivey, M. B. (1999). *Intentional interviewing and counseling: Facilitating client development in a multicultural society* (4th ed.). Pacific Grove, CA: Brooks/Cole.

Jourard, S. M. (1958). A study of self-disclosure. *Scientific American, 198*(5), 77–82.

Jourard, S. M. (1959). Healthy personality and self-disclosure. *Mental Hygiene, 43*(4), 499–507.

Jourard, S. M. (1964). *The transparent self, self-disclosure and well-being*. New York: Van Nostrand Reinhold.

King, A. (2001). *Demystifying the counseling process: A self-help handbook for counselors*. Boston, MA: Allyn and Bacon.

Levin, F. M., & Gergen, K. J. (1969). Revealingness, ingratiation, and the disclosure of self. *Proceedings of the 77th Annual Convention of the American Psychological Association, 4*, 447–448.

Long, V. O. (1996). *Communication skills in helping relationships: A framework for facilitating personal growth*. Pacific Grove, CA: Brooks/Cole.

Martin, D. G. (1983). *Counseling and therapy skills*. Prospect Heights, IL: Waveland Press.

Miars, R. D., & Halverson, S. E. (2001) The helping relationship. In D. Capuzzi & D. R.

Gross (Eds.), *Introduction to the counseling profession* (3rd ed., pp. 50–68). Boston, MA: Allyn and Bacon.

Okun, B. F. (2002). *Effective helping: Interviewing and counseling techniques* (6th ed.). Pacific Grove, CA: Brooks/Cole.

Patterson, C. H. (1985). *The therapeutic relationship: Foundations for an eclectic psychotherapy*. Pacific Grove, CA: Brooks/Cole.

Sue, D. W., Ivey, A. E., & Pedersen, P. B. (1996). *A theory of multicultural counseling and therapy*. Pacific Grove, CA: Brooks/Cole.

Welch, I. D. (1998). *The path of psychotherapy: Matters of the heart*. Pacific Grove, CA: Brooks/Cole.

Welch, I. D., & Gonzalez, D. M. (1999). *The process of counseling and psychotherapy: Matters of skill*. Pacific Grove, CA: Brooks/Cole.

Chapter 18

Responding with Concreteness and Focus

"She could look through muddy water and see dry land" (Hill, 1972, p. 33). Brother Blue (Hugh Hill), a poet who performs his works, recited that line years ago. Yet, his words remain with me to this day as a startlingly clear example of what concreteness means in psychotherapy. "If you don't have the narrative straight, the client isn't likely to have it clear either" (Ivey & Ivey, 1999, p. 120). Clients often are confused, unclear, desultory, and even inarticulate in trying to tell their stories. One of the primary tasks of a therapist becomes seeing through the muddy water of chaos and confusion to reasonable order and clarity.

DEFINITIONS

Concreteness and focusing has been defined in the following ways:

> The task of the counselor to help the client clarify the pieces of the puzzle and fit them together so that the whole makes sense to the client. (Miars & Halverson, 2001, p. 62)

> The helpees' pinpointing or accurately labeling feelings and experiences. (Gazda, Asbury, Balzer, Childers, & Walters, 1984, p. 15)

> Specific feelings, specific thoughts, and *specific examples of actions*. (Ivey & Ivey, 1999, p. 161 [emphasis added])

> Clarifying a word, statement, or concept that is otherwise vague, abstract, or unclear. It means helping your clients speak in terms of the specific rather than the general way they speak of thoughts, feelings, and behaviors. (Long, 1996, p. 209)

> Clarifying facts and feelings specifically. (Okun, 2002, p. 42)

> A process of defining, honing, and hemming up the vague and undifferentiated aspects of the client's life into a more precise knowledge of what the problem is, why it is a problem, and *how to deal effectively and efficiently with it.* (Welch & Gonzalez, 1999, p. 185 [emphasis added])

CONCRETENESS VERSUS FOCUSING

These definitions lead one to view therapy as a strategy of getting to the point and nailing things down. Clients' narratives are heard and sorted into relevant points and outlined clearly for them. Oh my! We are early in this chapter and already it is time for a caution. I have described the therapeutic process as including exploration, understanding, and action. In this model of the counseling process, one of the goals of early sessions is exploration, or *elaboration*. Ivey and Ivey (1999) caution us about the dangers of concreteness: "There are times, nevertheless, when concreteness is not the most appropriate response. Some problems are best discussed in more general and abstract terms, and some cultural groups tend to be subtler. Cultural differences of expression in empathy, respect and warmth, and concreteness must always be kept in mind" (p. 161). Young (2001) advises that "early in the relationship, the helper does not try to narrow the field of discussion, but dares the client to go deeper and disclose more" (p. 199).

If you go back and examine the definitions above you will see two sorts. The first has to do with clarifying thoughts, feelings, and behaviors. The second has to do with taking action. This chapter is entitled "Responding with Concreteness *and* Focus." The way to figure out of this seeming clash of definitions is to recognize that concreteness has two rather different definitions in psychotherapy. To distinguish them, I have divided them, rather arbitrarily, into the terms *concreteness* and *focusing*. As I am using the term here, "concreteness" means identifying and clarifying feelings, linkages, confusions, and connections, for example, in the client's narrative. It is based in empathy and the goal, at least early in therapy, is to help the clients explore and elaborate issues, concerns, problems, and dilemmas in their narratives.

Focusing has a different meaning and use. Long (1996), for example, suggests that "just as focusing in photography involves getting a clear image, in the context of a helping relationship it means helping clients see clearly their issues, challenges, direction, and goals" (p. 187). This difference is highlighted in the definitions above in italics. In the model of exploration, understanding, and action, focusing is a way of moving the client toward the action stage. Gazda, Asbury, Balzer, Childers, and Walters (1984) label this concept a "transition dimension." Young (2001) describes the frustration of inexperienced therapists in training as they reach a place in their relationship with clients where the facilitative conditions of empathy, genuineness, and warmth have led them to a doorway. Then, they recognize that they don't know what to do next. "Where do I go from here?" they ask. Young (2001) teaches that "once the relationship is firmly established [then] the helper begins to change the focus of counseling sessions from the introduction of new topics and assessment to the identification of the most crucial issues to be addressed in later sessions" (pp. 198–199). Welch and Gonzalez (1999) describe this action phase of therapy as "a matter of pinning down the action that the client wants to take, defining a plan, and moving toward implementation" (p. 185). This transition leads to the development of another set of skills. "The skills at the goal-setting stage are methods for narrowing down the information into a few specific tasks and goals" (Young, 2001, p. 199).

MULTICULTURAL AND DIVERSITY CONCERNS

Techniques such as directness, confrontation, and concreteness should be used with sensitivity and awareness. Sue, Ivey, and Pedersen (1996) identify one of the multicultural competencies as the awareness of "how their own cultural background/experience, attitudes, values, and biases influence psychological processes" (p. 46). They also write, "Culturally skilled counselors possess knowledge about their social impact upon others. They are knowledgeable about communication style differences, how their style may clash or facilitate the counseling process with minority clients, and how to anticipate the impact it may have on others" (p. 46). One other competence seems appropriate as well. "Culturally skilled counselors are able to engage in a variety of verbal/nonverbal helping responses. . . . When they sense that their helping style is limited and potentially inappropriate, they can anticipate and ameliorate its negative impact" (Sue, Ivey, & Pederson, 1996, pp. 48–49). These multicultural counseling competencies can be used to develop our sensitivity to clients who come from cultures different from our own and to learn from both experience and training how and when to intervene in concrete and specific ways.

CONCRETENESS

In the early sessions of therapy, concreteness takes the form of clarifying and making connections that the client might not see initially. Vanessa is a young African American woman who has come to therapy because of interpersonal struggles in her life. She is a college graduate and one of her sources of interpersonal tension is at work.

> Cl: Well, at work . . . I'm not sure what I'm feeling. I know I'm angry but I don't know why. I'm the only African American and the only woman in the office. I'm just confused.
>
> Th: Angry, and the confusion is . . . I think three different things came to

me. . . . Let me write them out here [therapist moves chair beside the client and writes and continues talking]: "Confused if it's anger you are bringing to work or something being done at work that angers you." Then, "Not sure if it's connected to being a woman." Then, maybe "confusion if the anger comes from feelings of being an African American in a white workplace."

The therapist has done two different and helpful things here. The client's feelings of anger and confusion are general and, while related to work, aren't well defined. First, the therapist has introduced possible sources of the anger as a way of helping the client clarify her feelings and confusion. Second, the therapist has written them so they are clear and can be discussed one at a time. There isn't any implication that one or the other of these is true or more important than another.

Gazda, Asbury, Balzer, Childers, and Walters (1984) note that "when helpers respond with clear, concise, detailed statements regarding [clients'] problems, [clients'] are reinforced in their attempts to clarify their own problems" (p. 146). The use of a concrete intervention in this early session has the effect of helping the client explore her feelings and doesn't narrow the therapy.

Responding concretely can serve several important functions in therapy. The following were adapted from Gazda, Asbury, Balzer, Childers, and Walters (1984):

- It alerts the client that you genuinely are listening to them and can help build the relationship
- It helps focus the therapy in the present
- It keeps the therapist focused on the client's feelings and experiences
- It permits the therapist to understand the client more accurately
- It allows corrections and misunderstandings to be made
- It helps the client clarify and attend to issues and concerns

Table 18.1 provides guidelines for helping clients tell their stories more concretely and clearly. These suggestions can help you help clients who are struggling to tell their stories and provides structure without taking the lead from them.

FOCUSING

Focusing transposes the client from discussing thoughts, feelings, and behaviors to action. Long (1996) defines focusing as "the intentional directing by the helper of attention toward specific aspects of client communication for the purpose of facilitating clarification, insight, and understanding" (p. 217). These "concrete and specific responses help clients become more specific, help them

Table 18.1
Guidelines for Helping Clients Be More Concrete

Sometimes, with a little structure, a client who is struggling to tell his or her story in a coherent and orderly way can be helped with a few simply prompts. Consider these suggestions as you work with clients who ramble or have difficulty with a clear presentation of their life struggles, situations, events, and the people who play a role in their therapy.

1. Use prompts, encouragers, paraphrases, and summaries to help bring out the story: "Tell me the story . . ."
2. Draw out the client with prompts such as, "The first thing that happened was . . ."; "Next? . . . and the result was . . . ?"
3. Help the client to elaborate by asking, "And is there anything else I should know?"
4. Summarize the story with the client to make sure both client and you have it accurately.

Adapted from A. E. Ivey & M. B. Ivey (1999).

move from vagueness to clarity and focus upon reality, upon the practical; thus they are helped to move from feeling to action" (Patterson, 1985, p. 110).

Locke and Latham (1984) view this process of focusing through the lenses of goal setting. Goal setting is one means of empowering clients. Clients are empowered because goals

- focus their attention,
- focus their action,
- energize them,
- increase their effort,
- increase the search for strategies to cope, and
- increase persistence.

As a client's story unfolds, "focusing adds precision to client observation through selective attention to certain aspects of client talk" (Ivey & Ivey, 1999, p. 226). As the client talks, "selective attention" may be given to aspects of the story that strike the therapist as more central than others. As we have seen in the first section of this book, the I/F principle helps therapists identify those parts of clients' stories that are more important. Therefore, the possible focus will be different depending upon the content of the client's narrative. The therapy will go in different directions depending upon the focus brought to the session. A number of different areas of focus can be used in therapy, including:

- The client—focuses on intrapersonal issues or concerns
- The main theme or problem—focuses on issues that are factual or situational
- Others—focuses on interpersonal concerns
- Family—focuses on systems issues
- Mutuality—focuses on the positive aspects of the relationship
- The therapist—focuses on issues of immediacy or other problems in the therapy
- Cultural/environmental/contextual issues—focuses on multicultural issues including racial or sexual oppression, other social justice issues, and such concerns as finances and vocation (Ivey & Ivey, 1999).

Gendlin (1978, 1981) has developed a therapeutic style and system that uses focusing as its central method. "Central to this method is the idea of a 'felt sense.' A felt sense is a physical sensation or a bodily awareness that can help us get to the heart of a problem" (Young, 2001, p. 293). Martin (1983) indicates that Gendlin's method emphasizes "that emotional growth requires both cognitive and experiential involvement" (p. 56). Gendlin's method is presented in Table 18.2 for your consideration.

Whether we use a particular method such as Gendlin's or whether we gravitate toward personally developed methods of helping clients move from discussing thoughts, feelings, and behaviors to developing a plan of action, focusing is a necessary and crucial step in the therapeutic process.

SUMMARY

Concreteness, in which the therapist helps clients clarify thoughts, feelings, and behavior, and focusing, in which the therapist helps the client develop a concrete plan of action, are ways of responding that represent a transition in therapy. The client has spent time exploring and elaborating and finding an understanding to the problem. Focusing on specific aspects of the issue or concern allows the client to come up with plans for addressing the concern.

There is a danger in the techniques of concreteness and focusing that includes multicultural issues and, perhaps, the therapist's tendency to try to move to solutions before any genuine understanding of the issues, problems, or dilemmas is developed by the client or the therapist. In the model of therapy that includes exploration, understanding, and action, the role of concreteness is viewed as an elaboration technique early in therapy in which the therapist's goal is to help the client clarify and explore issues brought into the therapy. In focusing, the therapist's goal is to help the client develop plans and methods of implementation to address well-understood issues, problems, and dilemmas.

The positive outcome of concreteness is that what was vague and confusing

Table 18.2
Gendlin's Focusing Strategy

This method is one that some clients will appreciate and others might find intimidating or unusual. Some care should be given to its use and you might practice on yourself to get a sense of how the method works with you before you use it with clients.

Step 1—Prepare. Sit quietly and relax as you prepare to go through the process.

Step 2—Center (Focus) Your Thoughts and Feelings. Thoughts, feelings, and problems begin to emerge. Simply let them come without analyzing them. Let them "stack up" and practice viewing them in a detached and distant way.

Step 3—Use a "Felt Sense." As you view the problems from a distance, consider which one *feels* the most important. This is a kinesthetic sensation in the body. Do not analyze, but let your body sense the problem. How does your body feel about the problem? This might take some time and concentration, but do not rush; allow yourself to experience your feelings about the problem.

Step 4—Identify the Core (Crux). Focus on the problem and try identify one aspect of it that is central or that feels the worst. Do not search for an answer but wait to see if something emerges. At this stage, do not attach any words to your experience: continue to feel and experience it.

Step 5—Label. This is the stage at which you will label the problem. Keep your focus on the core feeling and allow words (or images) to emerge.

Step 6—Focus. Young (2001) describes this step: "Place the words you have come up with next to your feelings or bodily sensations about the problem. Do they match? Make sure they fit precisely. If they are correct, you will have a physical experience of completeness or a confirming sensation" (p. 294). After focusing you might record your experience in a journal for future reference.

Adapted form Gendlin (1978, 1981).

can become clear and understood. The positive outcome of focusing is that a client is empowered and learns to cope effectively with what previously was considered unmanageable and threatening.

REFERENCES

Egan, G. (1998). *The skilled helper: A problem-management approach to helping* (6th ed.). Pacific Grove, CA: Brooks/Cole.

Gazda, G. M., Asbury, F. S., Balzer, F. J., Childers, W. C., & Walters, R. P. (1984). *Human relations development: A manual for educators* (3rd ed.). Boston, MA: Allyn and Bacon.

Gendlin, E. T. (1978, 1981). *Focusing*. New York: Bantam Books.

Hill, H. (1972, fall). Miss Wunderlich. *Colorado Journal of Educational Research, 12*, 33.

Ivey, A. E., & Ivey, M. B. (1999). *Intentional interviewing and counseling: Facilitating client development in a multicultural society* (4th ed.). Pacific Grove, CA: Brooks/Cole.

Locke, E. A., & Latham, G. P. (1984). *Goal setting: A motivational technique that works.* Englewood Cliffs, NJ: Prentice-Hall.

Long, V. O. (1996). *Communication skills in helping relationships: A framework for facilitating personal growth.* Pacific Grove, CA: Brooks/Cole.

Martin, D. G. (1983). *Counseling and therapy skills.* Prospect Heights, IL: Waveland Press.

Miars, R. D., & Halverson, S. E. (2001). The helping relationship. In D. Capuzzi & D. R. Gross (Eds.), *Introduction to the counseling profession* (3rd ed., pp. 50–68). Boston, MA: Allyn and Bacon.

Okun, B. F. (2002). *Effective helping: Interviewing and counseling techniques* (6th ed.). Pacific Grove, CA: Brooks/Cole.

Patterson, C. H. (1985). *The therapeutic relationship: Foundations for an eclectic psychotherapy.* Pacific Grove, CA: Brooks/Cole.

Sue, D. W., Ivey, A. E., & Pedersen, P. B. (1996). *A theory of multicultural counseling and therapy.* Pacific Grove, CA: Brooks/Cole.

Welch, I. D., & Gonzalez, D. M. (1999). *The process of counseling and psychotherapy: Matters of skill.* Pacific Grove, CA: Brooks/Cole.

Young, M. E. (2001). *Learning the art of helping: Building blocks and techniques* (2nd ed.). Upper Saddle River, NJ: Merrill/Prentice-Hall.

Chapter 19

Responding with Confrontation

Confrontation is laden with risks and is potentially harmful for clients. This is especially true if you understand confrontation to mean the "clashing of forces or ideas" (*Webster's Ninth New Collegiate Dictionary*, 1983). "Most people seem to use confrontation to mean that the therapist is pointing out discrepancies in the client's thinking and presenting alternative views that the client hasn't seen or can't see for himself or herself" (Martin, 1983, p. 52). The "usual meaning carries an aggressive, shake-'em-up-good connotation that implies that the therapist is the expert who has to guide the client toward truth" (Martin, 1983, p. 59).

PROBLEMS WITH DIRECT CONFRONTATION

The 1960s were a time of demythologizing and stripping psychotherapy of its authoritarianism. It was a time of striving to make psychotherapy, and even daily life itself, a more honest and straight-ahead endeavor. One of the outcomes of that notion of honest psychotherapy was an increasingly confrontational style in which the therapeutic thing to do was to tell the truth—sometimes no matter how brutal or even painful. The outcome was, as Carkhuff and Anthony (1979) put it, that "far too many helpers have made frequent and often harmful use of confrontation" (p. 116).

Carkhuff and Anthony (1979) take a strong position on the use of confrontation. They state flatly that "confrontation is neither a necessary nor a sufficient condition of helping!" (p. 116).

Take note that the references above are not recent. They give us a flavor of the shift from a time when the very nature of therapy was being redefined and some of the excesses were being reexamined. Confrontation was one of those excesses. Some argued that counselors and psychotherapists had misunderstood and that confrontation was "not a personal confrontation of the client by the therapist" (Patterson, 1985, p. 76). Carkhuff (1979) argued that "no helper confronts a [client] when there is an alternative approach that promises [client] gains" (p. 119). So why is there a chapter on confrontation here? It is a legitimate question. It is here because clients come to counseling and psychotherapy with confusions, gaps, distortions, and discrepancies in the descriptions they give of themselves, others, and the events of their lives.

CLIENT RESPONSES TO CONFRONTATION

Confusions, gaps, distortions, and discrepancies—these words constitute a fair description of psychological defenses. A substantial amount of work in therapy has to do with clients looking freshly at their experiences and wrestling with old patterns of behavior that have not served them well. Some of that work, of course, means engaging their defenses in order to look at aspects of their behavior and lives that have been neglected. Clients ward off information that would dispute presently held beliefs and behaviors, whether they come from others or themselves, in many different ways.

It isn't unusual for us as humans to slip and slide, dodge and weave, when we face uncomfortable aspects of ourselves. Because anxiety is uncomfortable and because we mostly want to avoid it, patterns of avoidance, or psychological defenses, are common. These include the following, which are adapted from Egan (1998):

1. Counterattack. The client meets the perceived threat by attacking back, and "some attempt is made to point out that [the other person] is no better than anyone else" and has no right to bring up the uncomfortable topic (Egan, 1998, p. 165).
2. Persuasion. The client might argue that they have been misunderstood and try to persuade the other person to change his or her point of view.
3. Rationalization. The client might try to convince her- or himself that the issue isn't that important or significant or worthy of spending much time over. "Bitter grapes" and "sweet lemons" are forms of rationalization in which one argues that a positive effort isn't really good or that a negative behavior might, after all, have positive features to it.
4. Co-option. The clients might seek support for his or her behavior or beliefs from others and attempt to convince the therapist that he or she is wrong. The client might move from therapist to therapist until he or she finds one who agrees (colludes) with him or her.
5. Cooperation (false). The client might appear to be involved in self-challenge within sessions, but make no honest effort to use what he or she develops in therapy in daily life.

NEW UNDERSTANDINGS

In the face of these defenses, it is no surprise that counselors and psychotherapists can become frustrated and impatient. They want to make progress and break through the defenses to more productive work in the therapy. Yet at least a part of our training is in understanding that emotional issues are not often open to direct investigation. Ivey and Ivey (1999) argue that "confrontation is not a direct, harsh challenge" (p. 196). In fact, as counselor educators and other mental health trainers struggle with this issue of dealing with defenses and client confusion, distortion, and discrepancies, they have wiggled uncomfortably with the use of the word "confrontation." Patterson (1985) suggests that a better meaning of confrontation is "to set side by side for comparison, or to place before" (p. 76). He argued that "confrontation can be viewed as the attempt to bring to awareness the presence of cognitive dissonance or incongruence in the client's feelings, attitudes, beliefs, perceptions, or behaviors" (p. 76). Sommers-Flanagan and Sommers-Flanagan (1993) maintain than the goal is "to help clients perceive and deal with reality more effectively" (p. 93). In an effort to teach beginning therapists how to better deal with and manage client confusions, distortions, and discrepancies, counselor, psychologist, and social work trainers have struggled with what to call the process. Egan (1982) insists that some behaviors and beliefs need to be challenged and states that this needs to be done with accurate empathy. Ivey and Ivey (1999) invite us to "think of confrontation as a supportive challenge" (p. 196). Martin (1983) argues that when a counselor or psychotherapist feels the need to confront, the problem lies in the therapist and not in the client. He argues for a response that strives for "evocatively empathic" therapy in which the therapist pushes him- or herself even harder to understand the client's point of view. Long (1996) agrees with this assessment to some degree and states that confrontation "is a form of empathic focusing and a specific type of implicit empathy" (p. 221). Brammer (1988) recognizes that the emotional effects of confrontation can be "challenge, exposure, or threat" (p. 80). Brammer (1988) names his approach "constructive confrontation" (p. 80). Lauver and Harvey (1997) are so uncomfortable with the term "confrontation" that they have labeled it "collegial confrontation" to reflect their concerns that "confrontation" implies judgmentalness and superiority of the helper. This collegial approach has three characteristics:

1. It is a genuine expression of listener confusion
2. It reiterates the facts
3. It is the counselor's understanding of the information that is being clarified. (Lauver & Harvey, 1997, p. 87)

Each of these authors is striving to blend three realities. First, clients do have defenses and these can confuse, distort, and create discrepancies in their narratives. Second, defenses seem to be well prepared to deal with direct treatment and little is gained by this approach. Third, calling attention to distortions or discrepancies is not meant to attack the person and, despite frustrations and annoyance, there is no therapeutic gain in doing so.

MULTICULTURAL AND DIVERSITY CONCERNS

Any approach that brings up various forms of discrepancies to clients is fraught with peril. "All confrontation runs the risk of threatening the client" (Patterson, 1985, p. 77). This urge to sensitivity is emphasized by Welch and Gonzalez (1999):

> One helpful rule for all psychotherapists, whether new or old, is to be tough on defenses and tender with persons. . . . [I]t is important to remember that people in therapy are vulnerable and that a confrontation of a client's "personness" stands little chance of successfully elaborating a situation, provide understanding, or moving the client toward action. On the other hand, defenses should be encountered with strength and resolve. Observers must gauge not only timing and strength but whether the counselor is trying in some way to sway the client, especially if a value is being confronted. (Pp. 199–200)

It is in the matter of value that diversity and multicultural concerns can be most sensitive. A therapist's awareness of the client's worldview is an important consideration in multicultural competency. "Culturally skilled counselors are aware of their negative emotional reactions toward other racial/ethnic groups that may prove detrimental to their clients in counseling. They are willing to contrast their own beliefs and attitudes with those of their culturally different clients in a nonjudgmental fashion" (Sue, Ivey, & Pedersen, 1996, p. 47). It is important to recognize that "some people are truly victimized by the systems of society. They can be helped by people willing to fight for the rights of others and by structural changes in society" (Egan, 1998, p. 159). It is becoming increasingly recognized that advocacy is an important role for counselors and psychotherapists, especially by feminist therapists, the multicultural movement, and others who are willing to bring social justice issues into counseling and psychotherapy. The victims of hatred, violence, and exploitation can be aided by therapists who are "willing to fight for the rights of others." Sue, Ivey, and Pedersen (1996) list another competence that directly addresses this new attitude of advocacy: "Culturally skilled counselors are able to exercise institutional intervention skills on behalf of their clients. They can help clients determine whether a 'problem' stems from racism or bias in others (the concept of healthy paranoia) so that clients do not inappropriately personalize problems" (p. 49).

The goals of multicultural competences include gaining a better recognition of the differences between cultures, respect for these differences, and better recognition from all counselors and psychotherapists of the fact that the urge to confront might be rooted in a cultural assumption of what is "right" and proper. In fact, Messer and Winokur (1980) suggest that confrontation could "reflect a North American cultural bias" (p. 818). Ivey and Ivey (1999) point out that "confrontation needs to be used with great sensitivity to individual and cultural differences. Within the United States and Canada, we have a variety of cultures and people who may object to strong confrontations. . . . [D]irect, blunt confrontations are likely to be especially culturally inappropriate for Asian, Latina/Latino, and Native American clients" (p. 201). It seems especially important when considering bringing a discrepancy or confusion into the therapy that sensitivity to multicultural concerns be considered among the primary reasons for caution and tentativeness.

THE SKILLS OF CONFRONTATION

Given these cautions, it still remains true that clients come to therapy with issues and concerns that are ladened with defenses—denial, distortion, discrepancies—that need to be dealt with in ways that are effective, productive, and growth oriented. Discrepancies, incongruities, and double messages are common in therapy. Please see Table 19.1 for a list of thoughts, feelings, and behaviors that can call for confrontation. These skills are both attitudinal and behavioral. One of the first understandings is that confrontation is not a facilitative skill to be used early in the therapeutic relationship. Any challenge or confrontation, whether based in empathy or not, must be built on a foundation of trust. A guiding principle is that that the earlier in the therapy, the more tentative one should be in using confrontation. It takes time to establish a relationship of trust, a bond and a connection with clients.

Egan (1998) proposes several attitudes and behaviors necessary before one begins to challenge clients. First, understand the "games" and defenses clients might use to deflect dealing with incongruities and discrepancies in their therapy. This understanding needs to come without one becoming calloused or cynical about working with people's defenses. Second, become comfortable with the idea that you are an influence in the lives of clients. Confrontation needs to be built on both an understanding of one's power and a heartfelt sincerity to hold that power in check for the positive benefit of clients. It is the delicate relationship between calling an incongruity to a client's attention without insinuating any corrective action. Third, recognize that confrontation is a normal part of the counseling process and incorporate it seamlessly into one's counseling style. Resist the urge to become a "confrontational specialist." Fourth, work on one's assertiveness skills in order to overcome the tendency not to bring up bad news (the MUM effect—"the tendency to withhold bad news even when it is in the [client's] best interest to hear it") (Egan, 1998, p. 166). Fifth, challenge yourself to overcome excuses not to bring up discrepancies and incongruities in the client's narrative. The sixth, and final, recommendation is, perhaps, the most

Table 19.1
What Should Be Confronted?

This is a selected listing of what others have seen in counseling interviews that they believe should be confronted. "*Incongruities*, *discrepancies*, and *double messages* are nearly universal in counseling interviews. They are often at the root of a client's immobility and inability to respond creatively to difficult life situations" (Egan, 1998, p. 56).

"distorted views of others, the world, and themselves" (Sommers-Flanagan & Sommers-Flanagan, 1993, p. 93).

"The discrepancy or contradiction is usually one of the following types:
1. A discrepancy between what clients say and how they behave
2. A contradiction between how clients say they feel and how their behaviors suggest they are feeling.
3. A discrepancy between two verbal messages of the client" (Hackney & Cormier, 1994, p. 118).

There are three general areas of human behavior that often need to be challenged—dysfunctional mind-sets and perspectives, self-limiting internal actions, and problematic external actions. These are *blind spots*—that is, self-limiting ways of thinking and acting that clients fail to see or don't want to see (Egan, 1998 p. 150).

"A counselor-perceived *discrepancy* in client behavior is the cue for counselor confrontation" (Lauver & Harvey, 1997, p. 86).

"Invite clients to challenge themselves to change ways of thinking and acting that keep them mired in problems situations and prevent them from identifying and developing opportunities. If they do not accept the invitation, then challenge them directly to change" (Egan, 1998, p. 147).

"(1) discrepancy between the clients' expressions of what they are and what they want to be (real self, self-concept versus ideal self); (2) discrepancy between clients' verbal expressions about themselves (awareness or insight) and their behavior as it is either observed by the therapist or reported by the clients; and (3) discrepancy between clients' expressed experience of themselves and the therapist's experience of them. A fourth category might be added to cover discrepancy between clients' experiences of themselves and others as reported at different times, either in the same session or in different sessions" (Patterson, 1985, p. 76).
Ellis argues that one of the most important interventions a therapist can make is to challenge clients' irrational beliefs. Some of these irrational beliefs are:

> I must always be loved and approved by the significant people in my life.
>
> I must always, in all situations, demonstrate competence, and I must be both talented and competent in some important area of life.
>
> I must have my way, and my plans must always work out.
>
> People who do anything wrong, especially those who harm me, are evil and should be blamed and punished.

Table 19.1 (continued)

If anything or any situation is dangerous in any way, I must be anxious and upset about it.

Things should not go wrong in life, and if by chance they do, there should be quick and easy solutions.

Other people and outside forces are responsible for any misery I experience. No one should ever take advantage of me.

It is easier to avoid facing life's difficulties than to develop self-discipline; making demands of myself should not be necessary.

What I did in the past, and especially what happened to me in the past, determines how I act and feel today.

I can be happy by avoiding, by being passive, by being uncommitted, and by just enjoying myself (Ellis, 1987a; Ellis, 1987b; Ellis, 1991).

Confrontation invites clients to look at discrepancies in their thinking, feelings, or behaviors, and reassess their perspective. As a result, confrontation helps them gain greater clarification of underlying issues.

"In verbal and nonverbal behavior, these might include discrepancies

1. between two statements . . .
2. between two behaviors . . .
3. between a statement and a behavior . . ." (Long, 1996, p. 222).

"Discrepancies in thoughts, feelings, and behaviors might occur

1. between stated thoughts and feelings . . .
2. between stated thoughts and behavior . . .
3. between stated feelings and behavior . . ." (Long, 1996, p. 222).

"Discrepancies in perceived reality and actual reality might include

1. discrepancies in observed reality,
2. polarized thinking, and
3. failure to acknowledge choices." (Long, 1996 p. 223).

difficult: Take on a continuing task of being an effective therapist by coming to terms with your own shortcomings, imperfections, and "blind spots," both as a therapist and as a person. Sometimes this means being involved in therapy yourself; sometimes it means to become a "supervisor of the self" and provide an ongoing critique of your performance in sessions. Welch (1998) proposes that one of the positive outcomes of psychotherapy is that clients become "therapists of the self" and that they can begin to do for themselves what they have learned from the therapeutic relationship. It seems equally possible that a therapist can become a supervisor for the self and put into practice the skills and knowledge gained in the supervisory relationship.

Guidelines for Effective Confrontation

Effective counseling and psychotherapy is rooted in the therapist's empathic capacity and communication. The skills of confrontation are no different and if not rooted in empathy are deeply suspect. Like many skills of therapy, these guidelines begin with the therapist:

1. The recognition and acceptance of and the willingness to act on feelings in the self are prerequisites for confrontation (Brammer, 1988; Lauver & Harvey, 1997). There was a time some years ago when the prominent model of training was based in a denial of or "suspension" of the self. The therapist was trained to be aloof from and indifferent to his or her own feelings. In more modern times, that model has given way to the "self as instrument" approach in which therapists are trained to use their feelings, attitudes, beliefs, and values as guides for understanding and entering the relationship with clients. This has manifested itself in such facilitative practices as self-disclosure and, to some extent, has brought about newer understandings of confrontation. Using the recognition of feelings in the self as a guide, therapists can relate their confrontation not in terms of some client failure but within the therapist's feelings of confusion or lack of understanding.
2. The foundation of confrontation lies in a solid therapeutic relationship (Egan, 1998; Sommers-Flanagan & Sommers-Flanagan, 1993; Welch & Gonzalez, 1999). Confronting clients, as mentioned above, must be rooted in empathy. Empathy is a process that grows in the relationship. In one respect, the right to confront a client is earned in the building of a solid therapeutic relationship. Egan (1998) proposes four processes in earning the right to confront. First, build a working, therapeutic relationship. Second, base the confrontation in empathy, in understanding the client. Third, stay open to being challenged by the client so that you do not respond defensively and are open to owning that you have made a mistake or misunderstood in some crucial way. Fourth, remember that your own life is in process and that you are continuing to refine your skills as a therapist and to develop as a human being.
3. Confrontation is integrated into the helping process (Egan, 1998). Confrontation is not something that is special to the helping process. It is one skill among many that can be integrated into the therapy. In this sense, confrontation is no different than responding with any other statement in therapy. Just as with any intervention, there are cautions and concerns that must be met. Part of the therapist's task, as discussed above, is to become comfortable with the idea of influence, of challenge, and of being a force in the client's life. It is important to know that the confrontation is not based in a moralistic judgment or some implied need for the client to

change. It is stated so that apparent incongruities can be examined and evaluated by the client.

4. Effective confrontation is tentative without being apologetic (Egan, 1998; Welch & Gonzalez, 1999). Confrontation is tentative because it is seated in a lack of clear understanding by the therapist. What appears to be inconsistent or discrepant might well be integrated by the client in ways that the therapist initially doesn't see. In this sense, the confrontation needs to be phrased tentatively so that it invites the client to examine what appears incongruent to the therapist. While all confrontations have the potential of being threatening, tentativeness eases this threat to a degree.
5. Confrontation describes client thoughts, feelings, or behaviors (Brammer, 1988; Egan, 1998; Hackney & Cormier, 1994; Lauver & Harvey, 1997; Sommers-Flanagan & Sommers-Flanagan, 1993). Effective confrontation is not harsh. It isn't condemning. It isn't even prescriptive. It is descriptive. An effective confrontation describes what is confusing or not understood by the therapist in nonjudgmental, noncorrective, and nonprescriptive terms. It does not contain an accusation, an evaluation, or a solution. Most important, the focus is on the thought, feeling, or behavior and not on the person. This is a time in therapy to present evidence or the facts as they are understood in sufficient degree to demonstrate what is confusing or discrepant. The purpose is to invite the client to examine, side by side, two apparent incongruities in thoughts, feelings, or behavior.
6. The confrontation is mediated in some way (Brammer, 1988; Egan, 1998; Ivey & Ivey, 1999; Lauver & Harvey, 1997). "Simply labeling the incongruity through a nonjudgmental confrontation may be enough to resolve a situation" (Ivey & Ivey, 1999, p. 199). Egan (1998) recommends that the focus here be on the client's strengths rather than weaknesses. He recommends four strategies. First, build on the client's past successes. Second, make sure that your confrontation is coming from a solid understanding of the client. Third, make certain you are respectful of the client's values and cultural traditions. Fourth, deal empathically with the client's *defenses*. Lauver and Harvey (1997) suggest another part of the process in what they call "valuing." This involves the client determining for him- or herself the value of the poles of the discrepancies to see if, in fact, one is more important than the other. An examination of value can have the effect of ranking thoughts and beliefs and removing any apparent contradiction.
7. The purpose of confrontation is to encourage self-challenge (Egan, 1998; Welch, 1998). Clients have lives outside of therapy, and at least one goal of the therapist is to end therapy with the client. It is not necessarily a goal of counseling and psychotherapy that the client leave therapy problem free. What is a more likely goal is that the client leave more prepared to cope with the issues and concerns in his or her life. In this sense, a part

of confrontation is the goal of teaching the client to confront her- or himself. If clients learn to confront their own recognized incongruities, then they are significantly more prepared to cope more effectively and efficiently in their lives.

Regulating the Intensity of the Confrontation

Gazda, Asbury, Balzer, Childers, and Walters (1984) provide a systematic discussion of how to regulate the intensity of a confrontation and the outcomes of too weak or too strong an intervention. The following description of the effect of confrontation and recommended strategies is based upon Gazda's and his colleagues' work.

Mild Confrontation. In the early sessions of therapy, confrontation should be mild if one decides to confront discrepancies at all. These approaches will lessen the intensity of a confrontation:

1. Before any confrontation, build the therapeutic relationship. Ensure that the relationship is working on a foundation of trust.
2. Generalize the confrontation. Rather than specifically discussing the client's discrepancy, talk about people in general and how the discrepancy you see might affect people in general.
3. Use vague and imprecise language. Use language such as "sometimes," "maybe," "perhaps," or "it may be that. . . ." This is not accusatory language.

Undesirable Outcomes from Weak Intervention.

1. Clients can lose respect for you as the therapist. They may believe you lack courage.
2. The intervention can have no effect. The client may miss the intent of your intervention or it may "bounce off" without effect.
3. A feeble intervention can have the effect of strengthening the behavior.

Stronger Confrontation.

1. Personalize the confrontation. Speak specifically about the client and his or her behavior.
2. Use evidence in the confrontation. Be concrete and specific so that, as much as possible, you are describing facts rather than your opinion.
3. Deal with events immediately rather than waiting until a later session. Pointing out the discrepancy or conflict immediately makes the events less likely to be denied or avoided.
4. Deal with actions over words whenever possible. Actions have a tangible

immediate quality that words lack. It is easier to defend and deny words than a behavior.

Undesirable Outcomes of a Strong Intervention.

1. The intervention is so threatening that it provokes defensiveness.
2. The client abandons the therapy.
3. The intervention provokes anger and the client counterattacks.
4. The intervention results in dishonesty. The client may pretend to accept the confrontation but makes no changes.
5. The intervention may create dependency. The client is defeated and feels helpless and seeks comfort from the stronger therapist.

The therapist has to make a judgment about whether to confront and how intense that confrontation will be based upon a number of factors. These includes how strong the relationship is, gender and cultural concerns, the nature of the client, and the relevance of the discrepancy or distortion. The guidelines above provide a rough map of how to proceed once you have made a decision to use confrontation in therapy.

Judging the Effectiveness of a Confrontation

Ivey and Ivey (1999) have developed a Confrontation Impact Scale (CIS) to measure the effectiveness of therapists' challenges of clients' discrepancies. They suggest that

> you will find that your clients talk and think about change in various ways. Identifying where they are in the change process can help you identify the effectiveness of your interventions and help you plan with the client for further exploration. . . . anytime a client is working through change, you will find clients talking about their issues with varying levels of awareness. Using this scale while in the interview can be helpful in following client movement both during a single session and over a series of interviews. (Pp. 208–209)

The Liekert-like scale has five points along the continuum.

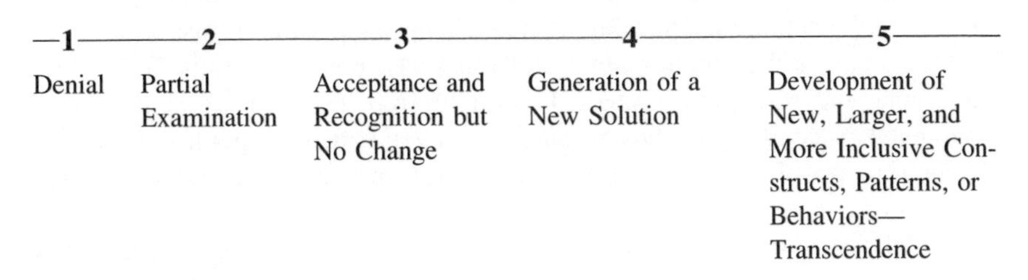

Table 19.2
The Effective Confrontation Checklist

Confrontation should reflect the goal of a therapeutic helping relationship. Does your confrontation meet the principles below?

The Three Rs—Reflecting Attitudes of:

_____ Rights—Do you honor your client's right to be where they are, including having defenses, and choice as to when they are ready to move?

_____ Respect—Do you present the confrontation in such a way that it is *not* judgmental or patronizing?

_____ Responsibility—Do you allow the client the ultimate responsibility for choice and rate of change?

Facilitative Dimensions

_____ Genuineness—Are you genuine and honest?

_____ Positive Regard—Do you verbally and nonverbally communicate acceptance of your client?

_____ Empathic Focusing—Do you focus on the client's perspective rather than your own, sincerely trying to understand the client's point of view?

Communication Style

_____ Tentative Communication—Do you communicate to the client that you are putting the discrepancy in front of them to consider and assess, not telling them how to act, think, or feel? Do you avoid giving advice?

Adapted from Long (1996).

Ivey and Ivey (1999) report that Martin Heesacker and Shawn Prichard of the University of Florida have developed a paper-and-pencil form of this scale. Factor analysis revealed that the points along the continuum do exist as separate factors.

Long (1996) has developed a checklist for effective confrontation. Please see Table 19.2 for an adaptation of the checklist. Long (1996) believes that "confrontation is empathic focusing on discrepancies to help the client gain self-understanding through clarifying underlying issues. Confrontation should reflect the goal of the helping relationship: to help clients understand themselves better" (p. 223). Long further suggests that ineffective confrontation results from three identifiable and correctable factors. First, a confrontation can fail because it is judgmental. Second, it can fail because the therapist doesn't point out the discrepancy to the client. Third, it can fail because the therapist provides a prescription or conclusion for the client.

Whether you use a formal scale or a checklist to evaluate the effectiveness of your interventions, it is important to "measure" the impact and effectiveness of the confrontation just as it is with any intervention in therapy. Whether you ask a question, make a statement, or use confrontation, it is important to continue to understand the client's feelings, thoughts, meanings, and attributions. In chapter 20, the use of questions in therapy is discussed. This is a point in therapy where a question can be used to good effect. You as the therapist can ask the client to evaluate the impact of the intervention for him- or herself. You might ask, "What did you get from that activity?" or "What did you learn from that?" Either of these open-ended questions can provide you with a measure of the impact and effectiveness of the confrontation. Then you can make an adjustment or follow up with other responding skills to advance the therapy.

SUMMARY

Over the years, I have come to have less and less confidence in direct and strong confrontation. One of my dilemmas stems from a philosophical problem of separating nonjudgmentalness from any strong confrontation. It seems to me that when one person strongly confronts another, there is likely a conflict of values. This has become more apparent to me as I have considered the multicultural competences that have received more and more attention in the last few years. Nevertheless, clients come to counseling and psychotherapy with confusions, gaps, distortions, and discrepancies in the descriptions they give of themselves, others, and the events of their lives. As we struggle with the ever-present pushes and pulls of a critical and quickly judging culture, it demands both training and discipline to confront clients empathically and nonjudgmentally.

There are inherent problems with the concept of confrontation if one takes it to mean "a clash of values and ideas." In such an understanding, the demands of nonjudgmentalness seem nearly impossible to achieve. A number of authors have struggled to redefine the tasks of confrontation in more empathic, collegial, and constructive understandings.

The guidelines for effective use of confrontation in therapy include the recommendation that confrontation not be used if another responding skill can provide a therapeutic outcome. Further, it is recommended that confrontation is not a skill to be used early in the therapy. An effective confrontation demands that a firm, solid therapeutic relationship be formed prior to any confrontation. This is especially true if the therapist intends to confront a client strongly. Increasingly, the focus of confrontational skills has focused on the therapist's lack of understanding of the client's point of view, and the intervention has focused more and more on exploration and clarification.

Clients respond to ineffective confrontation, whether too weak or too strong, with defensive behaviors that range from counterattacks to trying to persuade or co-opt the therapist and false cooperation. The effectiveness of any therapeutic intervention is always a matter of concern, and methods of evaluating the impact and effectiveness of confrontation include Liekert-like scales, paper-and-pencil instruments, and checklists.

While direct confrontation must be considered seriously before its use, in general, counselors and psychotherapists must find ways of coping with client discrepancies, distortions, incongruities, and inconsistencies. Guidelines for using confrontation effectively are provided in this chapter as an integrated aspect of therapy in the same way any responding skill would be used in therapy.

REFERENCES

Brammer, L. M. (1988). *The helping relationship: Process and skills* (4th ed.). Englewood Cliffs, NJ: Prentice-Hall.

Carkhuff, R. R., & Anthony, W. A. (1979). *The skills of helping*. Amherst, MA: Human Resource Development Press.

Egan, G. (1982). *The skilled helper: Model, skills, and methods for effective helping* (2nd ed.). Monterey, CA: Brooks/Cole.

Egan, G. (1998). *The skilled helper: A problem-management approach to helping* (6th ed.). Pacific Grove, CA: Brooks/Cole.

Ellis, A. (1987a). The evolution of rational-emotive therapy (RET) and cognitive behavior therapy (CBT). In J. K. Zeig (Ed.), *The evolution of psychotherapy*, pp. 69–78. New York: Brunner/Routledge.

Ellis, A. (1987b). Integrative developments in rational-emotive therapy (RET). *Journal of Integrative and Eclectic Psychotherapy, 6*, 470–479.

Ellis, A. (1991). The revised ABCs of rational-emotive therapy (RET). *Journal of Rational-Emotive and Cognitive-Behavior Therapy, 9*, 139–192.

Gazda, G. M., Asbury, F. S., Balzer, F. J., Childers, W. C., & Walters, R. P. (1984). *Human relations development: A manual for educators* (3rd ed.). Boston, MA: Allyn and Bacon.

Hackney, H., & Cormier, S. (1994). *Counseling strategies and interventions* (4th ed.). Boston, MA: Allyn and Bacon.

Ivey, A. E., & Ivey, M. B. (1999). *Intentional interviewing and counseling: Facilitating client development in a multicultural society* (4th ed.). Pacific Grove, CA: Brooks/Cole.

King, A. (2001). *Demystifying the counseling process: A self-help handbook for counselors*. Boston, MA: Allyn and Bacon.

Kottler, J. A., & Brown, R. W. (1985). *Introduction to therapeutic counseling*. Pacific Grove, CA: Brooks/Cole.

Lauver, P., & Harvey, D. R. (1997). *The practical counselor: Elements of effective helping*. Pacific Grove, CA: Brooks/Cole.

Long, V. O. (1996). *Communication skills in helping relationships: A framework for facilitating personal growth*. Pacific Grove, CA: Brooks/Cole.

Martin, D. G. (1983). *Counseling and therapy skills*. Prospect Heights, IL: Waveland Press.

Messer, S. B., & Winokur, M. (1980). Some limits to the integration of psychoanalytic and behavior therapy. *American Psychologist, 30*, 818–827.

Okun, B. F. (2002). *Effective helping: Interviewing and counseling techniques* (6th ed.). Pacific Grove, CA: Brooks/Cole.

Patterson, C. H. (1985). *The therapeutic relationship: Foundations for an eclectic psychotherapy*. Pacific Grove, CA: Brooks/Cole.

Sommers-Flanagan, J., & Sommers-Flanagan, R. (1993). *Foundations of therapeutic interviewing*. Boston, MA: Allyn and Bacon.

Sue, D. W., Ivey, A. E., & Pedersen, P. B. (1996). *A theory of multicultural counseling and therapy*. Pacific Grove, CA: Brooks/Cole.

Webster's ninth new collegiate dictionary. (1983). Springfield, MA: Merriam-Webster.

Welch, I. D. (1998). *The path of psychotherapy: Matters of the heart*. Pacific Grove, CA: Brooks/Cole.

Welch, I. D., & Gonzalez, D. M. (1999). *The process of counseling and psychotherapy: Matters of skill*. Pacific Grove, CA: Brooks/Cole.

Chapter 20

Responding with Questions

"Clients are often searching for meanings in their lives that they can live with, but through experience seasoned psychotherapists have learned that the underlying causes of life, the motivations that push or pull us, are not open to direct investigation" (Welch & Gonzalez, 1999, p. 201). Herein lies the principal difficulty with asking questions in psychotherapy. While it is certainly true that "questions can encourage or discourage client talk" (Ivey & Ivey, 1999, p. 55), the use of questions as an effective way of responding to clients is limited.

CONTROVERSY

The use of questions constitutes something of a mild controversy in counseling and psychotherapy. Patterson (1985) is blunt: "Never ask a question—except when you don't understand what a client is saying" (p. 106). "We suggest that beginning interviewers completely eliminate the questions from their repertoire," say Sommers-Flanagan and Sommers-Flanagan (1993, p. 92). King (2001), on the other hand, is convinced "that the counselor who has learned to ask questions effectively is the counselor who will be the most facilitative" (p. 41). Along this continuum of controversy lies an approach to responding that is optimally therapeutic.

THE *WHY* QUESTION

What is not controversial is the rejection of *why* questions. "Why?" you might ask. Good question.

> "Why" questions are especially troublesome because they may put clients on the defensive or leave them feeling they must provide a logical explanation for their behavior. (Miars & Halverson, 2001, p. 59)

> Why questions are especially accusatory and are difficult to answer candidly. (Brammer, 1988, p. 75)

> Why questions are usually avoided because clients rarely know the answer. (Hackney & Cormier, 1994, p. 84)

This sampling gives you the flavor of why *why* questions aren't effective in counseling and psychotherapy. Think of those times when someone has demanded of you, "Why did you do that?" I suspect that you have felt defensive, challenged, and even attacked. It is difficult indeed to escape the judgmental and accusatory implications of asking why someone did something.

It is worthwhile to consider that asking why is also disrespectful for clients. Put plainly, if clients knew why they were acting as they are, then they wouldn't be in therapy. People aren't stupid. If we know our motivations, then we can act effectively to cope. It is when we are confusing, distorting, and denying that we are ineffective and inefficient in our behavior. It is a psychological principle that clear purposes lead to decisive behavior. Vague and undifferentiated purposes lead to ineffective and inappropriate behavior. Counselors and psychotherapists are the professionals in our society who are expected to know psychological principles of behavior. This leads us to a *why* question. Why would psychotherapists ask *why* questions? The answer isn't pretty. It may well be that counselors and psychotherapists who routinely and typically ask such probing questions are acting more out of their own needs—or, more graciously, out of a lack of training—than any concern for client welfare. Hackney and Cormier (1994) don't give much quarter here. They suggest three reasons: First, curiosity that might border on voyeurism; second, a form of narcissism in which the therapist wants to look good and appear expert; third, an approach that presses painful questions, which might approach sadism. There is a straightforward and effective way to manage *why* questions in counseling and psychotherapy: Don't ask them.

THE PROBLEM OF QUESTIONING

We are a nation of "askers." We question strangers in brief encounters. "Where are you from?" "What do you do?" "Have any kids?" If a friend asks for help, a North American will question and then give advice. These social habits intrude into the counseling relationship, especially for inexperienced therapists who ask more questions than experienced ones.

Martin (1983) labels this "Perry Mason" counseling in which "the therapist sets out looking for the evidence, asking lots of questions" (pp. 80–81). The problem is it is "very difficult to ask questions that clearly place the focus on [the] client" (Hackney & Cormier, 1994, p. 83).

In responding to clients, statements have a significantly greater probability of building a therapeutic relationship, obtaining important information, and empowering the client. Okun (2002) states clearly that "at the beginning of any interview or session, you can better draw out the helpee and get more information by making responsive listening statements than by asking questions" (p. 94). While, as we will see later, there are uses for questioning, they are limited and specific.

Disadvantages of Asking Questions

There are a number of problems with the inappropriate use of questions. There are disadvantages for both the therapist and for the client.

Disadvantages for the Therapist. First is the problem of control. A therapist who asks many questions seizes control of both the content and direction of therapy sessions. The client is prevented from telling his or her story and instead is forced to respond to the therapist's questions. While the questions may be of some importance to the therapist, they may be of little interest to the client and may actively interfere with the client's needs. The therapist's questions set the direction of the therapy. The clients may or may not follow the lead set by the therapist's questions, but the danger of this approach is that the client's need may never be addressed. Clients may drop out or, since they are vulnerable, continue to answer the therapist's questions because they believe the therapist is an expert and that they should be doing what the therapist asks them to do.

Second is the problem of power. Clients are vulnerable and, to some extent, are people who have exhausted their personal store of options. They are people who, to some degree, have lost their personal sense of decisiveness. In a word, they have lost their sense of power. "A questioning counselor can appear to have all the power in the relationship" (Miars & Halverson, 2001, p. 59). One of the unstated, but widely accepted, goals of therapy is defeated when the therapist, intentionally or not, seizes power in the therapeutic relationship. When questions are overused, the therapist controls "the session, focus and direction" of therapy (Long, 1996, p. 172). If clients come to therapy in part because they have lost touch with their sense of power, then one measure of successful counseling and psychotherapy is the degree to which they feel empowered as a result of it. The question of power in the therapeutic relation can be a complex one. For a further discussion of power in therapy, see Welch's *The Path of Psychotherapy: Matters of the Heart* (1998) and Welch and Gonzalez's *The Process of Counseling and Psychotherapy: Matters of Skill* (1999). A questioning style, the overuse of questions, or probing questions can all empower the therapist to the detriment of the client.

Third is the problem of multiculturalism. Sue, Ivey, and Pedersen make a powerful statement in their book, *A Theory of Multicultural Counseling and Therapy* (1996). They say that "it will be important to remember that the counseling/therapy clientele of the future is a globally defined population" (p. 261). It goes without saying that people are different. What must be said, however, and what must be repeated, is that those differences must be acknowledged and respected. Since people are different, their reactions to questions will be different as well. There are cultures in which the North American style of direct questioning is offensive. There are other cultures in which a reflective, passive approach is viewed as unhelpful. The point of multicultural competence is to acknowledge, respect, and adapt one's counseling approach to the cultural differences of particular clients. Even those cultures that appreciate a more direct approach may not appreciate the overuse of questions. "Interviews in which the client is responding to the therapist are not therapy interviews but interrogations, usually" (Patterson, 1985, p. 106). Blunt, but it makes the point. Okun (2002) suggests that even when information is needed, especially sensitive or emotional information, "you can turn a question into a statement that will produce more information than the question would have" (p. 96). What is suggested here is that it is possible to be direct (as opposed to directive), straightforward, decisive, and purposive without "grilling," or overusing questions. Here is an example: A young, male client might report feelings of being held down by other family members and yet experience guilt at going against family wishes.

> Cl: I have things that I want to do with my life . . . but . . . but my family expects me to follow their direction . . . to do what they expect of me.
>
> Th: What is expected of you?

This seems to me to be an example of at least three therapeutic mistakes. First, the therapist has now taken the lead and has focused the client on family expectations. It isn't clear, at least to me, that the client's intentions are at all pointed in that direction. Second, there is no recognition of affect, personal meaning, or emotion. There is obviously feeling in this client's statement. Third, it strikes me that the question is, at least to some degree, premature at best, and irrelevant at worst. Others might disagree, but I'm not sure the expectations of the family, at least at this point, are important to the therapy.

How might a statement have been different?

> Cl: I have things that I want to do with my life . . . but . . . but my family expects me to follow their direction . . . to do what they expected of me.
>
> Th: You are in a painful place. You have dreams of your own . . . and . . . you don't want to be disrespectful to your family . . . your parents. And yet . . .

This statement acknowledges at least the apparent feeling of the client, the dilemma, and allows the client to continue exploring the life decision. It leaves the direction of the therapy open to the client and yet is focused enough that some possibility of advancing the therapy is apparent. What do you think as you compare the two possible responses? There are many cultures in the world in which loyalty to family interests clashes with American individualism. Probing questions too often can be infused with cultural assumptions even unintentionally. The wiser course of action seems to be change questions into statements.

Fourth is the problem of manipulation. Questions can be insidious. One of my pet peeves is the question that begins, "Don't you think. . . ." My immediate reaction is that I'm about to hear in a disguised form what the questioner thinks. I suspect this is "sneaky manipulation." Schubert in his "The Therapeutic Interview" (1977), an unpublished manuscript at the University of Regina, reports that one form of questioning can be identified as "manipulative questions" in which "the questioner is not interested in the answer but in getting the other person to admit [he or] she is wrong or inadequate" (cited in Martin, 1983, p. 80). The danger is that questions can be disguised and lead the client in directions the therapist considers important. "Manipulation" is an ugly word in therapy. Manipulation is an ugly act in therapy. It goes to what is in the heart of the therapist; what are his or her intentions. Questions, especially questions of a probing and closed-ended nature, run the risk of unintentionally (in the worse case scenario—intentionally) manipulating the client into the therapist's interests and needs.

Fifth is the problem of the lazy therapist. It isn't difficult to ask questions. It is an intellectual exercise. It doesn't actually require any real understanding of another person's feelings, meanings, or needs. So, someone can ask questions of another without any investment or involvement with him or her. Even open-ended questions don't risk much on the therapist part. If a client tells you they have a fear that their marriage is breaking up and you respond by asking, "How do you feel about that?" then we have not risked much, invested much, or even thought much. "When helpers feel that they can always ask [clients] for clarification of a statement or feeling, they often pay less attention to the [clients] and thus miss many cues . . . —the greater the number of questions, the less likelihood that the helper can assist the [client]" (Gazda, Asbury, Balzer, Childers, & Walters, 1984, p. 145). In other chapters of this book such responses as empathy, genuineness, focusing, and self-disclosure are presented. These skills require something of the therapist. They require training and commitment. They require unlearning some of our cultural assumptions and habitual ways of responding to others and replacing them with therapeutic interaction. Effective questioning also requires training and discipline. Part of the discipline, of course, is limiting our use of questions to those times and situations in therapy in which they are useful.

In all honesty, it doesn't take much to ask questions. The danger of using a question-asking style is, naturally, that the client may fall into a pattern of merely responding to questions. When you start asking questions, "the client will give minimum answers and then wait for the next question" (Hackney & Cormier, 1994, p. 83). As we shall see below, the information gained from a question-asking style tends to suffer from a number of flaws. It may be intellectual, false, and superficial. When the therapist has not risked much, he or she has limited the client from risking much as well. As we will see, the judicious use of questions can be effective, but a style of routine questioning is a low-risk, low-energy, and ineffective approach to responding.

Disadvantages for the Client. First is the problem of responsibility. When a therapist engages in a question-asking style, the client can come to expect that once the information is gathered the therapist will provide a solution to his or her issue, problem, or dilemma. "When the [therapist] asks a direct question . . . the message is that the [therapist] is the expert and will offer a solution once the question is answered" (Gazda, Asbury, Balzer, Childers, & Walters, 1984, p. 143).

We talked above about the problem of the lazy therapist. A number of problems of question asking can lead to a lazy client. After a number of questions, a client may assume that the responsibility of the therapy rests with the therapist and wait for further instructions or questions. The control, direction, and focus of the therapy are now the responsibilities of the therapist and not of the client. This is, indeed, a disadvantage for the client.

Second is the problem of dependence. When the counselor or psychotherapist asks direct questions of the client, he or she creates a relationship of dependence. The therapist has assumed a position of power, of authority, and of expertise that can create an expectation of resolution. The client can come to expect that the therapist will solve or cure the issue, problem, or concern. In our discussion of power above, it is indicated that this defeats one of the metapurposes of counseling, which is to empower the client. Question asking that leads to an expectation of a therapist-generated solution does not empower clients. Rather, it weakens them further. They already doubt their capacity and ability to find solutions or resolutions to their concerns, and now the therapist has confirmed their doubts. Clients in such a dynamic are at risk for becoming dependent upon the therapist.

Third is the problem of expectations. This triad of responsibility, dependence, and false expectations obviously are linked closely. It is important for clients to respect the competence of their psychotherapist. Confidence in the therapist's ability to be a good servant and a skilled facilitator is essential to a successful outcome in therapy. What is equally important is that a client builds, or rebuilds, increasing confidence in his or her own ability to cope effectively with the issues and concerns of life. A pattern of routine questioning can do just the opposite. It can reduce the client to a mere responder to therapist inquires. In such a passive role, the expectation can develop that it is the therapist who has the answer to the client's life concerns and it is the therapist who is the expert and who should be consulted in life's decisions. The false expectation of a therapist-guided life weakens the client, and, rather than progressing toward a sense of personal competence, the client abdicates responsibility and slides into a dependent relationship.

Fourth is the problem of resentment. "Facilitative responses *give* something . . . questions demand something" (Gazda, Asbury, Balzer, Childers, & Walters,

1984, p. 144 [emphasis in original]). In an atmosphere of questioning, especially probing questions, clients can fear that they will be forced to reveal something of themselves they presently are not prepared to disclose. They may come to resent the questioning, and thus the therapeutic relationship is damaged and the predictions for a successful outcome are diminished greatly. Frankly, it seems difficult to build a therapeutic relationship in which one party is asking questions and the other is expected to answer. Such an encounter seems much more like Patterson's (1985) "interrogation" than a counseling relationship. In the ask-and-respond set, it is not unreasonable to expect that, sooner or later, the responder will become resentful. This seems even more likely in a therapeutic relationship of which it seems reasonable to assume that the therapist will give something back to the client. In the chapter on self-disclosure we see how therapist risk and disclosure can contribute to effective counseling and psychotherapy. It may well be that a question-asking style can be viewed as aloof and withholding, which surely can lead to resentment.

Fifth is the problem of involvement. Clients who come to expect that the therapist will take the lead by asking questions can become passive clients. It is possible that they become less and less involved in their own therapy and instead follow the lead of the therapist, wherever that may take them. It is possible, of course, that the therapist might lead the client in a productive and helpful exploration of personal issues. But, if we ask the question of probability, then it is less probable that a leading therapist will be consistently effective in helping clients learn effective coping skills for presently felt issues and concerns. What such a questioning therapist consistently will create is a passive and dependent client who obediently answers questions but doesn't actively offer clinically important insights into the therapy.

Sixth is the problem of self-exploration. "Once the response set—helper question followed by [client] answer—is established, it becomes difficult to turn over the initiative to the [client]" (Gazda, Asbury, Balzer, Childers, & Walters, 1984, p. 144). The client becomes reluctant to introduce anything into the therapy, waiting instead to be prompted by the therapist. Thus, direct questioning "tends to interfere with depth self-exploration" (Gazda, Asbury, Balzer, Childers, & Walters, 1984, p. 144). It is possible, of course, for a therapist to ask important and exploratory questions. What is unlikely, however, is that there will be many of these. Instead, after a few pertinent inquires, questions frequently become "hit-or-miss," and the client's self-initiated explorations tend to become more and more related to important personal issues if not hindered by frequent questions.

Seventh is the problem of deception. In response to frequent questioning, clients may begin to provide "socially acceptable answers rather than honest ones" (Brammer, 1988, p. 75). It is possible, perhaps even probable, that clients want to be liked and seen as worthwhile, and thus may try to please the therapist. Clients might try to read the therapist's intentions, "read between the lines," and give an answer they think is what the therapist wants. This might not be intended deception, but it provides false and misleading information in the therapy. This is a danger that making empathy statements avoids. The power of a statement is that it places the responsibility for understanding the client on the therapist. If the statement is incorrect, then the client has the opportunity to correct it. It is the accuracy-checking quality of empathy-based statements that both clarifies issues and empowers clients. Question asking has the quality of a therapist-led therapy in which the client assumes a role of follower. A question followed by an answer followed by another question has none of this accuracy-checking balance. Misunderstandings and misinformation can flourish in such a question-and-answer style.

These problems and disadvantages for therapists and clients are meant to dissuade you from adopting questioning as a primary style in therapy. The overuse of questions is the principle fault to be avoided. "It can be argued that questions are one of the most commonly used and abused clinical interviewing techniques" (Sommers-Flanagan & Sommers-Flanagan, 1993, p. 182). I'm hopeful that the arguments above have convinced you that, of the many ways of responding to clients, question asking has limited effectiveness. But, of course, there is a place for questions in therapy. After this discussion of the perils of asking questions, it might be difficult to believe, but there are times and situations in which asking a question is appropriate and effective. Used sparingly and prudently, questions can become one more effective tool in therapy.

THE APPROPRIATE USE OF QUESTIONS

It has been said that there is a time and a place for everything. There are times and situations in which questions can be used effectively to progress therapy. I have said that the role of questions in therapy should be limited and purposive. There seem to me to be five specific instances when questions are appropriate and effective. These are (1) during the intake interview, (2) for assessment, (3) in opening and closing sessions, (4) for clarifying something that is not understood, and (5) during the action phase of therapy in which it is important to focus and address concretely the actions that come from exploration and insight. We will take up these specific uses of questions below. But first let's look at some general guidelines for using questions in counseling and psychotherapy.

Guidelines for Using Questions

One of the principal predictors of the successful outcome of psychotherapy is the quality of the relationship between the therapist and the client. Discussed above were the dangers of a question-asking style, including client resentment and lack of involvement. These guidelines for using questions increase the probability that the therapeutic relationship will be established.

Prepare Clients for Questions. It is recommend that you prepare clients for your questions. It is important to introduce questions using language suggested in the example below to help establish the relationship and to let the client know that question asking is not the format that will be routinely followed in the therapy. Sommers-Flanagan and Sommers-Flannagan (1993) suggest the following introduction:

> There is some specific information I need to obtain, so for the next few minutes I'll primarily be asking you specific questions designed to help me get that information. Some of the questions may seem odd or may not make much sense to you. If you want, afterward I can explain why I asked the types of questions I asked. (P. 189)

This example might be a bit wordy, but it does a couple of important things. First, it tells the client that question asking is not routine. Second, it empowers the client to explore anything that is confusing or odd. This is also a good beginning for establishing the sort of therapeutic relationship that can lead to a successful outcome. It teaches that this is not a power relationship, there are no secrets, and that the client has rights.

Ask Open-Ended Questions Whenever Possible. Open-ended questions are those that permit clients to explore and take the session in the direction they believe is important. Closed questions are questions that have a specific answer and can be answered with a yes or no response. Here are some examples of open-ended and closed questions.

Cl: I am just so angry at my roommate!

Th: What are the situations and events that make you angry? (closed)

or

Th: How are you going to deal with your anger? (open—while this question has the effect of focusing the interview on the anger and doesn't tend to open the client to other emotions, it is still an open-ended question)

Another example:

Cl: I don't know why I came. I'm don't really know where to start.

Th: Do you think therapy can be helpful to you? (closed)

or

Th: Hard to know where to begin? As you have thought about it, how do you think I can be helpful to you? (open—allows the client to take the therapy where he or she wants and may open up doubts and reservations about therapy)

Limit the Use of Questions. While questions may be used effectively, they are like any other counseling response: If they are used too frequently or overused, then they lose their effectiveness. There are specific times and situations in which questions may be effective. The difficulty with questions is that even when a question is an appropriate response, there are few questions that are effective, pertinent, and stimulating. After these few questions are exhausted, then questions become repetitive, probing, and vague. It is important to avoid using questions as your principle responding style.

Approach Sensitive Life Events and Situations Cautiously. When dealing with sensitive life information, questions are unlikely to be the most effective approach. There is the danger of seeming to probe and poke too deeply into an area before a client is ready or properly prepared. When dealing with sensitive areas of a client's life, even open-ended questions should be phrased carefully so that they do not go too deeply too quickly.

> Cl: I'm not sure how to get into this—I know I want to talk about it, but I'm not sure . . .
>
> Th: What are the fears you have about talking about it? (leaves open the danger both of forcing the client to talk in a way that he or she may fear will hurt the therapist's feelings because it might have to do with trust, and of exposing content before the client feels ready)

or

> Th: Take the time you need—how can I be of help as you wrestle with getting your concerns out in the open? (combines a statement with a question, provides support and encouragement with an open-ended question that permits the client to go at her or his own rate, and asks the client to be of help to the therapist, which can have the effect of empowering the client)

These four guidelines can help you use questions effectively in counseling and psychotherapy. Now let's look at those times and situations in which questions can be used effectively.

Using Questions

There seem to me to be five instances or situations in psychotherapy where questions may be used effectively. As mentioned above, these are: intake, assessment, opening and closing a session, clarifying, and action stage.

The Intake Interview. There are two primary purposes for the intake interview. First, it is a time to begin to build the therapeutic relationship. The impressions the client forms early on contribute to the ultimate outcome of the therapy. Second, it is a time to gather information. Intake forms require a good bit of specific information, including such things as name, address, telephone numbers, insurance information, names of and information about family members, previous counseling experience, and use of medications. Typically, this information is collected by a series of closed questions that elicit specific answers. There are dangers in this procedure that were pointed out above. There is the danger that a rapid-fire–questioning technique could be offensive or unsettling for the client. There is the danger that the questioning could create a response set in the client, which could lead to unreasonable expectations that the therapist always will take the lead and, once the questions are answered, provide a solution to the client's issues and concerns.

Some practitioners have tried to avoid the problem of asking repeated questions by having the client fill out the Intake Form privately before the first session. This approach deals with the problem of question asking, but it detracts somewhat from the relationship-building advantages of interacting with clients as they respond to important clinical information on the form.

Another approach has been to give clients a copy of the Intake Form and let them respond to the questions while the therapist writes and interacts. Another has been to position the chairs side by side so the client can see clearly what is being written and what the next piece of needed information is. The advantage of this procedure is that the therapist gets all the needed information, is able to interact with the client, and needs only to ask the first few questions before the client picks up what the next question is and responds without being asked. Tongue-in-cheek, I suggest that we change the name of the Intake Form to "Relationship-Building Device" because each of the questions on the form offers a chance to interact with clients and build on connecting points, such as family names in common or a similar birthday. These opportunities for "small talk" are therapeutically important in the beginning of trust building and establishing a therapeutic alliance.

All of these alternatives notwithstanding, the intake interview is one time during the counseling process when questions are appropriate and useful. Even closed questioning has its place in this information-gathering session.

Assessment. Clients may need to take a variety of assessment instruments, ranging from intelligence assessments to standardized personality instruments and projective techniques. The standardized assessment instruments, of course, are formatted with many closed questions, and some of these are administered verbally. Often clients are administered some form of a Mental Status Examination, and the nature of this clinical assessment demands closed questions dealing with cognition, affect, memory, reasoning, and orientation. Standardization forces the use of closed questions asked in a particular way. Projective techniques make more use of open-ended questions that permit the client to introduce their personal interpretation of what is being asked. This is a situation in therapy where question asking is necessary and appropriate.

Opening and Closing Sessions. Some soft structure permits clients to enter the therapeutic relationship with greater ease. A beginning strategy is often to ask an open-ended question. Some suggested openings include:

- How can I be of help today?
- As you were driving over, thoughts about what you were going to talk about today must have been running through your head. What were some of those thoughts? (Looks a bit like a closed question, but it still leaves the direction and content up to the client.)
- How shall we begin today?
- How has your week gone? (Again, this is a closed question that leaves the direction and content up to the client.)

These beginning questions are meant to be open so the client can feel free to introduce whatever he or she wants into the session.

Closing the session can also benefit from open-ended questions. Some examples are:

- What are you going to take away from today's session? (Summarizing)
- As you think back over today's session, are there things that remain unfinished? (Planning for the next session)
- As we wrap up today, where do you think we need to start next week? (Planning for the next session)
- Sometimes friends might ask what you did in therapy today. How would you answer them? (Summarizing)

Both opening and closing sessions with questions can serve to bring some gentle structure to therapy sessions. They can provide a way to ease into the special environment of therapy and back into the ordinary commerce of daily life.

Clarifying. Sometimes clients are vague or leave out important pieces of their story. Sometimes we just miss what a client says. There are times to clarify what is confusing for us, and a straightforward way of doing that is to ask a clarifying question. Consider the following situation:

Cl: I was over at my buddy's apartment and we were sitting around and we got into this argument—you know, about the game—usually we just do this for fun but for—I don't know, it got out of hand, you know . . . And so Jim, Mike, me, and Rob and a couple of other guys were arguing and he just up and hits me!

Th: Who hit you?

This is a clear clarifying question that is needed just to get a specific piece of important information. The client replies, is acknowledged, and then the therapist can follow with a statement that continues the client's narrative.

Another client might use words or slang that the therapist doesn't understand, as in the following example.

> Cl: Well, school is messed up—there just so many posers—they just make me want to puke—you know, throw up right in their face and so I tell 'em—yeah, that's the thing that is getting me into the most trouble at school—the posers.
>
> Th: So . . . you're in trouble at school because of the "posers." You know, I don't know what that is. What is a poser?
>
> Cl: You know, they're plastic—you know . . . uh, phonies.

The therapist wasn't able to connect with this client until the term "posers" was clarified. Then the understanding that the client was offended by people who came across as phony made sense, and the counseling session could progress.

The Action Stage. During the action stage of therapy, the therapist and client cooperatively search for solutions, resolutions, and action plans for the client so he or she can cope with their continuing life situations. This is a time to be specific and concrete in determining, detailing, planning, and implementing strategies for change. As below, a client might suggest several options but struggle to nail one down to practice or attempt.

> Cl: I have to talk to my dad about this but I'm not sure which way to do it. I can call him on the phone but I think I might be . . . uh, ummm—being chicken. So maybe a face-to-face is what I need to do. I'm not sure I really would be able to tell him either on the phone or face-to-face. Maybe I should write him a letter.
>
> Th: You know you have to communicate with your dad. You can do it by phone, in person, or write a letter. Which one is it going to be?

The therapist has been with the client through the exploration and understanding of the issues in his or her life. Options have been generated and the client is on the verge of selecting one. The therapist is forcing the issue with a closed question. This is a time in therapy when questions can prove useful. It is a time to be specific and concrete. Questions can pinpoint which action is necessary and the one the client wishes to try.

The intake interview, assessment, opening and closing sessions, clarifying missed or misunderstood information, and the action stage are appropriate times in which questions are appropriate and effective.

MULTICULTURAL AND DIVERSITY CONCERNS.

As we have reviewed multicultural counseling competences throughout this book, a reoccurring theme has been seeking out knowledge of the role of culture in a variety of therapeutic interventions. Questioning is one aspect of therapy where this advice seems most appropriate. Clients from different cultures will differ in their acceptance, appreciation and responses to direct questions. Some might appreciate the directness and apparent expertise of the therapist, while others might find such a direct approach to be invasive and disrespectful. Sue, Ivey, and Pedersen (1996) provide both a theory of multicultural counseling and therapy and an overview of gender-and ethnicity-based responses to the theory. While questioning isn't directly addressed in their text, one of the multicultural counseling competences does address the problem of being locked into one way of responding to clients:

> Culturally skilled counselors are able to engage in a variety of verbal/nonverbal helping responses. They are able to send and receive both verbal and nonverbal messages accurately and appropriately. They are not tied down to only one method or approach to helping, but recognize that helping styles and approaches may be culture-bound. When they sense that their helping style is limited and potentially inappropriate, they can anticipate and ameliorate its negative impact. (Pp. 48–49)

Such flexibility in skills is one that recommends itself well to using questions in therapy.

SUMMARY

Questioning in counseling and psychotherapy is something of a mild controversy. The range of recommendations is from Never to Highly recommended. King (2001) suggests, "Questions are the tools we use to explore, to clarify, to decide, and to plan. The right question can open a new vista for consideration or help to shut the door to an unproductive or unwanted scenario" (p. 41). Whatever approach a therapist takes, it should be taken with caution.

One question around which there seems to be widespread agreement is the question *why*. The seemingly unavoidable accusatory and judgmental nature of the question itself does not lend itself to effective use in therapy. The disadvantages of using questions as one's primary intervention style or of overusing questions, include disadvantages for both the therapist and the client. The disadvantages mentioned for the therapist include problems of control, power, multiculturalism, manipulation, and laziness.

The disadvantages for the client are problems of reduced responsibility, increased dependence, unreasonable expectations, resentment, reduced involvement, reduced self-exploration, and deception.

There are, of course, times when asking a question is an effective intervention in counseling and psychotherapy. The guidelines for using questions consist of preparing clients for questions, making the point that questions are not a routine part of the therapy; using open-ended questions rather than closed questions; limiting the use of questions and not using questioning as one's primary intervention style; and approaching sensitive areas cautiously.

Specific stages of therapy and particular instances lend themselves to using questions. These include the intake interview, assessment, opening and closing sessions, clarifying missing information or misunderstandings, and the action stage of therapy, in which it is necessary to be concrete and pin down plans for action.

The view presented here is that when there is an opportunity for a therapist to replace a question with a statement, then that is the wiser and more therapeutic course.

REFERENCES

Brammer, L. M. (1988). *The helping relationship: Process and skills* (4th ed.). Englewood Cliffs, NJ: Prentice-Hall.

Egan, G. (1998). *The skilled helper: A problem-management approach to helping* (6th ed.). Pacific Grove, CA: Brooks/Cole.

Gazda, G. M., Asbury, F. S., Balzer, F. J., Childers, W. C., & Walters, R. P. (1984). *Human relations development: A manual for educators* (3rd ed.). Boston, MA: Allyn and Bacon.

Hackney, H., & Cormier, S. (1994). *Counseling strategies and interventions* (4th ed.). Boston, MA: Allyn and Bacon.

Ivey, A. E., & Ivey, M. B. (1999). *Intentional interviewing and counseling: Facilitating client development in a multicultural society* (4th ed.). Pacific Grove, CA: Brooks/Cole.

King, A. (2001). *Demystifying the counseling process: A self-help handbook for counselors*. Boston, MA: Allyn and Bacon.

Lauver, P., & Harvey, D. R. (1997). *The practical counselor: Elements of effective helping*. Pacific Grove, CA: Brooks/Cole.

Long, V. O. (1996). *Communication skills in helping relationships: A framework for facilitating personal growth*. Pacific Grove, CA: Brooks/Cole.

Martin, D. G. (1983). *Counseling and therapy skills*. Prospect Heights, IL: Waveland Press.

Miars, R. D., & Halverson, S. E. (2001). The helping relationship. In D. Capuzzi & D. R. Gross (Eds.), *Introduction to the counseling profession* (3rd ed., pp. 50–68). Boston, MA: Allyn and Bacon.

Okun, B. F. (2002). *Effective helping: Interviewing and counseling techniques* (6th ed.). Pacific Grove, CA: Brooks/Cole.

Patterson, C. H. (1985). *The therapeutic relationship: Foundations for an eclectic psychotherapy*. Pacific Grove, CA: Brooks/Cole.

Sommers-Flanagan, J., & Sommers-Flanagan, R. (1993). *Foundations of therapeutic interviewing*. Boston, MA: Allyn and Bacon.

Sue, D. W., Ivey, A. E., & Pedersen, P. B. (1996). *A theory of multicultural counseling and therapy*. Pacific Grove, CA: Brooks/Cole.

Welch, I. D. (1998). *The path of psychotherapy: Matters of the heart*. Pacific Grove, CA: Brooks/Cole.

Welch, I. D., & Gonzalez, D. M. (1999). *The process of counseling and psychotherapy: Matters of skill*. Pacific Grove, CA: Brooks/Cole.

Chapter 21

Responding Nonverbally

The hand points the way to the heart. As counselors and psychotherapists, we recognize the importance of clients' nonverbal behavior. We have been taught that a significant portion of human communication is through nonverbal signals. Ivey and Ivey (1999) report that "some authorities claim that 85% or more of communication is nonverbal" (p. 82). Gorden (1992) reviews studies that suggest approximately 65 percent of verbal meaning is determined through one's nonverbal gestures.

What's good for the goose is good for the gander. As counselors and psychotherapists, we recognize the importance of client's nonverbal messages. It is equally true that client's recognize our nonverbal messages and are "interpreting and reacting to the nonverbal messages of the helper" (Young, 2001, p. 80). We cannot point simultaneously to the importance of clients' nonverbal communication and fail to recognize it in ourselves. Our silence, our gestures, our facial expressions, our posture, and our eye contact "speak," and the client listens and interprets. As Young (2001) reminds us "you cannot *not* communicate" (p. 80).

THE THERAPIST'S NONVERBAL MESSAGE

Welch and Gonzalez (1999) describe the nonverbal behaviors counselors and psychotherapists need to avoid: "Counselors who lounge. Therapists who sit behind desks. Counselors who sit stiffly with their arms crossed. Therapists who do not make eye contact or seem to be 'shifty-eyed' or nervous, agitated, or bored. All these people display behavior that can confuse and put off clients. Hand gestures that put up a barrier between the client and the therapist . . . interfere with the open flow of information between a client and a therapist" (p. 204).

Young (2001) offers suggestions for establishing a positive nonverbal climate indicating that, "from the beginning, helpers try to present the most welcoming,

Table 21.1
Helpful Nonverbal Counselor Behaviors

Helpful Nonverbal Counselor Behaviors
Good eye contact maintained
Occasional head nodding
Facial animation
Occasional smiling
Occasional hand gesturing
Close physical proximity [to client]
Moderate rate of speech
Leaning body [toward client]
Occasional touch, as appropriate
Relaxed, open posture
Confident vocal tone

Adapted from B. F. Okun (2002, p. 33).

nonthreatening, and facilitative nonverbals that encourage the client to talk and do not interfere with the client's telling of the story" (p. 80). The overall goal is that "nonverbal behavior should indicate a clear-cut willingness to work with the client" (Egan, 1998, p. 65). A list of helpful therapist nonverbal behaviors is presented in Table 21.1.

GUIDELINES

There are two guidelines for therapists' nonverbal behavior. The first is awareness. While it is probably true that we do not control consciously *all* our nonverbal behavior, we can become aware of its impact on others and control, at least, *some* of it. An analogy might be that we can learn to control the words we use, selecting those that seem most appropriate. In just the same way, we can learn to use nonverbal communication to communicate more accurately our therapeutic intentions.

The second is congruence. "We tend to trust people when their nonverbal messages seem consistent with the words they utter. On the other hand, we are wary of people whose words say one thing while their faces, tone of voice, or gestures say something else; their words register as insincere" (Lauver & Harvey, 1997, p. 57). Some years ago, I was supervising a beginning therapist who reported he was having difficulty with one of his clients. He reported that the client seemed not to want to "open up" even though the therapist reported verbally inviting the client to "feel free to talk about anything you want to here." As we reviewed the videotape together, the problem became clear. As the therapist had spoken these words, he had extended his arm with his hand palm out, in much the way a traffic cop would halt traffic! The therapist's words said one thing and his nonverbal gesture communicated something entirely different. One of the phenomena of human communication seems to be that when words say one thing and the body says another, we believe the body. The client was unwilling to open up with a person who was incongruent and clearly signaling "to stop and go no further." Take a look back at Table 8.1 for a list of effective and ineffective nonverbal behaviors for a number of the core conditions.

Awareness can lead to congruence. It requires two processes. First, it requires intentionality. Second, it requires practice. Given good intentions, the willingness to practice, a knowledgeable observer, and videotaped sessions, becoming aware of and congruent in nonverbal communication is a skill well within our competence. Table 21.2 presents a scale, which you and/or your observer may use in reviewing your sessions, may guide you toward improvement and development of your nonverbal behavioral competence.

The outcome of our intention to become aware of and congruent in our therapeutic nonverbal communication can bear sweet fruit. "To adjust our nonverbal behavior so the other person knows us more accurately raises the level of genuineness. . . . To remove the ineffective patterns that intrude or distract increases the level of respect. . . . To put effort into our observation of the nonverbal signals of another person shows caring" (Gazda, Asbury, Balzer, Childers, & Walters, 1984, p. 71).

A WELCOMING ENVIRONMENT

Often a client's first impression of counseling and psychotherapy comes from the environment in the office. Just as our personal nonverbal presentation should be open and welcoming, it is important that the climate in which therapy is conducted be open and welcoming as well. This is an often-neglected aspect of effective psychotherapy. As it is with many things, problems can occur from an office that is overly Spartan or overly lavish. Table 21.3 gives you a checklist to measure your therapy room's degree of welcoming.

THE ROLE OF CULTURE

Therapists' nonverbal behavior has taken on more importance in recent times due to the recognition of the multicultural influences in counseling and psychotherapy (Egan, 1998; Sue, Ivey, & Pedersen, 1996). Patterson (1985) recognizes the difficulty of nonverbal communication in general: "This is a difficult area in working with clients from the same culture. . . . With clients from other cultures the problem is greater, since nonverbal behaviors may have different, even opposite, meanings in different cultures" (p. 191). Eye contact might be a source

Table 21.2
Nonverbal Behavior Rating Scale

Instructions: Rate the therapist's behaviors on a scale of 0 to 3.0 = did not occur, 1 = occurred but needs improvement, 2 = occurred and is adequate, 3 = therapist especially strong on this point. The therapist will not use all behaviors in every session, but, over a period of time, the ratings will indicate nonverbal behaviors that need further development.

1. The therapist maintained eye contact with the client.

   0 1 2 3

2. The therapist varied facial expressions during the interview.

   0 1 2 3

3. The therapist responded to the helpee with alertness and facial animation.

   0 1 2 3

4. The therapist sometimes nodded his or her head.

   0 1 2 3

5. The therapist had a relaxed body position.

   0 1 2 3

6. The therapist leaned toward the client to encourage the client.

   0 1 2 3

7. The therapist's vocal pitch varied when talking.

   0 1 2 3

8. The therapist's voice was easily heard by the client.

   0 1 2 3

9. Sometimes the therapist used one-word comments, such as "mm-hm" or "uh-huh" to encourage the client.

   0 1 2 3

10. The therapist communicated warmth, concern, and empathy by smiling and using other gestures.

    0 1 2 3

Adapted from B. F. Okun (2002, pp. 299–300).

of difficulty with some clients. "In some situations such as the military and with some cultural groups, direct eye contact can be considered an act of defiance, rude gesture, a sexual invitation, or a sign that you consider yourself to be superior" (Young, 2001, p. 80).

In considering the skills related to therapist nonverbal behavior, Sue, Ivey,

Table 21.3
Checklist of Environmental Factors for a/the Therapist's Office

Lighting (not too bright or dim)	______
Chair Arrangement (placement, distance)	______
Appropriate Chairs (comfortable but not overly stuffed)	______
Neat, Clean	______
Casual	______
Warm	______
Cheerful (appropriately decorated, not overly childlike, odd, or "bizarre")	______
Desk or Other Barrier	______
"Throne" for Counselor (not a noticeably larger chair, or "power chair")	______
Lack of Needed Materials	______
Inappropriate Seating (for children—counselor at eye level, for multiple clients—counselor not separating clients)	______

Adapted from I. D. Welch & D. M. Gonzalez (1999).

and Pedersen (1996) consider one multicultural counseling competency to be the ability to be knowledgeable, flexible, and adaptive:

> Culturally skilled counselors are able to engage in a variety of verbal/nonverbal helping responses. They are able to send and receive both verbal and nonverbal messages accurately and appropriately. They are not tied down to only one method or approach to helping, but recognize that helping styles and approaches may be culture-bound. When they sense that their helping style is limited and potentially inappropriate, they can anticipate and ameliorate its negative impact. (Pp. 48–49)

This multicultural counseling competence provides another motivation for increasing our awareness of the role, importance, impact, and ambiguity of nonverbal behavior in counseling and psychotherapy. It seems a daunting task to master the skills of therapy, and when we add in the issues of diversity, it can seem overwhelming. The guidelines above, including intentionality and a willingness to practice, are enhanced by sound advice from Ivey and Ivey (1999): "Take on the skills, be aware and respectful of cultural differences, but also make sure that you are yourself" (p. 36). The task, after all, is to enter into a genuine relationship.

THE SPECIAL CASE OF TOUCH

Touch in psychotherapy has a long and important history. We might trace its roots to indigenous healers throughout history who have used touch to aid incantations and other healing practices. In the practice of psychotherapy, Freud's "pressure technique"—in which he laid his hand on the forehead of a client to encourage "free association"—may mark its presence in modern psychotherapy (Smith, Clance, & Imps, 1998). Many contend that research supports the use of touch in psychotherapy, even though it has become more controversial (Willson & Masson, 1986, Goodman & Teicher, 1988; Hunter & Struve, 1997; Cronise, 1993; Halbrook & Duplechin, 1994; Horton, Clance, Sterk-Elifson, & Emshoff, 1995; Kertay & Reviere, 1993; Suiter, 1984). Frankly, I invite you to research this topic for yourself so that you can come to an understanding of the role and importance of touch as well as the cautions important in the practice of effective counseling and psychotherapy.

It may be that we live in a hypersensitive time regarding relationships between men and women, differences in cultures, and the vagaries of individual preferences. "This diverse country is one in which the range of values, beliefs, and opinions on any subject can boggle the mind and defeat nearly any widely pleasing resolution. When to touch, how to touch, where to touch, who to touch, and even the meaning of touching have all been the source of debate in our society" (Welch & Gonzalez, 1999, p. 164).

There are some straightforward guidelines to follow as you consider the importance of touching in the therapeutic relationship. A general guideline is to make sure that what is in your heart, what your intentions are, is therapeutic. This is the message that will be communicated. Bluntly, if you are having sexual feelings, or are even generally attracted to a client, it is best to restrict touch to the standard level of touch reserved for greeting and saying goodbye—a handshake, for example. Given this essential caution, these guidelines can be helpful:

1. Touch should be appropriate. It should be a gesture of friendship, of welcoming, and of reassurance. It should not be erotic, sensual, or suggestive. It should not be used negatively, dismissively, or patronizingly.
2. Touch should not impose greater intimacy than the client can tolerate. There are important cautions regarding clients who have been victimized physically, including abused, tortured, and raped. These clients should be touched cautiously and with permission. It follows that it is inappropriate, no matter the circumstances, to touch certain parts of the body in a therapeutic relationship including genital areas or any of the erogenous parts of the body. This extends to a therapist patting or touching a client on the leg or knee. Handshakes, pats on the arms or shoulders, and even a hug around the shoulders can all be appropriate and important uses of touch in psychotherapy (Fisher, Rytting, & Heslin, 1976).

In spite of the cautions, touch in psychotherapy is an important part of nonverbal communication and, used appropriately, communicates warmth and acceptance to clients. Stated in the negative, the importance of touch is clear. What would be our understanding of a therapist who refuses to touch clients? Certainly, put this way it raises suspicions about why one person would *not* want to touch another appropriately. A final guideline for touch in psychotherapy is to use touch, at minimum, in the way touch is used in the larger society. It seems reasonable that this guideline would permit counselors and psychotherapists to extend their hand in greeting, kneel down to take the hand of a child, or take the arm of an elderly or infirm client to help them stand or sit. Be respectful, be yourself, and respond as one would in a natural, socially appropriate way.

SUMMARY

Nonverbal signals for clients form the basis for much of our understanding of their intended message. It is equally important for us to understand that our nonverbal messages are being read and interpreted by clients. While we may not be able to control all of our nonverbal signals, it is certainly the case that we can become aware of and control important nonverbal signals in order to become more effective psychotherapists.

The path to the effective use of nonverbal communications in therapeutic relationships lies in developing awareness and in our willingness to practice, leading to congruence. Learning to understand how to communicate nonverbally with clients who are much like us is one thing. But the skill is complicated by clients who come from different cultures and backgrounds. This is one of the major contributions of the emphasis on diversity and multicultural counseling. It highlights the need to become aware not only of differences, but also of a variety of skills necessary to permit us to be flexible and adaptive when faced with clients who have worldviews predominantly different from our own.

Touch is an important part of being a human being. Touch, or its lack, carries important emotional messages for all of us. The research is generally supportive of touch in psychotherapy, but there are important cautions, including erotic or suggestive touching, and those regarding timing for clients who have been victimized physically and/or sexually. Touch is an aspect of therapy that has received a good deal of research attention, and I invite you to research this area of nonverbal behavior for yourself so that you can come to an understanding of the importance and use of appropriate touch in counseling and psychotherapy.

REFERENCES

Barrett, M. S., & Berman, J. S. (2001, August). Is psychotherapy more effective when therapists disclose information about themselves? *Journal of Consulting & Clinical Psychology, 69*, 597–603.

Cronise, J. G. (1993, August). The taboo of touch in psychotherapy. *Dissertation Abstracts International, 54*(2-B), 1090–1091.

Egan, G. (1998). *The skilled helper: A problem-management approach to helping* (6th ed.). Pacific Grove, CA: Brooks/Cole.

Fisher, J. D., Rytting, M., & Heslin, R. (1976). Affective and valuative effects of an interpersonal touch. *Sociometry, 39*, 416–421.

Gazda, G. M., Asbury, F. S., Balzer, F. J., Childers, W. C., & Walters, R. P. (1984). *Human relations development: A manual for educators* (3rd ed.). Boston, MA: Allyn and Bacon.

Goodman, M., & Teicher, A. (1988). To touch or not to touch. *Psychotherapy: Theory, Research and Practice, 25*, 492–500.

Gorden, L. R. (1992). *Basic interviewing skills*. Itasca, IL: F. E. Peacock.

Halbrook, B., & Duplechin, R. (1994). Rethinking touch in psychotherapy: Guidelines for practitioners. *Psychotherapy in Private Practice, 13*, 43–53.

Horton, J. A., Clance, P. R., Sterk-Elifson, C., & Emshoff, J. (1995, fall). Touch in psychotherapy: A survey of patient's experiences. *Psychotherapy, 32*, 443–457.

Hunter, M., & Struve, J. (1997). *The ethical use of touch in psychotherapy*. Thousand Oaks, CA: Sage.

Ivey, A. E., & Ivey, M. B. (1999). *Intentional interviewing and counseling: Facilitating client development in a multicultural society* (4th ed.). Pacific Grove, CA: Brooks/Cole.

Kertay, L., & Reviere, S. L. (1993, spring). The use of touch in psychotherapy: Theoretical and ethical considerations. *Psychotherapy, 30*, 32–40.

Lauver, P., & Harvey, D. R. (1997). *The practical counselor: Elements of effective helping*. Pacific Grove, CA: Brooks/Cole.

Okun, B. F. (2002). *Effective helping: Interviewing and counseling techniques* (6th ed.). Pacific Grove, CA: Brooks/Cole.

Patterson, C. H. (1985). *The therapeutic relationship: Foundations for an eclectic psychotherapy*. Pacific Grove, CA: Brooks/Cole.

Smith, E.W.L., Clance, P. R., & Imps, S. (1998). *Touch in psychotherapy*. New York: Guilford.

Sue, D. W., Ivey, A. E., & Pedersen, P. B. (1996). *A theory of multicultural counseling and therapy*. Pacific Grove, CA: Brooks/Cole.

Suiter, R. L. (1984, February). A comparison of male and female professionals' and nonprofessionals' evaluations of the use of touch in psychotherapy. *Dissertation Abstracts International, 44*(8-A), 2422.

Welch, I. D., & Gonzalez, D. M. (1999). *The process of counseling and psychotherapy: Matters of skill*. Pacific Grove, CA: Brooks/Cole.

Willson, B. G., & Masson, R. L. (1986). The role of touch in therapy: An adjunct to communication. *Journal of Counseling and Development, 64*, 497–500.

Young, M. E. (2001). *Learning the art of helping: Building blocks and techniques* (2nd ed.). Upper Saddle River, NJ: Merrill/Prentice-Hall.

Appendix: Practice Exercises for Listening and Responding

The exercises and activities in this section are best done with a small training group. I recommend triads in which one partner plays the role of a helper, one a client, and the other an observer who provides feedback and/or compares experiences. It is possible, of course, to complete many of the exercises and activities alone, it is just that the interaction and feedback of others provides a variety of perceptions that enhance learning.

There are three rules to learning new skills. The first rule is practice. In order to develop a new skill, we have to go through the awkward stage of abandoning an old habit and replacing it with new habits and responses. So, that takes practice. That brings us to the second rule. The second rule is practice. See, it takes repetition to replace old habits with new. This brings us to the third rule. The third rule is practice. Stop me when you have heard enough! In order to learn the skills of listening and responding, you have to know what to do and then practice, practice, practice.

These exercises and activities are meant to provide basic lessons in learning the skills of listening and responding. The surest way, naturally, is to work directly with clients, under supervision, videotaping your sessions for review and discussion. Prior to seeing clients, however, it is effective and important to practice basic listening and responding skills. Since clients take some comfort in the ease and competence of the therapist, the naturalness with which we listen and respond can make a difference in the building relationship. That is the spirit in which these exercises and activities are offered.

Listening for Content—I

This exercise is designed to provide practice in listening for the characters and events of a story. In a group of three, have one member tell a short (perhaps a minute or two) narrative of a real, but not overly revealing, event in his or her life. Here are three examples of possible stories:

—A time I was embarrassed in public

—A time when I was afraid

—Dealing with an employee for whom "customer service" is an unknown concept

As the speaker tells his or her story, record:

Who are the characters in this narrative? ______

What is the plot/theme of the narrative? ______

When does the narrative take place? ______

Where does the narrative take place? ______

Why does the client say she feels this way (her explanation)? ______

How did the client get to where she/he is in her/his development? ______

As the story is told, record your impressions.

Have the two listeners compare their impressions.

Finally, the hard part: Paraphrase your understanding of the story. You might use the incomplete sentence below to help.

Last: *(when)*, you and *(who)* were in *(where)*, then *(how, what)* because *(why)*.

Listening for Content—II

The following exercises are just for practice:

—Something you can do individually to sharpen your listening skills is to watch a short segment of a television program (videotape, audio recording) and record your impressions in the categories below.

—As you observe other counselors-in-training, use the categories below to help follow the content of the session (clients might tell several stories in a session, so record your impressions of each one).

—As you review your own counseling sessions record the content in the categories below.

Who are the characters in this narrative? ______________________________

____

What is the plot/theme of the narrative? ______________________________

____

When (the time of the story)? ______________________________

Where (the setting)? ______________________________

Why (the client's explanation)? ______________________________

____

How (did the client get to where he or she is in his or her development)?

____

Listening for Intensity and Frequency

Sometimes clients themselves are confused about what occupies their thoughts and troubles them the most. One of the reasons clients come to therapy is to sort out the many troubling thoughts and events that prevent them from more satisfying lives. Clarifying these priorities is a helpful intervention in itself. Intensity and frequency are clues to the priority events and situations hold in a client's life. Here is a story a client told in therapy. In a group of three (or, individually) read the story and identify the frequency and the intensity of the events in the client's narrative. Beatrice is a woman in her sixties whose husband died about one year before she came for counseling.

> I . . . umm . . . I know I need to be here . . . but, . . . well, I . . . I don't know where to start. I am a widow. My husband, Bert, died last year. He had cancer and . . . he died quickly. . . . I mean, . . . he was diagnosed and lived only six months after the diagnosis. I'm lost without him. Just lost. He was my buffer. I relied on him. I'm not good with people . . . and he . . . was. We had a small business and he was the one who dealt with the people and I did paper work, books, ordering and we were a wonderful team. Now I have to talk to people on my own and I hate it. I don't know how to be social. He was the social one and now I'm trying to be social but I'm lost and angry. It was like he was the master of ceremonies and I was just able to hide out in the wings. Why did he have to die before me! He would have been fine without me, but I don't know what to do without him—I'm just confused, and angry. I'm alone and just don't know what to do.

Now that you have read the story, compare your individual understandings with the other members of your group to see agreement and differences. Take some time to discuss how you arrived at your understandings.

Listening for Drama, Affect, Metaphor, and Symbol

Read Beatrice's story again. This time, again in a group of three, read the story and look for instances of drama, of affect (emotions or strong feelings), metaphor, and symbol. A metaphor is a word or image that replaces another word to suggest a similarity or analogy between them ("His words were daggers in my heart," for example, would mean a painful experience. Another word for the same concept). A symbol is using one image to stand for another (the heart is a symbol for love).

Drama ______________________________

Affect ______________________________

Metaphor ______________________________

Symbol ______________________________

In your group, discuss your agreements and differences. It is important here to discuss also what meanings these emphases in speech could have for the client.

Listening and Responding

Often we take listening for granted. Here is a class exercise that teaches that listening and understanding is more difficult than it might seem. In a class, or a group of six to eight, make an agreement that no one can speak until he or she has paraphrased the previous speaker's point—to the satisfaction of the previous speaker. This rule is surprising in that it shows how difficult it really is to get the full intention of a speaker; it forces people to listen harder to rephrase their first understanding. Try it; it's hard!

Gossip

This one is both fun and enlightening. This game is called "Gossip," or sometimes "Telephone." The entire class sits in a circle and someone begins by whispering a short message to the person on the right. The person then whispers the message as he or she understood it to the person on his or her right, and this process is continued until the message makes the entire circle. The first person then tells the original message and the last person tells the message he or she received. It is amazing the distortions that take place in this game. It is fun and funny.

Now, repeat the game, only this time, after the message is whispered, have each listener check with each speaker to make sure the message was understood before he or she passes it along. Repeat until the message circles the entire class. Then, have the originator tell the starting message and the last person tell the message as he or she understood it. Compare the accuracy of the two methods. While it may not be entirely correct, the prediction is that the second method will result in a more accurate message. This is the importance of an accuracy check with clients' messages as well. When we make sure we understand, then distortions are reduced.

A Test for Language Style

LANGUAGE STYLE CHECKLIST*

The Language Style Checklist can help identify the dominance of each of your major sensory modalities—auditory, visual, and kinesthetic. Each item below has three choices. All of the choices may not apply to you. If a choice seems like you, then score that choice: If a choice does not seem like you at all, score a 0; score a 3 for the choice that is most typical of you; a 2 to the second choice; and a 1 to the final choice, if it applies.

1. When I am learning something new, I usually
   a. ( ) like to have someone explain it to me.
   b. ( ) like to read the instructions in a manual or book.
   c. ( ) like to make a model or try it out.
2. At social events, I
   a. ( ) have a conversation with two or three people at once.
   b. ( ) am a people watcher.
   c. ( ) am active and dance or play games, etc.
3. If I were in community theater in a musical, I would
   a. ( ) play in the orchestra or sing in the cast.
   b. ( ) design the costumes, paint the scenery, or work the lighting effects.
   c. ( ) make the costumes, build the sets, or take an acting role.
4. When I am angry, I usually
   a. ( ) talk about it, tell somebody off, or make jokes about it.
   b. ( ) fantasize or daydream about revenge.
   c. ( ) hit the wall, throw things, or get physical with people.
5. When I dream about a success in life, I dream of
   a. ( ) hearing the applause of a huge crowd.
   b. ( ) seeing my picture in the morning newspaper.
   c. ( ) winning a sporting event.
6. I prefer a teacher to
   a. ( ) lecture, use explanations, and encourage discussion.
   b. ( ) use the chalkboard, overheads, and assign readings.
   c. ( ) require in-class activities, poster presentations, and practice.
7. When I talk, I
   a. ( ) use my voice for expression.
   b. ( ) use facial expressions for emphasis.
   c. ( )"talk" with my hands.

*Adapted from Nancy A. Haynie (copyright 1981).

8. When I have to remember something, I
   a. ( ) repeat it aloud, tell it to someone else, or tape it.
   b. ( ) like to visualize it, draw a picture, or write myself a note.
   c. ( ) tie a ribbon on my finger or do something physical to help me remember.
9. When I cook, I
   a. ( ) like to have the recipe explained to me.
   b. ( ) read the recipe from a book.
   c. ( ) experiment and taste test.
10. I like to
   a. ( ) go to musical concerts, listen to the radio, or talk on the telephone.
   b. ( ) read, go to the movies, or watch television.
   c. ( ) play sports, exercise, or just take a walk.

Scoring

Total all A choices	Auditory	= preference for sounds and hearing
Total all B choices	Visual	= preference for visual images
Total all C choices	Kinesthetic	= preference for physical activity

If the scores are within four points of one another, you have a mixed style and can process information in any sensory modality with balanced ease. If there are five points or more between any of the scores, you have a relative preference for one style over the others. You may have two styles that seem stronger than the other one. This means you express yourself more naturally in the style with the higher score(s).

If you find that you have a strong preference for one style, then a part of your practice can be to develop the ability to respond so that you are able to match the client's language style more easily.

Listening for Nonverbal Messages

In triads, watch a segment of one of your therapy sessions (or, videotape a role play in class). Using the checklist below, identify the nonverbal behaviors of both the client and the counselor-in-training. Note the time on the video so you can return during the discussion to observe the behavior.

	Counselor	**Client**
Appropriate Eye Contact	________	________
Appropriate Facial Expressions	________	________
Inappropriate Facial Expressions	________	________

Appropriate Head Nodding	________	________
Facilitative Nonverbal Gestures	________	________
Distracting Nonverbal Gestures	________	________
Appropriate Tone of Voice	________	________
Critical or Mocking Tone of Voice	________	________
Nonverbal Warmth & Attentiveness	________	________
Boredom, Fidgeting, or Inattention	________	________

At the end of the segment, compare your ratings and discuss your agreements and differences. What effect did the nonverbal behavior you observed have on the session?

Charades

Play a game of charades with your training group for fun and for sensitivity to the idea that messages, sometimes even complex messages, can be conveyed without words. One other significant aspect of Charades, by the way, is that it teaches the importance of checking one's guess with the performer—it is in this process of guessing and checking that the solution is found. You can convey emotions such as the global categories: mad, bad, sad, and glad. Or you can try to solve more complex messages such as psychoanalytic theory, person-centered counseling, or "Just because you're paranoid doesn't mean they aren't out to get you!"

Building a Nonverbal Vocabulary

There is another exercise in this section dealing with building a verbal affective vocabulary. This activity is intended to help you build a nonverbal affective vocabulary in order to recognize common nonverbal behaviors and gestures and their common meanings. You may do this individually or in a small group. Using the global affective feelings (mad, bad, sad, and glad), identify five gestures or other nonverbal behaviors for each global feeling.

Mad	**Bad**	**Sad**	**Glad**
Clinched Fist	Drooping Head	Frown	Smile
_____	_____	_____	_____
_____	_____	_____	_____
_____	_____	_____	_____
_____	_____	_____	_____
_____	_____	_____	_____

As you develop an affective vocabulary, you might repeat this exercise with more specific feelings to see if specific gestures might correspond more directly with specific feelings (i.e., raised arms might correspond more to triumph, while gesturing down with the arm and fist might signal relief after a success).

Diversity and Multicultural Competencies Program Checklist*

Use this checklist to assess the degree to which your program is preparing you to work effectively in diverse and multicultural settings. It provides the basic, fundamental, and minimum level of program support not only for academically teaching diversity and multicultural issues, but also for modeling the importance of these issues in our profession. You might consider that seven of ten categories is a minimum level of compliance. If your program does not meet this standard, then you can be an agent of change to increase programmatic multicultural competence.

______ Ethnic and racial minority faculty are members of the full-time faculty.

______ Ethnic and racial minority students are enrolled in the program.

______ The program requires a diversity and multicultural studies course.

______ Diversity and multicultural issues are integrated into all coursework.

______ The program has an active diversity and multicultural issues committee.

______ Training opportunities are available for working with diverse clients.

______ Invited speakers about diversity and multicultural issues are a regular part of the intellectual climate of the program.

______ Diversity and multicultural issues are welcomed as research topics.

______ The library provides holdings and support for diversity and multicultural topics.

______ Diversity and multicultural issues are assessed in course evaluations and comprehensive examinations.

Personal Diversity and Multicultural Concerns

Here is a checklist for you to use as you develop your personal skills in working in diverse and multicultural settings. It is a way to track your development through the program and a way to set personal goals for yourself in order to enhance your knowledge and skills of diverse and multicultural counseling competencies. The checklist provides a guide for your personal development as you seek to become more competent in diversity and multicultural

*Adapted from J. G. Ponterotto, C. M. Alexander, & I. Grieger (1995). A multicultural competency checklist for counseling training programs. *Journal of Multicultural Counseling and Development, 23*, 11–20. See this article for a fuller treatment of program competencies.

issues. It provides guidelines for assessing your personal cultural values and biases, your awareness of clients' culture and values, and your development of appropriate counseling skills and strategies.

Diversity and Multicultural Counseling Competencies Checklist*

Personal Values and Biases

I am: ______ Developing knowledge of my culture and how it affects my personal and professional understanding of what is normal and of the process of psychotherapy.

______ Developing knowledge of how social injustices, oppression, racism, sexism, stereotyping lifestyles, and discrimination affects me personally and professionally.

______ Exploring my personal negative reactions to other races/ethnicities, genders, and sexual orientations and am willing to discuss and understand other worldviews.

______ Exploring educational and training experiences that increase my understanding and effectiveness in working with diverse and multicultural clients.

______ Striving to understand the influence of culture and lifestyle and actively working to develop a nonracist identity.

Clients' Cultures and Values

I am: ______ Developing knowledge of how social injustices, oppression, racism, sexism, stereotyping lifestyles, and discrimination affects others and how these forces affect life choices and the appropriateness or inappropriateness of counseling interventions.

______ Actively seeking specific knowledge of groups with whom I might most likely work and learning strategies for seeking out information about groups with whom I am unfamiliar.

______ Becoming aware of the role of family, neighborhood characteristics, and community resources for individual clients.

______ Developing a willingness to become involved with minority persons outside the counseling setting—in community organizations, celebrations, events, friendships, and social issue groups, for example.

Counseling Skills and Strategies

I am: ______ Developing knowledge of how traditional counseling practices may clash with the cultural values and beliefs of different racial, ethnic, religious, and cultural groups.

______ Developing knowledge of institutional practices that might interfere with minority individuals seeking therapeutic help (e.g., language, staff, setting).

*Adapted from D. W. Sue, A. E. Ivey, & P. B. Pedersen (1996). *A theory of multicultural counseling and therapy*. Pacific Grove, CA: Brooks/Cole.

______ Developing my ability to respond in a variety of verbal and nonverbal ways that increase my flexibility in working with different genders and cultures when one approach is ineffective or inappropriate.

______ Becoming aware of the inappropriateness for many linguistic and cultural groups of traditional assessment instruments that are designed to measure intelligence, personality, and pathology.

______ Developing a willingness to use community and institutional interventions as therapeutic strategies in addition to traditional one-on-one counseling approaches.

______ Exploring and developing a willingness to work to eliminate discrimination and other forms of social injustice as forces of psychopathology in the lives of the clients with whom I work.

Building an Affective Vocabulary*

I can make an assumption about students enrolled in graduate programs in counseling, social work, and psychology: I can assume that each holds a well-developed cognitive vocabulary. In fact, you would not be in a graduate program if you did not. We know the language of the intellect. What may not be as well developed, and my experience as a supervisor of many therapists-in-training affirms this, is a vocabulary useful in describing the feelings and emotions of clients. Our affective vocabulary lags behind our intellectual vocabulary. This exercise is meant as a stimulus to increase your knowledge and use of affective language. For each of the global feeling categories (mad, bad, sad, and glad), list a minimum of ten words under each category. I have given an example under each category. Push yourself. Compare your lists with others in your training group in order to add words to your list. Here is a tip: Use a thesaurus or, even easier, your word processor on the computer to check the word list in the spell-check tools. They often provide synonyms.

Mad	**Bad**	**Sad**	**Glad**
Angry	Confused	Depressed	Happy
______	______	______	______
______	______	______	______
______	______	______	______
______	______	______	______
______	______	______	______
______	______	______	______
______	______	______	______
______	______	______	______
______	______	______	______

*For a well-developed Affective Word List, also see I. D. Welch & D. M. Gonzalez (1999). *The process of counseling and psychotherapy: Matters of skill.* Pacific Grove, CA: Brooks/Cole.

The Empathy Chain

This exercise has two purposes. First, it aids in building an affective vocabulary and second, it teaches that there might be a number of facilitative responses that encourage a client to continue his or her narrative. This is a group exercise that works best with five or six participates. One of the group members role plays a therapy situation (e.g., a roommate problem, anger at a coworker, a crumbling relationship). After the client talks for about one minute, each of the other members offers their understanding of the feelings or meanings communicated by the client. Here is an example:

Cl: I'm just going nuts with the guy in my office. He is so obnoxious.

Th 1: Just feeling angry.

Th 2: Aggravated.

Th 3: Offended.

Th 4: Insulted.

Th 5: Mad.

After each of the team members has responded, the client selects the response that most fits what he or she was trying to communicate and continues with another sentence or two. Then, the process is repeated for a minimum of three times. This will generate a number of affective words for each member of the team to hear and will provide some insight into the therapy process. Different responses take the client in different directions. This is one of the reasons that checking our perceptions is so critical. We want to ensure that we are going in the direction the client leads us rather than taking the client in a direction of our suggestion.

Empathy Ladders

When we respond to a client, we might not exactly match the level of feeling they are trying to express. We might overstate or understate their feelings. In order to understand the client accurately, we have to be able to modify our understandings. This requires that we have some sense and understanding of the degrees of meaning for different levels of emotional intensity. Here is a practice exercise to force us to learn graduated meanings for affective words. Begin by selecting a feeling word and placing it in the middle of a "ladder" (see below). For two spaces above find a word that is stronger than the middle word and for two spaces below find a word that is weaker. Here is an example:

______	Enraged
______	Furious
Angry	**Angry**

______ Irritated
______ Miffed

If you really push yourself, you then can take each of the other words you generate and produce a ladder for each of them. One more tip: One way to increase your affective vocabulary is to force yourself to use different words in therapy. I use a rule that says that if I have tried a word three times in a therapy session, then I forbid myself from using that word in the session again until the summary. After all, if I have used the same word three times, then that signals that the session is not advancing and I am becoming routine in my responses and need to give the client something more with which to work. Again, let me remind you of the word processor spell-check function and the thesaurus in your word processor.

A Basic Counseling Response

While this basic counseling response may seem simplistic and mechanical (it is), it has the benefit of capturing both the content and the feeling, emotions, and/or meaning of the client's communication. This is something to practice over and over until you are able to formulate statements instantly and naturally (repeat—instantly and naturally).

Here is a direct client statement. Read it and then complete the basic counseling response below.

- I have to go to the dentist and it is something I have put off and put off. "You feel (affective word), when (content)." (An example of a basic counseling response might be, "You feel nervous when you even think about going to a dentist.")
- I have been fighting with my husband more and more lately. "You feel ______________, when ______________."
- My roommate is driving me crazy. "You feel ______________, when ______________."
- I am not sure about what to say in counseling. "You feel ______________, when ______________."
- I am so shy, and I know that is one of the reasons I don't go out much. "You feel ______________, when ______________."
- Do you think you can help me? (This one will be hard. It is tough to resist direct questions! A tip: How would you have to feel to ask a question like this?) "You feel ______________, when ______________."
- I wish I could stop thinking about her. I just have to accept that she doesn't

love me.
"You feel ______________________, when ______________________."

- I'm failing econ and I don't know what my parents are going to think.
  "You feel ______________________, when ______________________."
- I know it's stupid to be so upset about a cat. But, I can't seem to get over her dying.
  "You feel ______________________, when ______________________."

After you believe you have mastered the basic counseling response, you can drop the stem and simply use the affective descriptions. So instead of saying "You feel ______, when ______," you can simply state the affective description: "Angry when you think about him." Many experienced therapists have learned to drop content statements and know that an accurate empathy statement communicates understanding of content as well.

Responding with Self-Disclosure

Therapeutic self-disclosure isn't about telling stories to clients. It is a facilitative strategy to help clients find ways of coping with their troubling life situation. It is in the therapeutic and facilitative purpose that self-disclosure's effectiveness may be measured, discussed, and improved. Gazda et al (1984) provides a scale for determining the level of therapeutic self-disclosure. Such scales are used typically in research studies and may be used for training as well. The purpose here is to practice recognizing the level of self-disclosure and formulating therapeutic self-disclosing statements.

Self-Disclosure Scale*

(1 is unhelpful, even harmful; 4 is effective and specific)

1. The therapist is detached and aloof or reveals personal information only in an attempt to meet his or her own needs exclusively. This reverses the roles of therapy and alters the focus of therapy from the client to the therapist.
2. The therapist responds only to direct questions, revealing only what is requested by inquiries from the client. Even then, questions are answered "hesitantly and briefly." Self-disclosure is not used as a facilitative strategy.
3. The therapist reveals general, surface disclosures that clearly are meant to be facilitative. The client knows a little about the general and surface

*Adapted from G. M. Gazda, F. S. Asbury, F. J. Balzer, W. C. Childers, & R. P. Walters (1984). *Human relations development: A manual for educators* (3rd ed.). Boston, MA: Allyn & Bacon.

experiences of the therapist in order to cope with his or her own understanding in dealing with his or her life situation.

4. The therapist responds in clearly facilitative self-disclosing ways that are specific and detailed and that reveal the uniqueness of the therapist. This involves risk and vulnerability and is clearly relevant to the client's issues and concerns.

1.	**2.**	**3.**	**4.**
Detached; Aloof Witholds	*Withholds until Asked*	*Volunteers General Information*	*Volunteers Specifics*

Step 1. In your training group (a triad is recommended) use this scale to review a therapy session and rate the level of disclosure of the therapist. This might be one of your own sessions or one of the many professionally produced demonstrations of therapy.

Step 2. After discussion of your ratings, review those therapist responses that were scored at 2 or below. Now formulate a therapeutic self-disclosing response that is 3 or above.

Focusing and Concreteness

Here is a technique for helping to focus your counseling sessions. It requires 8½-by-11-inch paper (or larger, so that it that can be taped to a wall) and pen or pencil. I prefer to use colored markers for each section. Work in triads: One member acts as a client, one as the therapist, and one as an observer. Select a therapy issue to role-play. The client begins by talking in general terms for two or three minutes (remember, this is a role play; in therapy you might use this activity for ten or fifteen minutes in order to help focus the client). Then, the therapist says, "We have been talking in general ways about this. Let's focus in on it." Write the following headings across the top of the page:

Issue	**Feelings**	**Desired Outcome**	**Block**
	(Major emotion)	(What you want)	(What's stopping you)

The therapist passes the marker to the client and asks, "How would you label the issue you have been talking about?" Next, "What feeling do you have about the issue?" Next, "What do you want to happen?" And then, "What is preventing you from getting what you want?"

The therapist may then follow with other issues and repeat the process until the client has listed their most important issues. After the "chart," is completed, the observer provides feedback on the therapist's use of the technique. Then the client, therapist, and observer discuss the overall effectiveness of the strategy.

This provides an "agenda" not only for the present therapy session, but also for others. This is a strategy that seems to work well with clients who are not highly verbal. Practice so that each member of the group has an opportunity for each role.

Index

About the Author

IRA DAVID WELCH is Dean of Professional and Graduate Studies at Chadron State College in Nebraska. He is recognized as a Diplomate in Counseling Psychology by the American Board of Professional Psychology.